The
Secret
Lives of
Color

Kassia St. Clair is a freelance writer and
a former assistant books and arts editor
at *The Economist*, and writes regularly
for *Elle Decoration*. Her popular column
on color there sparked the idea for
this book.

www.kassiastclair.com

The
Secret
Lives of
Color

Kassia St. Clair

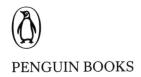

PENGUIN BOOKS

PENGUIN BOOKS
An imprint of Penguin Random House LLC
375 Hudson Street
New York, New York 10014
penguin.com

First published in Great Britain by John Murray (Publishers),
an imprint of Hodder & Stoughton Ltd.
Published by arrangement with Hodder & Stoughton Ltd.
Published in Penguin Books 2017

LIBRARY OF CONGRESS CATALOGING-IN-PUBLICATION DATA

Names: St. Clair, Kassia, author.
Title: The secret lives of color / Kassia St. Clair.
Description: New York : Penguin Books, 2017. | Includes
  bibliographical references and index.
Identifiers: LCCN 2017014300 | ISBN 9780143131144 (hardback)
Subjects: LCSH: Color—Psychological aspects—History. |
  Color—Social aspects—History. | Symbolism of colors—History. |
  BISAC: ART / History / General. | ART / Color Theory. | ART /
  Techniques / Color.
Classification: LCC BF789.C7 S64 2017 | DDC 155.9/1145—dc23
LC record available at https://lccn.loc.gov/2017014300

Printed in the United States of America
10   9

Set in Kings Caslon

For Fallulah

The purest and
most thoughtful
minds are those
which love color
the most.

**John Ruskin, *The Stones of Venice*
(1851–3)**

Contents

38

62

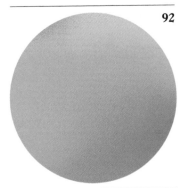

92

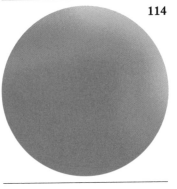

114

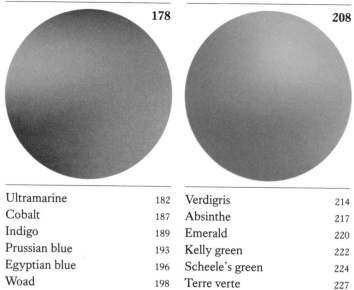

134

158

178

208

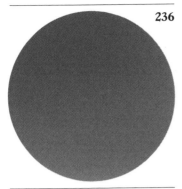

236

260

Preface

I fell in love with colors in the way most people fall in love: while concentrating on something else. Ten years ago, while researching eighteenth-century women's fashions, I would drive down to London to gaze at yellowing copies of *Ackermann's Repository*, one of the world's oldest lifestyle magazines, in the Victoria and Albert Museum's wood-clad archive. To me, the descriptions of the latest fashions of the 1790s were as mouthwatering and bewildering as the tasting menu of a Michelin-starred restaurant. One issue described "[a] Scotch bonnet of garnet-colored satin, the ends trimmed with a gold fringe."

> That worst and vilest of all colors, pea-green!
>
> **Arbiter Elegantiarum, 1809**

Another recommended a gown of "puce-colored satin" to be worn with a "Roman mantle of scarlet kerseymere." At other times, the well-dressed woman would be nothing without a pelisse in hair brown, a bonnet trimmed with coquelicot-colored feathers or lemon-colored sarcenet silk. Sometimes there were colored plates accompanying the descriptions to help me decipher what hair brown could possibly look like, but often there were not. It was like listening to a conversation in a language I only half understood. I was hooked.

Years later, I had an idea that would allow me to write about my passion month in, month out, turning it into a regular magazine feature. Each issue I would take a different shade and pull it apart at the seams to discover its hidden mysteries. When was it fashionable? How and when was it made? Is it associated with a particular artist or designer or brand? What is its history? Michelle Ogundehin, the editor of the *British Elle Decoration*, commissioned my column and in the years since I have written about colors as ordinary as orange and as recherché as heliotrope. These columns provided the germ for this book and I am profoundly grateful. *The Secret Lives of Color* is not intended to be an exhaustive history. This book is broken down into broad color families and I have included some—black, brown, and white—that are not part of the spectrum as defined by Sir Isaac Newton.[1] Within each family I have picked out individual shades with particularly fascinating, important, or disturbing histories. What I have tried to do is provide something between a potted history and a character sketch for the 75 shades that have intrigued me the most. Some are artists' colors, some are dyes, and others are almost more akin to ideas or sociocultural creations. I hope you enjoy them. There are many wonderful stories that I didn't have room for here, so I have included a glossary (or color swatch) of other interesting hues along with suggestions for further reading.

I don't believe there are "off-putting" colors.

David Hockney defending another shade of green—olive, 2015

Light is therefore color, and shadow the privation of it.

J. M. W. Turner, 1818

Color vision
How we see

Color is fundamental to our experience of the world
around us. Think of hi-vis jackets, brand logos, and the
hair, eyes, and skin of those we love. But how is it,
precisely, that we see these things? What we are really
seeing when we look at, say, a ripe tomato or green paint,
is light being reflected off the surface of that object and
into our eyes. The visible spectrum, as you can see from
the diagram on page 14, makes up only a small proportion
of the entire electromagnetic spectrum. Different things are
different colors because they absorb some wavelengths of
the visible light spectrum, while others bounce off. So the
tomato's skin is soaking up most of the short and medium
wavelengths—blues and violets, greens, yellows and
oranges. The remainder, the reds, hit our eyes and are
processed by our brains. So, in a way, the color we perceive
an object to be is precisely the color it *isn't*: that is, the
segment of the spectrum that is being reflected away.

When light enters our eyes it passes through the lenses
and hits the retinas. These are at the backs of our eyeballs
and are stuffed with light-sensitive cells, called rods and
cones because of their respective shapes. Rods do the
heavy lifting of our vision. We have about 120 million
in each eye; they are incredibly sensitive and principally
distinguish between light and dark. But it is the cones
that are most responsive to color. We have far fewer
of these: around six million in each retina, the majority
huddled together in a small, central spot called the macula.
Most people have three different types of cone,[2] each tuned
to light of different wavelengths: 440 nm, 530 nm, and
560 nm. About two-thirds of these cells are sensitive to
longer wavelengths, which means we see more of the warm

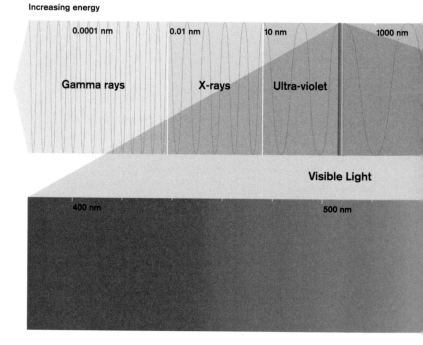

colors—yellows, reds, and oranges—than the cooler colors
in the spectrum. Around 4.5 percent of the world's
population are color-blind or deficient because
of faults in their cone cells. The phenomenon is not
completely understood, but it is usually genetic and is
more prevalent in men: around 1 in 12 men are affected
compared to 1 in 200 women. For people with "normal"
color vision, when cone cells are activated by light,
they relay the information through the nerve system
to the brain, which in turn interprets this as color.

This sounds straightforward, but the interpretation
stage is perhaps the most confounding. A metaphysical
debate over whether colors really, physically exist or
are only internal manifestations has raged since the
seventeenth century. The squall of dismay and confusion
on social media over the blue and black (or was it white
and gold?) dress in 2015 shows how uncomfortable we

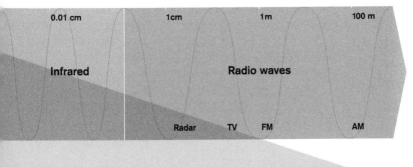

are with the ambiguity. This particular image made us
acutely aware of our brain's post-processing: half of us saw
one thing, the other half something completely different.
This happened because our brains normally collect and
apply cues about the ambient light—whether we are in full
daylight or under an LED bulb, for example—and texture.
We use these cues to adjust our perception, like applying
a filter over a stage light. The poor quality and lack of
visual clues like skin color in the dress image meant that
our brains had to guess at the quality of the ambient light.
Some intuited that the dress was being washed out by
strong light and therefore their minds tuned the colors
to darken them; others believed the dress to be in shadow,
so their minds adjusted what they were seeing to brighten
it and remove the shadowy blue cast. That is how an
Internet full of people looking at the same image saw
very different things.

Whiteness and
all gray Colors
between white
and black, may
be compounded
of Colors, and
the whiteness of
the Sun's Light
is compounded
of all the primary
Colors mix'd in
a due Proportion.

Sir Isaac Newton, 1704

Simple arithmetic
On light

In 1666, the same year that the Great Fire of London
consumed the city, a 24-year-old Isaac Newton began
experimenting with prisms and beams of sunlight.
He used a prism to prize apart a ray of white light to reveal
its constituent wavelengths. This was not revolutionary
in itself—it was something of a parlor trick that had
been done many times before. Newton, however, went
a step further, and in doing so changed the way we think
about color forever: he used another prism to put the
wavelengths back together again. Until then it had been
assumed that the rainbow that pours out of a prism in the
path of a beam of light was created by impurities in the
glass. Pure white sunlight was considered a gift from God;
it was unthinkable that it could be broken down or,
worse still, created by mixing colored lights together.
During the Middle Ages mixing colors at all was a taboo,
believed to be against the natural order; even during
Newton's lifetime, the idea that a mixture of colors could
create white light was anathema.

Artists would also have been puzzled by the idea
that white is made up of lots of different colors, but for
different reasons. As anyone who has ever had access
to a paint set knows, the more colors you mix together,
the closer you approach to black, not white. It has been
suggested that Rembrandt created the complex, dark,
chocolaty shadows in his paintings simply by scraping
together whatever happened to remain on his palette and
blending that directly onto the canvas, because so many
different pigments have been found within their depths.[3]
The explanation for the fact that mixing colored
light makes white, while mixing colored *paint* makes

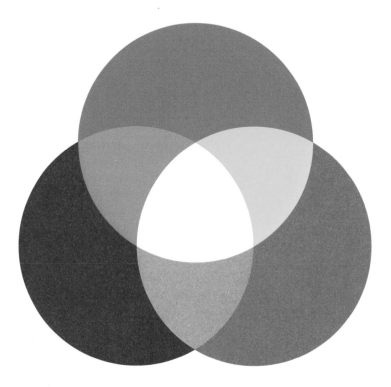

Additive Color Mixing
Colors are created by mixing
different colored lights.
Combining the three primaries
produces white.

black, lies in the science of optics. Essentially, there are two different types of color mixing: additive and subtractive. With additive mixing, different light wavelengths are combined to create different colors, and when added together the result is white light. This is what Newton demonstrated with his prisms. However, the opposite happens when paints are mixed. Since each pigment only reflects back to the eye a proportion of the available light, when several are mixed together more and more wavelengths are subtracted. Mix enough together and very little of the visible spectrum is reflected, so we will perceive the mixture to be black, or very close to it.

For painters with a limited range of impure pigments at their disposal, this is a problem. If they want to create a pale purple, for example, they have to mix together at least three—a red, a blue, and a white—but they might have to add even more to get the precise violet they're after. The more colors they blend, the more likely it is that the end result will be murky. But the same is true even for simple colors like green and orange: it's better to use a single pigment rather than mixtures that will inevitably absorb more of the available light wavelengths, sucking the luminosity from the painting. The search for more and brighter colors is fundamental to the story of art, from prehistory to today.

Without paint in
tubes there would
have been . . .
nothing of what
the journalists
were later to call
impressionists.

Pierre-Auguste Renoir, date unknown

Building the palette
Artists and their pigments

Pliny the Elder, a Roman naturalist writing in the first
century A.D., claimed that painters in classical Greece used
only four colors: black, white, red, and yellow. He was
almost certainly exaggerating—the Egyptians had
discovered a way of manufacturing a bright, clear blue
[page 196] at least as early as 2500 B.C. But it is true that
early artists were restricted, for the most part, to a small
range of pigments they could extract from the ground or
from plants and insects.

Humanity has been well served with earthy red- and
yellow-toned browns from the beginning. The earliest
pigment use that we know of is from the Lower Paleolithic
period, about 350,000 years ago. Prehistoric peoples could
render a deep black from the ashes from fires [page 274].
Some whites could be found in the ground; another was
produced by early chemists from around 2300 B.C. [page 43].
Although pigments had been discovered, traded, and
synthesized throughout recorded history, the process
accelerated dramatically in the nineteenth century due to
the burgeoning Industrial Revolution. More and more
chemicals were being produced as by-products of industrial
processes, and some made excellent pigments and dyes.
William Perkin, for example, stumbled across the purple
dye mauveine [page 169] while trying to synthesize a cure
for malaria in 1856.

The availability of some pigments and the introduction
of others has helped to shape the history of art. The palm
prints and bison on the walls of prehistoric caves owed
their somber palette to the pigments that the earliest artists
could find in the world around them. Fast-forward several
thousand years to illuminated medieval manuscripts, and

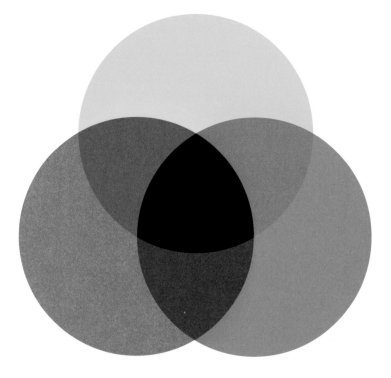

Subtractive Color Mixing
By mixing a limited set of colors,
many others can be created.
A perfect mixture of primaries
will yield black.

the black and white remained unchanged, but flat fields of gold and several brilliant colors like red and blue had been added. Centuries later, the paintings of Renaissance artists or old masters benefited as much from a broader range of pigments as they did from realistic representations of perspective and sophisticated ways of dealing with light and shade. Some works from this time remain unfinished, with a single figure left as a simple sketch, because the artist couldn't afford the expensive pigments needed to complete the canvas. The clear blue ultramarine [page 182], for example, was so dear that the commissioning patrons often had to buy it themselves: the artists couldn't afford it. And customers often felt the need to specify, in written contracts, how much of the expensive paints they expected artists to use in the finished work, and which figures should be clothed in which colors, fearful that hard-up painters would use a cheaper alternative.[4]

For their part, early artists had a very different relationship with their colors than modern artists. Because some colorants reacted with others, artists had to plan their compositions bearing potentially ruinous combinations in mind, ensuring that none overlapped or appeared next to each other. Most pigments were made by hand, either by the artists themselves or with the help of apprentices in their studios. Depending on the pigment, this could require grinding down rocks to powder, or the handling of technically challenging or poisonous raw ingredients. Pigments could also be obtained from specialists, including alchemists and apothecaries. Later, those who produced and traded in colors were known as colormen, and procured rare pigments from across the globe.

It was only relatively late in the nineteenth century that artists really benefited from a proliferation of ready-made

pigments (and even then these weren't always reliable).
Cheap compounds, such as cerulean, chrome orange, and
cadmium yellow, freed artists from either pestles or
unscrupulous colormen who sold unstable mixes that
would discolor within weeks or react with other colors, or
the canvas itself. Coupled with the invention of collapsible
metal paint tubes in 1841, the new colors allowed artists
to work outside and douse their canvases with the
brightest pigments anyone had ever seen. It is small
wonder critics were initially unsure: this was color as it
had never been seen before, and it was dazzling.

Too often histories of color—what few there are—are limited to the most recent periods and to artistic matters, which is very reductive. The history of painting is one thing, the history of colors is another—and altogether more vast.

Michel Pastoureau, 2015

Vintage paint charts
Mapping color

In the dying years of the seventeenth century, a Dutch
artist called A. Boogert made a concerted attempt to pin
all known colors down. In a volume containing over 800
hand-painted swatches glossed with spidery black labels,
Boogert described how to mix an array of watercolor tints,
from the palest sea foam to deepest viridian. He is far
from the only person to have attempted to catalog all
known tints, shades, and hues. Scientists, artists, designers,
and linguists have all spent time trying to chart courses
through color space, and assign plot points with names,
codes, or grid references. Pantone's index-card-style chips
are the most famous modern solution to the problem of
locking precise shades across linguistic and cultural divides,
but it is only one in a long line of such efforts.

Because colors exist as much in the cultural realm as
they do physically, such attempts are somewhat Sisyphean.
Take, for example, the idea that colors can be grouped into
two camps, warm and cool. We would unhesitatingly say
that red and yellow are warm, and green and blue are cool,
but this division can only be traced back to the eighteenth
century. There is evidence that in the Middle Ages blue
was considered hot, even the hottest of colors.

There are also discrepancies between the name a
society gives a color and the actual color, and these can
shift over time, like tectonic plates. Magenta [page 167],
which is now considered a pink but was originally more
purple-red, is one example. Others can be found among
the wonderfully abstruse definitions in Merriam-Webster's
Third New International Dictionary, published in 1961.
Begonia is "a deep pink that is bluer, lighter, and stronger
than average coral, bluer than fiesta, and bluer and stronger

than sweet William." Lapis lazuli blue is "a moderate blue that is redder and duller than average copen and redder and deeper than azurite blue, Dresden blue, or pompadour." The intention of these descriptions was not to send the reader on a wild definition-chase through the dictionary; they were probably the work of color expert Isaac H. Godlove, a consultant hired by the editor of Webster's *Third* and the director of Munsell, a color-mapping company.[5] The problem is that, fun as these entries are now, average coral, fiesta, and copen have largely lost their cultural currency—they don't get the reader one iota closer to knowing what the color being defined actually looks like. By the same token, someone reading about avocado green in 100 years' time might be equally mystified: Is it the dark color of the skin that's meant? Or the clay green of the outer flesh? Or the butter tint near the seed? But for people today, avocado green [page 230] still has meaning.

Over the course of time the margin for error becomes ever greater. Even when the documentary evidence, such as a painting, remains, we are often seeing it in lighting conditions entirely different from the ones it was created in. It's the difference between looking at a house-paint sample on your computer screen, in the can at your local hardware store, and then on the walls in your home. Also, since many stable dyes and paints are recent innovations, the colors themselves may have deteriorated. Colors, therefore, should be understood as subjective cultural creations: you could no more meaningfully secure a precise universal definition for all the known shades than you could plot the coordinates of a dream.

Savage nations,
uneducated people,
and children have
a great predilection
for vivid colors.

Johann Wolfgang von Goethe, 1810

Chromophilia, chromophobia
Politics of color

A certain distaste for color runs through Western culture
like a ladder in a stocking. Many classical writers were
dismissive. Color was a distraction from the true glories
of art: line and form. It was seen as self-indulgent and,
later, sinful: a sign of dissimulation and dishonesty.
The bluntest expression of this comes from the nineteenth-
century American writer Herman Melville, who wrote
that colors "are but subtle deceits, not actually inherent
in substances, but only laid on from without; so that all
deified Nature absolutely paints like a harlot."[6] But
arguments like these are very old indeed. The Protestants,
for example, expressed their intellectual simplicity, severity,
and humility in a palette dominated by black and white;
bright colors like red, orange, yellow, and blue were
removed both from the walls of their churches and from
their wardrobes. The pious Henry Ford steadfastly refused
for many years to bow to consumer demand and produce
cars in any color other than black.

In art, the tussle over the respective merits of *disegno*
(drawing) versus *colore* (color) raged on through the
Renaissance and, although somewhat muted, continues
into the present day. *Disegno* represented purity and
intellect; *colore*, the vulgar and effeminate. In an imperious
essay from 1920, tellingly entitled "Purism," the architect
Le Corbusier and his colleague wrote:

[I]n a true and durable plastic work, it is form *which comes first, and
everything else should be subordinated to it ... [Cézanne] accepted without
examination the attractive offer of the color-vendor, in a period marked by a
fad for color-chemistry, a science with no possible effect on great painting. Let
us leave to the clothes-dyers the sensory jubilations of the paint tube.*[7]

Even among those who accepted the value of color, the ways in which they were conceptualized and ordered had an impact on their relative importance. The ancient Greeks saw colors running along a continuum from white to black: yellow was a little darker than white and blue was a little lighter than black. Red and green were in the middle. Medieval writers had great faith in this light-to-dark schema too. It was only in the seventeenth century that the idea emerged of red, yellow, and blue as primary colors, and green, orange, and purple as secondary ones. Most iconoclastic of all was Newton and his spectrum, an idea that he wrote about in 1704 in *Opticks*. This was hugely influential: suddenly white and black were no longer colors; the spectrum no longer ran from light to dark. Newton's color wheel also imposed order on the relationship between complementary colors. These were color pairs—for example, green and red, blue and orange—that were found to resonate strongly with each other when placed side by side. The idea of complementary colors would prove to have a profound effect on the art that followed; artists including Vincent van Gogh and Edvard Munch used them to give structure and add drama to their paintings.

As colors came to take on meanings and cultural significance within societies, attempts were made to restrict their use. The most notorious expression of this phenomenon was through the sumptuary laws. While these were passed in ancient Greece and Rome, and examples can be found in ancient China and Japan, they found their fullest expression in Europe from the mid-twelfth century, before tailing off again in the early modern period. Such laws could touch on anything from diet to dress and furnishings, and sought to enforce social boundaries by encoding the social strata into a clear visual system:

the peasants, in other words, should eat and dress like
peasants; craftsmen should eat and dress like craftsmen;
and so on. Color was a vital signifier in this social
language—dull, earthy colors like russet [page 246] were
explicitly confined to the meanest rural peasants, while
bright, saturated ones like scarlet [page 138] were the
preserve of a select few.

It is the best possible sign of a color when nobody who sees it knows what to call it.

John Ruskin, 1859

Colorful language
Do words shape the shades we see?

It was a stern-faced British politician who first noticed
something awry with the colors in ancient Greek
literature. William Ewart Gladstone was a devotee of
the poet Homer and it was while he was preparing the
definitive tract on his hero in 1858 that he stumbled across
some psychedelic oddities. Brows could certainly be
black metaphorically—in rage—but was honey really
green? Or the sea "wine-dark," the same color, bizarrely,
as oxen, while sheep were violet? He decided to survey
the Greek writer's entire oeuvre for color references.
Melas (black), it turned out, was by far the most frequently
used, with around 170 mentions, and there were about
100 mentions of white. Next—a steep drop in frequency—
erythros (red), which was used only 13 times, while
yellow, green, and purple were all referenced fewer than
10 times. Blue was not mentioned once. To Gladstone it
seemed there was one possible explanation: that the
Greeks were, in effect, color-blind. Or, as he put it, more
sensitive to the "modes and forms of light, and of its
opposite . . . darkness" than they were to color.

    In fact, humans evolved the capacity to see in color
several millennia earlier, so color blindness is not to
blame. And it isn't only the ancient Greeks who seem
to talk about color in ways that feel unfamiliar. A decade
later Lazarus Geiger, a German philosopher and
philologist, began to examine other ancient languages.
He pored over the Koran and the Bible in its original
Hebrew; he studied ancient Chinese stories and Icelandic
sagas. All exhibited the same muddled references to color
and, as he noted in one much-quoted passage on Vedic
chants from India, the same omission.

*These hymns, of more than ten thousand lines, are brimming with
descriptions of the heavens. Scarcely any subject is evoked more
frequently. The sun and reddening of dawn's play of color, day and
night, cloud and lightning, the air and ether, all these are unfolded
before us, again and again in splendor and vivid fullness. But there
is one thing no one would ever learn from those ancient songs who did
not already know it, and that is that the sky is blue.*[8]

When the word did appear, it evolved out of the
words that had previously served either for green or,
more commonly, black. Geiger believed he could trace
humanity's seeming sensitivity to different colors
through the evolution of their languages. All started
out with words for light and dark (or white and black);
next came red, and then yellow, then green, then blue.
A wider study conducted in the late 1960s by Brent
Berlin and Paul Kay confirmed a similar sequence.
This, it was believed, meant two things: the first was
that color categories were innate; the second was that
if we didn't possess a word for a color, it affected our
perception of it.

However, a broader survey, conducted in the 1980s,
revealed many exceptions: languages that didn't
necessarily "develop" in this way, and some that divide
up color space entirely differently. Koreans, for example,
have a word that distinguishes yellow green from regular
green; Russians have different words for light and dark
blue. A classic example is Himba, a language spoken
by a tribe in southwest Africa, which splits the color
spectrum into five slices. Another is Rennell-Bellona,
a Polynesian language spoken on an atoll in the Solomon
Islands, which roughly divides the spectrum up into white,
dark, and red, where dark includes blue and green, and red
includes yellow and orange.[9]

The subsequent literature on the relationship between language, color, and culture is maddeningly inconclusive. One camp—the relativists—say that language influences or even shapes perception and that without a word for a color we don't see it as distinct. The universalists, following Berlin and Kay, believe that basic color categories are universal and rooted, somehow, in our biology. What we can say for sure is that the language of color is tricky. Children who can discern the difference between a triangle and a square with ease may still struggle differentiating pink from red or orange. We also know that not having a separate word for something does not mean we can't distinguish it. The Greeks, of course, could see colors perfectly; perhaps they just found them less interesting than we do.

Lead white
Ivory
Silver

Isabelline
Chalk
Beige

White

"For all these accumulated associations, with whatever
is sweet, and honorable, and sublime, there yet lurks
an elusive something in the innermost idea of this hue,
which strikes more of panic to the soul than that redness
which affrights in blood." So wrote Herman Melville
in the forty-second chapter of *Moby-Dick*. Entitled "The
Whiteness of the Whale," the passage is a veritable homily
on the troubling, bisected symbolism of this color.
Because of its link with light, white has laid deep roots
in the human psyche and, like anything divine, can
simultaneously inspire awe and instill terror in the
human heart.

Like the eponymous albino leviathan of Melville's
novel, white has an otherness to it. If colors were people,
it would be admired, but it probably wouldn't be popular:
it is just a little too exclusive, autocratic, and neurotic.
For a start, it's tricky to make. You can't reach it by mixing
together other colored paints, you have to begin with
a special white pigment. And anything you add to that
pigment will only take it in one direction: toward black.
This is due to the way our brains process light. The more
pigments there are in a mixture, the less light is reflected
back into our eyes, and the darker and sludgier it becomes.
Most children will, at some stage, try mixing all their
favorite paints together expecting to make an extra special
color. They will gather fire-engine red, sunny-sky blue,
and perhaps some Care Bear pastels and begin stirring.
That such a mixture results not in something beautiful
but in an irretrievably murky dark gray is one of life's
first hard truths.

Fortunately, artists have always had relatively easy
access to white thanks to one of the most popular pigments
known to man: lead white [page 43]. Pliny the Elder
described the process of making it in the first century,

and it continued to be the white of choice in art for
centuries, despite being highly toxic. In the eighteenth
century Guyton de Morveau, a chemist and politician,
was asked to find a safer alternative by the French
government. In 1782 he reported that a lab technician
by the name of Courtois was synthesizing a white called
zinc oxide at the Dijon Academy. But although it wasn't
toxic and didn't darken when exposed to sulfurous gases, it
was less opaque, dried slowly in oils, and, most important,
was about four times the price of lead white. It was also
brittle—the fine tracery of cracks in many paintings of the
era can be laid at its door. (Winsor & Newton did
introduce it as a watercolor pigment in 1834—under the
name Chinese White, to make it sound exotic—but it
didn't take off. Of 46 English watercolorists questioned in
1888, only 12 admitted to having used it.)[1] A third
metal-based white was more successful. Titanium white,
first mass-produced in 1916, was both brighter and more
opaque than its rivals, and by the end of the Second World
War it had conquered 80 percent of the market.[2] Now,
everything from the markings on tennis courts to pills and
toothpaste uses this sparkling pigment, while its older
sibling languishes on the sidelines.

White has long been intricately connected with money
and power. Fabrics, including wool and cotton, had to be
heavily processed in order to appear white. Only the very
wealthy, supported by battalions of staff, could afford to
keep the fresh lace and linen cuffs, ruffs and cravats worn in
the sixteenth, seventeenth, and eighteenth centuries pristine.
This connection still holds true. Someone wearing a snow-pale
winter coat telegraphs a subtle visual message: "I do not
need to take public transportation." In *Chromophobia*
David Batchelor describes going to the house of a rich art
collector that had been decorated entirely in the shade:

There is a kind of white that is more than white, and this was that kind of white. There is a kind of white that repels everything that is inferior to it, and that is almost everything... This white was aggressively white.[3]

As he points out later in the book, it is not shades of white that are the problem, but white in the abstract, because it is associated with tyrannical labels like "pure." Le Corbusier, for example, proclaimed in his 1925 book *L'art décoratif d'aujourd'hui* the Law of Ripolin: all interior walls should be whitewashed [page 52]. This, he argued, would act as a moral and spiritual cleansing for society.[4]

For many, however, white is seen as positive, or as having a transcendent, religious quality. It is the Chinese color of death and mourning. In the West and Japan, brides wear it because it is a color symbolic of sexual purity. The Holy Spirit has often been depicted descending onto benighted humanity as a white dove appearing in a rush of pallid golden light. In the early twentieth century, when Kazimir Malevich was completing his *White on White* series, he wrote:

[T]he blue of the sky has been defeated by the supremacist system, has been broken through and entered white, as the true, real conception of infinity, and thus liberated from the color background of the sky... Sail forth! The white, free chasm, infinity, is before us.[5]

High-end modernists and minimalists, from Tadao Ando, the famous Japanese architect, to Calvin Klein, to Jonathan Ive at Apple, have drawn on white's power and hauteur. (Steve Jobs was initially against the tide of white products that Ive began producing around the turn of the millennium. He eventually agreed to the signature headphones and keyboard in "Moon Gray" plastic.

We think of them as white; technically, however, they are very pale gray.)[6] And despite, or perhaps because, white so readily shows the dirt, it has also become associated with cleanliness. "White goods," tablecloths, and lab coats are all defiant in their spotless impracticality, daring users to even think about spilling anything. American dentists complain that in a quest for teeth that appear sparkling clean, customers are now asking for teeth to be bleached so unrealistically white that whole new teeth-whitening palettes have had to be produced.[7]

The foundations of the architectural idolization of white are built on a mistake. For centuries the bleached-bone color of classical Greek and Roman ruins provided the keystone for Western aesthetics. The inheritance of Andrea Palladio—the sixteenth-century Venetian architect who repopularized supposedly classical concepts—and his Palladian successors can be seen in every grand building in every major city in the West. It was not until the mid-nineteenth century that researchers discovered that classical statuary and buildings were usually brightly painted. Many Western aesthetes refused to believe it. The sculptor Auguste Rodin is said to have beaten his chest in sorrow and said: "I feel it here that they were never colored."[8]

Lead white

Today the tombs of the rulers of the Goguryeo region lie
inconveniently over the border between North Korea and
China. They were a tough people: the Goguryeo, one of
the Three Kingdoms of Korea, resisted the vast armies of
its northern neighbors to rule over the peninsula and some
of southern Manchuria from the first century B.C. until the
seventh century. But the occupant of Anak Tomb no. 3,
depicted in a giant portrait on the wall, doesn't look very
warlike at all. In the fine-lined mural, he sits cross-legged
in a litter wearing a dark robe decorated with bright red
ribbons, an outfit that precisely matches the litter's drapes.
His expression is benign to the point of looking slightly
tipsy: his lips curve up under a curlicue mustache and his
eyes are bright and a little unfocused. What is really
remarkable, though, is how fresh his image remains after
sixteen centuries in damp tomb air. The secret to his
longevity lies in the paint used by the artist as the base
layer to prime the cave wall: lead white.[1]

Lead white is a basic lead carbonate with a crystalline
molecular structure. It is thick, opaque, and heavy, and
there is strong evidence that it was being manufactured
in Anatolia from around 2300 B.C.[2] It has remained in
production the world over ever since, using roughly the
same method described by Pliny the Elder 2,000 years ago.
Strips of lead were placed in a compartment inside a
specially designed clay pot that was divided into two.
Vinegar was poured into the other half; then the pots were
surrounded with animal dung and placed inside a shed
with a tightly fitting door for 30 days. During that time,
a relatively simple chemical reaction would take place.
Fumes from the vinegar reacted with the lead to form
lead acetate; as the dung fermented it let off CO_2, which,
in turn, reacted with the acetate, turning it into carbonate
(a similar process is used when making verdigris [page 214]).

Lead white, continued.

After a month some poor soul was sent into the stench to fetch the pieces of lead, by now covered in a puff-pastry-like layer of white lead carbonate, which was ready to be powdered, formed into patties, and sold.

The resulting pigment was tremendously versatile. It was used in the enamel on ceramic dishes and bathroom fittings, in house paints and wallpapers, well into the twentieth century. Artists liked it because it was so opaque and adhered well to almost any surface, and, later, because it could work in oils (if the proportions of the mixture were right). It was also cheap—a key concern for any self-respecting artist. In 1471, when the well-known Florentine muralist Neri di Bicci was buying some pigments in his hometown, he paid two and a half times as much for a good azurite as for *verde azzurro* (probably malachite); *giallo tedesco* (lead-tin yellow, page 69) was one-tenth the price of the azurite; while lead white was a mere hundredth the cost.[3] Artists were so generous with their use of lead white that, today, when paintings are X-rayed, its dense outline can form a kind of skeleton within a painting, allowing technicians to see alterations and later additions.

Lead white, however, had a deadly flaw. Writing in the Royal Society's *Philosophical Transactions* journal in the winter of 1678, Sir Philibert Vernatti described the fate of those involved in the production of white lead:

The Accidents to the Workmen are, Immediate pain in the Stomack, with exceeding Contorsions in the Guts and Costiveness that yields not to Catharticks... It brings them also to acute Fevers, and great Asthma's or Shortness of Breath... Next, a Vertigo, or dizziness in the Head, with continual great pain in the Brows, Blindness, Stupidity; and Paralytick Affections; loss of appetite, Sickness and frequent Vomitings, generally of sincere Phlegm, sometimes mixed with Choler, to the extreamest weakning of the Body.[4]

Lead poisoning was not a newly witnessed phenomenon, either. Nicander, a Greek poet and physician, describing the symptoms in the early second century B.C., condemned "the hateful brew . . . whose fresh color is like milk which foams all over when you milk it rich in the springtime."

It wasn't just those grinding and producing the pigment that began showing the effects of lead poisoning. White lead had long been used as a cosmetic to make skin look smooth and pale. Xenophon wrote disapprovingly of women wearing a "plaster of ceruse (white lead) and minium (red lead)" [page 107] in Greece during the fourth century B.C., and there is evidence that their contemporaries in China were mixing a similar brew with rice powder to use as a foundation.[5] Japanese archaeologists and professors are still discussing the role that poisonous makeup may have played in undermining the Shogun regime, which collapsed after nearly 300 years in power in 1868. Some scholars argue that breast-feeding infants were ingesting lead worn by their mothers; bone samples show that the skeletons of children under the age of three contain over 50 times more lead than those of their parents.[6] Yet cosmetic ceruse or "Spirits of Saturn"— essentially a white-lead paste mixed with vinegar— remained alarmingly popular for centuries. While at least one sixteenth-century writer was already warning that it made the skin "withered and gray,"[7] women in Queen Elizabeth's court were painting blue veins over its parchment-pale base layer. In the nineteenth century ladies could still buy any number of lead-based skin brighteners with names like "Laird's Bloom of Youth," "Eugenie's Favorite," or "Ali Ahmed's Treasure of the Desert," even after well-publicized deaths, including that of the British society beauty Maria, the Countess of Coventry. Maria, a rather vain woman, who was known to be rather too

Lead white, continued.

heavy a user of white-lead foundation, died in 1760, aged just 27.[8]

The irony of generations of women slowly killing themselves in an effort to look their best is of the darkest kind. Lead white may have helped the painted occupant of the Goguryeo tomb remain fresh, but then he was already dead. The pigment has seldom been a friend to the living.

Ivory

In 1831, a farmer on the Isle of Lewis, in the Outer Hebrides, discovered treasure that had been hidden in a small stone chamber in a sandbank for 700 years. The hoard consisted of 78 chess pieces from different sets, 14 pieces for a game similar to backgammon, and a belt buckle.[1]

The Lewis Chessmen, as they are now known, are mysterious. No one knows who made them, or how they came to be hidden on an obscure island.

Each piece is a unique Romanesque sculpture, oozing expressive charm. One of the queens has a hand resting on her cheek, in dismay or in concentration; several of the rooks are biting their shields, and another looks nervously to the left, as if he's just heard an unexpected sound. Each figure sports a subtly different hairstyle, and their clothes hang in stylized rumpled folds. They look as though they could be conjured to life, and this is precisely what happened in their recent star turn as models for the wizards' chess set in the first Harry Potter film. They were probably carved from walrus ivory (called "fish teeth" in Icelandic sagas), in Trondheim in Norway between 1150 and 1200. And while traces remain of the red some of the pieces were originally painted with, the color has worn away to reveal the natural color of the ivory itself.[2]

Ivory, whether sourced from walruses, narwhals, or elephants, has long been prized. And when elephant hunts became a status symbol, ivory only grew in prestige. The color profited by association. Western wedding dresses were generally colorful until Queen Victoria wore ivory satin trimmed with British lace in 1840. Many brides eagerly followed suit. The September 1889 issue of *Harper's Bazaar* recommended "[i]vory white satin and lampas [a type of woven fabric] . . . for autumn weddings." Now it is more common than ever; the Sarah Burton–designed wedding dress worn by the Duchess of Cambridge was made of ivory duchess satin.

Ivory, continued.

Ivory itself was used for thousands of years to make costly decorative items, like the Lewis Chessmen, combs, and brush handles. Later it was used for piano keys, ornaments, and pool balls. Chinese craftsmen use it to make impossibly intricate sculptures, complete with trees, temples, and figures, which can sell for thousands of dollars. So fierce did demand become that by 1913 America alone was consuming around 200 tons of ivory annually. Because of their value, elephant tusks were called "white gold" and walrus tusks "Arctic gold."[3]

Demand for ivory took an inevitable toll on the animals supplying it. In 1800 there were an estimated 26 million elephants; before 1914 there were 10 million; by 1979, 1.3 million. A decade later, when the trade was finally banned in the West, 600,000 remained.[4]

Demand remains enormous, particularly in Thailand and China, although the latter has vowed to ban the trade of ivory entirely by the end of 2017. This ban, if effectively enforced, will have come in the nick of time. Illegal poaching is rife, and seems to be accelerating. It has been estimated that in the three years to 2014 around 100,000 elephants were killed for their ivory, and around 25,000 more tuskless carcasses are found each year. At this rate, the elephant could be extinct in the wild within a decade or so; walruses too are on the endangered species list.

A bizarre addition to the trade comes from an animal that became extinct nine thousand years before the Lewis Chessmen were carved. As the glaciers and icebergs melt across the Arctic tundra, woolly mammoth carcasses have emerged in the thousands. Exact figures are hard to come by—so much of the trade in ivory is conducted on the black market—but it has been estimated that over half of China's current supply of ivory may have come from woolly mammoth tusks. In 2015 a single carved tusk weighing 200 pounds was sold in Hong Kong for $3.5 million.

Silver

It is not unusual for mountains to attract legends, but few are as rich in lore as Cerro Rico de Potosí, a soaring red peak in Bolivia. It isn't its size that attracts attention—at just under 16,000 feet it is far from the largest mountain in the Andes—but what it contains. From root to summit, Cerro Rico is riddled with silver mines. According to tradition, its secret was discovered by a poor local man. While out searching for a lost llama in January 1545, Diego Huallpa built a fire to keep the chill of the alpine night at bay. As the fire burned, the ground beneath it began to ooze liquid silver, like blood from a wound.

Owing to its value as a precious metal, silver has long held an important position in human culture, and we have never stopped seeking it out and finding uses for it. In the twentieth century it was used to evoke the future, space travel, and progress. From the shiny, zipped-up suits of the "Mercury 7," the world's first space crew, to Paco Rabanne's metal minidresses and André Courrèges's foil fashion in the 1960s, it seemed that silver was the color we would all be wearing once we'd become accustomed to zero gravity.

But it has symbolic affiliations with old-fashioned superstitions as well as an imagined future. In Scottish folklore a silver branch, covered with white blossoms or bearing silver apples, could act as a kind of passport into the fairy otherworld.[1] The metal was also thought to be able to detect poisons, changing color if it came into contact with one. This belief became so widespread that silver tableware became fashionable and then the standard. The first recorded appearance of the silver bullet being used to dispatch the forces of evil is from the mid-seventeenth century, when the town of Greifswald in northeastern Germany became all but overrun with werewolves. As the population dwindled it seemed as if the

Silver, continued.

entire town might have to be abandoned, until a group of students made little musket balls from the precious metal. Silver is now firmly embedded in the semiotics of horror movies, effective against all manner of beings, from werewolves to vampires.[2]

Perhaps such superstitions stem from silver's link with the night. While its more illustrious sibling gold [page 86] is traditionally twinned with the sun, silver is equated with the moon. As a partnership this makes a great deal of sense. Silver also waxes and wanes in alternate cycles of polishing and tarnishing. One minute it is bright and reflective, the next it is eclipsed by a black film of silver sulfide. There is something in this imperfection that makes it more human: it seems to have a life cycle, and, just as we die, so its brilliance dies a little too.[3]

Although the metal occurs naturally—finding a piece glinting in the dirt must seem like finding a gift from the earth itself—it is more frequently mixed with other elements in subtly sheened ores and alloys, and must be extracted by smelting. In Egypt, silver beads and other small objects have been found that date back to the Neolithic era, and these became more common in the twentieth and nineteenth centuries B.C.[4] One Egyptian archaeological hoard contained 153 silver vessels, nearly 20 pounds of the metal in all.[5] It has been used ever since in jewelry, medals, decorative elements on clothes, and coins.

It was silver mined in South and Central America that allowed the Spanish Empire to flourish for nearly five hundred years. (The Spanish even named a country after it: Argentina's name is derived from the Latin *argentum*, meaning silvery.) Between the sixteenth and eighteenth centuries the conquistadors exported around 150,000 tons of the metal. This accounted for around 80 percent of the world's supply, and funded a series of wars and further

conquests, both colonial and against European rivals.
To extract silver ore from Cerro Rico, one of the two most
profitable mines in their empire, the Spanish exploited
indigenous labor. Using a version of the *mita* forced-labor
system the Inca had used to build temples and roads, the
Spanish insisted locals over the age of 18 put
in a year's work for subsistence wages. Accidents and
mercury poisoning were common. The Spanish boasted
that with the silver extracted from Cerro Rico, they
could have built a bridge across the Atlantic back to their
homeland, and still have had silver to carry across it.
For the locals, Cerro Rico had a rather different reputation.
To them, it was "the mountain that eats men."

Whitewash

In May 1894, fear swept through the narrow streets of
Hong Kong. Plague. The disease, in its third and final
grand pandemic, had been spreading sporadically through
mainland China for forty years before materializing on
the island.[1] There was no mistaking the symptoms: first,
flulike chills and fever, then headaches and muscle pain.
The tongue would swell and become covered with a pale
fur. The appetite would disappear. Vomiting and diarrhea—
often bloody—would swiftly follow, and, most tellingly,
smooth, painful swellings would develop in the lymph
nodes in the groin, neck, or armpits.[2] Death was common,
and agonizing.

With the precise cause and even the means of
transmission still unknown, those fighting the disease
despaired of stanching its course. Volunteers desperately
searched back alleys for bodies, tended the sick in swiftly
erected, camplike isolation hospitals, and began furiously
whitewashing the streets and houses in the infected areas.[3]

Whitewash is the cheapest of paints, made from
a mixture of lime (crushed and heated limestone) and
calcium chloride or salt, combined with water. In 1848,
when Britain was battling waves of influenza and typhus,
it was estimated that using it to paint a whole tenement,
inside and out, would cost seven pennies, five and a half
without labor.[4] Whitewash does the job, but not well:
it flakes and has to be reapplied each year, and if the
proportions of the constituent ingredients are not quite
right, it can transfer onto clothes. Its disinfectant qualities
mean that it has always been popular with dairy farmers,
who coat the interiors of their barns and sheds with it.
The saying "Too proud to whitewash and too poor to
paint," a phrase usually associated with poverty-riddled
Kentucky, gives a good impression of the medium's social
standing. Its literary star turn is as a foil for the cunning

of the eponymous hero of Mark Twain's *The Adventures of Tom Sawyer*, originally published in 1876. After Tom becomes very dirty in a fight, his Aunt Polly orders him to daub "[t]hirty yards of board fence nine feet high:"

Sighing he dipped his brush and passed it along the topmost plank; repeated the operation; did it again; compared the insignificant whitewashed streak with the far-reaching continent of unwhitewashed fence, and sat down on a tree-box discouraged.[5]

Tom, of course, manages to trick friends into finishing the job, but the symbolism of his punishment is telling.

Aunt Polly was not the first to use whitewash to retaliate against perceived sin. During the English Reformation, churches and parishioners used it to obscure colorful murals and altarpieces that depicted saints in ways they now deemed impious. (Over the years, as the paint wore thin, the faces began peeking through again.) This practice perhaps explains the origin of the phrase "to whitewash," which means to conceal unpleasant truths, usually political in nature.

For those engaged in fighting epidemics, though, blotting out the pestilence using a pail of milky, disinfectant lime must have been profoundly comforting, even ritualistic. Is it a coincidence that it was around this time that white coats were adopted by doctors, and would become a visual symbol of the medical profession?

Isabelline

Isabella Clara Eugenia was, by the standards of her day, exceedingly beautiful. Like her English near contemporary, Queen Elizabeth I, she was very pale, with fine, marmalade-colored hair, only the merest suggestion of the Hapsburg lip, and a high, wide forehead. She was also powerful, ruling a large tract of northern Europe called the Spanish Netherlands.[1] This makes it seem all the more unfair that her namesake in the color world is a dingy yellow-white. As the author of *A History of Handmade Lace* described it in 1900: "a grayish coffee color, or in plain English, the color of dirt."[2]

The story goes that in 1601 Isabella's husband, Archduke Albert VII of Austria, began the siege of Ostend. Isabella, believing the siege would be short-lived, vowed she would not change or wash her underwear until he won Isabelline is the color the queen's linens had become when the siege finally ended three years later.[3] Luckily for the poor queen, proof that this story is nonsense isn't difficult to find. The tale only appeared in print in the nineteenth century—an aeon in Chinese-whisper years— and two exculpatory dresses in the hue crop up in the wardrobe of Queen Elizabeth I. Inventories, one taken a year before the start of the siege, show she owned both an isabelline kirtell (a long dress or tunic; she had 126 in total) and a "rounde gowne of Isabella-color satten . . . set with silver spangles."[4]

Mud, however, sticks, so despite royal endorsement, the color's fashionable career was short-lived. But it has managed to carve out another niche in the natural sciences, particularly in descriptions of animals. Pale palomino horses and Himalayan brown bears are isabelline, and there are several species of bird, including the *Oenanthe isabellina* or isabelline wheatear, that owe their names to the color of their pale dun plumage.

"Isabellinism" is also the name of a genetic mutation that renders feathers that ought to be black, gray, or dark brown a pallid yellowish color instead. A handful of the king penguins on Marion Island in the Antarctic make up one prominent group of sufferers.[5] Among the huddled ranks on the island, the wan mutants are the highly visible odd men out, the weaklings, and anyone who has ever watched natural-history documentaries knows what usually happens to them. A dubious legacy indeed for the poor Archduchess Isabella.

Chalk

If you were to view a minute paint sample from an Old
Master painting under a microscope, you would likely
see something wholly unexpected and far older than the
paint itself: nannofossils, the ancient remains of one-celled
sea creatures called coccolithophores. How on earth did
they get there? Chalk.

Chalk is formed from marine ooze, largely consisting
of single-celled algae, that formed a sediment on the ocean
floor and was then compounded over millions of years to
create a soft, calcium carbonate rock.[1] There is a vast
deposit over the south and east of England—responsible
for the white cliffs of Dover—and northwestern Europe.
It is quarried in great blocks that are left to weather, which
helps to separate out any chips of flint. The stone is then
ground under water, washed, and left to settle in large vats.
When drained and dried, the chalk is separated into layers.
The top layer, the finest and whitest, is sold as Paris
white; the one beneath, slightly less fine, is extra gilder's
white. Both are used as artists' pigments. The coarsest
grade, used in cheaper paints and building materials, is sold
as commercial white.[2]

The chemist and colorist George Field was rather
sniffy about chalk. It is "used by the artist only as a crayon,"
he wrote in his *Chromatography* of 1835.[3] Others were
less supercilious. Arnold Houbraken, a Dutch artist and
biographer, wrote in 1718: "It is said that Rembrandt
once painted a picture in which the colors were so
heavily loaded that you could lift it from the floor by the
nose."[4] This was thanks to the chalk, which the artist used
to make his paints go further, to thicken them so that
they stood off the canvas, and to make glazing layers
more transparent—because it has a low refractive
index, chalk is almost completely translucent in oils.[5]
It was also frequently used as the base layer either by itself

or as part of a gesso mixture, a kind of plaster of Paris.[6] Although the grounds were hidden underneath the finished product, they helped ensure the artwork, particularly murals, did not degrade so fast the patron could demand his money back. The fifteenth-century writer Cennino Cennini dedicates many pages of his *Il libro dell'arte* to lovingly detailing the preparation of different grades of gesso. One, *gesso sottile*, took over a month of daily stirrings to prepare, but, as he assured his readers, the effort was well worth it: "it will come out as soft as silk."[7]

Even without such loving preparation, chalk has a long history of use in art. The Uffington White Horse, for example, is one of the stylized chalk figures created in Europe during the Late Bronze Age. It still prances high on a hillside on the edge of the Berkshire Downs in southern England. Amid fears that it might be used for target practice by the Luftwaffe, the horse was covered up during the Second World War. When the war was over, William Francis Grimes, a Welsh archaeology professor, was charged with disinterring it.[8] Grimes had believed, as many still do, that the figure was carved directly into the hillside. Instead he discovered that it had been painstakingly constructed by cutting shallow trenches and filling them with chalk. (This had actually been described in great detail by Daniel Defoe in the seventeenth century, but everyone had ignored him.)[9]

There is much that is still unknown about the White Horse. Why, for example, did the people who made it go to so much trouble to do so? And why, while so much else has changed, has it been "scoured," or cleaned and rechalked, by the local population at least once every generation in the intervening three millennia?[10] Microscopes may have revealed the preferred fundament of the Old Masters, but chalk still has hidden depths.

Beige

Dulux sells a Brobdingnagian array of paint colors to its nontrade customers. Beige lovers riffling through the thick color-card wads are in for a treat. If "Rope Swing," "Leather Satchel," "Evening Barley," or "Ancient Artifact" doesn't appeal, "Brushed Fossil," "Natural Hessian," "Trench Coat," "Nordic Sails," or any of several hundred others may well do. Those who are in a rush, however, and who don't want to trawl through lists of evocative names, may find themselves a little stuck: not one of these pale yellow-grays is actually called "beige."

Is this because the word, with its glutinous-voweled center, is unappealing? (Marketers have an ear for that kind of thing.) The word was loaned in the mid-nineteenth century from French, where it referred to a kind of cloth made from undyed sheep's wool. As has often happened, "beige" attached itself to the color too. It rarely seems to have incited strong passions. It was mentioned in *London Society* magazine as being in vogue in the late autumn of 1889, though this was only because it "combines pleasantly with the fashionable tones of brown and gold."[1] Nowadays it is rarely mentioned in fashion, having been cast aside by more glamorous synonyms.

It was the favorite tint of Elsie de Wolfe, the 1920s interior designer who is credited with inventing the profession. Upon seeing the Parthenon in Athens for the first time, she was enchanted, exclaiming: "It's beige! My color!" But while she was clearly not alone—it crops up in many of the twentieth century's key palettes—beige has chiefly been used as a foil for colors with more character.[2] When two scientists surveyed over 200,000 galaxies and discovered that the universe, taken as a whole, is a shade of beige, they immediately sought a sexier name. Suggestions included "big bang buff" and "skyvory," but in the end they settled on "cosmic latte."[3]

There is the nub of beige's image problem: it is unassuming and safe, but deeply dull. Anyone who has ever spent any time visiting rental properties soon comes to loathe it—a few hours in and all the properties seem to be merging together into a sea of determined inoffensiveness. A recent book about how best to sell your home goes so far as to advise against it completely. The chapter on color opens with a diatribe against its tyrannical hold over the property market. "It seems," the author concludes, "that somehow *beige* is interpreted as a *neutral*—an ambiguous color that everyone will like."[4] In fact the situation is even worse than that: the hope is not that everyone will *like* it, but that it won't *offend* anyone. It could be the concept-color of the bourgeoisie: conventional, sanctimonious, and materialistic. It seems strangely apposite, then, that beige has evolved from being sheep-colored to being the color adopted by the sheeplike. Is any other hue so redolent of our flock instincts for tasteful, bland consumerism? No wonder Dulux's color-namers wanted to shun it: beige is boring.

Blonde
Lead-tin yellow
Indian yellow
Acid yellow
Naples yellow
Chrome yellow
Gamboge
Orpiment
Imperial yellow
Gold

Yellow

Oscar Wilde was arrested outside the Cadogan Hotel in London in April 1895. The following day the *Westminster Gazette* ran the headline "Arrest of Oscar Wilde, Yellow Book Under His Arm." Wilde would be found officially guilty of gross indecency in court a little over a month later, by which time the court of public opinion had long since hanged him. What decent man would be seen openly walking the streets with a yellow book?

The sinful implications of such books had come from France, where, from the mid-nineteenth century, sensationalist literature had been not-so-chastely pressed between vivid yellow covers. Publishers adopted this as a useful marketing tool, and soon yellow-backed books could be bought cheaply at every railway station. As early as 1846 the American author Edgar Allan Poe was scornfully writing of the "eternal insignificance of yellow-backed pamphleteering." For others, the sunny covers were symbols of modernity and the aesthetic and decadent movements.[1] Yellow books show up in two of Vincent Van Gogh's paintings from the 1880s, *Still Life with Bible* and, heaped in invitingly disheveled piles, *Parisian Novels.* For Van Gogh and many other artists and thinkers of the time, the color itself came to stand as the symbol of the age and their rejection of repressed Victorian values. "The Boom in Yellow," an essay published in the late 1890s by Richard Le Gallienne, expends 2,000 words proselytizing on its behalf. "Till one comes to think of it," he writes, "one hardly realizes how many important and pleasant things in life are yellow." He was persuasive: the final decade of the nineteenth century later became known as the "Yellow Nineties."

Traditionalists were less impressed. These yellow books gave off a strong whiff of transgression, and the avant-garde did little to calm their fears (for them the transgression was half the point). In Wilde's *The Picture of Dorian Gray*, published in 1890, it is down the moral rabbit hole of such a novel that the eponymous antihero disappears, never to return. Just as the narrator reaches his defining ethical crossroads, a friend gives him a yellow-bound book, which opens his eyes to "the sins of the world," corrupting and ultimately destroying him. Capitalizing on the association, the scandalous, avant-garde periodical *The Yellow Book* was launched in April 1894.[2] Holbrook Jackson, a contemporary journalist, wrote that it "was newness in excelsis: novelty naked and unashamed . . . yellow became the color of the hour."[3] After Wilde's arrest a mob stormed the publishers' offices on Vigo Street, believing they were responsible for the "yellow book" mentioned by the *Gazette*.[4] In fact, Wilde had been carrying a copy of *Aphrodite* by Pierre Louÿs and had never even contributed to the publication. The magazine's art director and illustrator, Aubrey Beardsley, had barred Wilde after an argument—he responded by calling the periodical "dull," and "not yellow at all."

Wilde's conviction (and the failure soon after of *The Yellow Book*) was not the first time the color had been associated with contamination, and was far from the last. Artists, for example, had numerous difficulties with it. Two pigments they relied on, orpiment [page 82] and gamboge [page 80], were highly poisonous. It was assumed Naples yellow [page 76] came from Mount Vesuvius's sulfurous orifice well into the mid-twentieth century, and often turned black when used as a paint; gallstone yellow was made from ox gallstones, crushed and ground in gum water; and Indian yellow [page 71] was probably made from urine.[5]

In individuals, the color betokens illness: think of sallow skin, jaundice, or a bilious attack. When applied to mass phenomena or groups the connotations are worse still. Hitched to "journalism" it indicates rash sensationalism. The flow of immigrants into Europe and North America from the East and particularly China in the early twentieth century was dubbed the "yellow peril." Contemporary accounts and images showed an unsuspecting West engulfed by a subhuman horde—Jack London called them the "chattering yellow populace."[6] And while the star the Nazis forced Jews to wear is the most notorious example of yellow as a symbol of stigma, other marginalized groups had been forced to wear yellow clothes or signs from the early Middle Ages.

Perversely, though, yellow has simultaneously been a color of value and beauty. In the West, for example, blonde hair [page 67] has long been held up as the ideal. Economists have shown that pale-haired prostitutes can demand a premium, and there are far more blondes in advertisements than is representative of their distribution among the population at large. Although in China "yellow" printed materials like books and images are often pornographic, a particular egg-yolk shade [page 84] was the favored color of their emperors. A text from the beginning of the Tang dynasty (A.D. 618–907) expressly forbids "common people and officials" from wearing "clothes or accessories in reddish yellow," and royal palaces were marked out by their yellow roofs.[7] In India the color's power is more spiritual than temporal. It is symbolic of peace and knowledge, and is particularly associated with Krishna, who is generally depicted wearing a vivid yellow robe over his smoke-blue skin. The art historian and author B. N. Goswamy has described it as "the rich luminous color [that] holds things together, lifts the spirit and raises visions."[8]

It is perhaps in its metallic incarnation, however, that

yellow has been most coveted. Alchemists slaved for centuries to transmute other metals into gold, and recipes for counterfeiting the stuff are legion.[9] Places of worship have made use of both its seemingly eternal high sheen and its material worth to inspire awe among their congregations. Medieval and early modern craftsmen, known as goldbeaters, were required to hammer golden coins into sheets as fine as cobwebs, which could be used to gild the backgrounds of paintings, a highly specialized and costly business.

Although coinage has lost its link with the gold standard, awards and medals are still usually gold (or gold-plated), and the color's symbolic value has left its mark on language too: we talk of golden ages, golden boys and girls, and, in business, golden handshakes or goodbyes. In India, where gold is often part of dowries and has traditionally been used by the poor instead of a savings account, government attempts to stop people hoarding it have resulted in a healthy black market and an inventive line in smuggling. In November 2013, 24 gleaming bars, worth over $1 million, were found stuffed into an airplane toilet.[10] Le Gallienne noted in his essay that "yellow leads a roving, versatile life"—it is hard to disagree, even if this is probably not what the writer had in mind.

Blonde

Rosalie Duthé, the first person known as a dumb blonde,
was born in France in the mid-eighteenth century.
Famously beautiful, even as a child, she was sent to a
convent by her parents to keep her out of trouble. Before
long, however, she somehow caught the eye of a rich
English financier, the 3rd Earl of Egremont, and fled the
convent under his protection. When his money ran out
she became a courtesan as notorious for her stupidity as
for her willingness to pose for nude portraits. In June 1775
she found herself skewered at the Theatre de l'Ambigu in
Paris in a one-act satire called *Les Curiosités de la foire*.
After seeing the performance, Rosalie was so mortified
she is said to have offered a kiss to anyone who could
restore her honor, but no one did.[1]

Although probably more fact than fiction, the legend
of Rosalie illustrates the way that blondes, like most
minorities—it has been estimated just 2 percent of the
world's population is naturally blonde—are both reviled
and revered by society. In the mid-twentieth century,
Nazis held up the ideal of the blue-eyed, pale-haired Aryan
as the apogee of humanity. A chilling exhibit in the
Stadtmuseum in Munich contains a hair-color chart,
employed in one of the tests designed to help identify those
with the Aryan physical characteristics the Führer wanted
to propagate in his master race.

Blondes, particularly women, are often associated with
lust. In ancient Greece, high-class prostitutes—*hetairai*—
bleached their hair using noxious mixtures like potash
water and the juice of yellow flowers.[2] Roman prostitutes
were also said to dye their hair pale or wear blonde wigs.[3]
More recently, a 2014 survey of the prices that female
prostitutes charged per hour worldwide showed that those
with natural, or natural-looking, blonde hair could
command far more than those with any other hair color.[4]

Blonde, continued.

In paintings of the Fall, Eve, the Bible's original sinner, is more often than not depicted with flowing golden locks that conceal nothing; her counterpoint, the Virgin Mary, is usually a brunette, swaddled from throat to toe in rich fabric [page 184]. John Milton drew heavily on this symbolism in *Paradise Lost*, published in 1667. Eve's "unadornèd golden tresses" lie in "wanton ringlets," echoing the coils of the serpent lying in wait nearby.

Anita Loos, an American scriptwriter born in 1889, wasn't a fan of blondes either. It was a blonde who had stolen the journalist and intellectual H. L. Mencken from under her nose. Her revenge came in the form of a magazine column, which became a novel in 1925, then a stage show, and finally the film starring Marilyn Monroe in 1953. The plot is simple: eye-catching Lorelei Lee, antiheroine of *Gentlemen Prefer Blondes*, blunders from one millionaire to the next. Although she is no fool when it comes to financial gain—"I can be smart when it's important," she says, eyeing up a diamond tiara—she is decidedly birdbrained when it comes to everything else. On board the boat to Europe, she seems uninformed about the birds and the bees: "Most of the sailors seem to have orphans which they get from going on the ocean when the sea is very rough."[5]

Goddesses, fairy-tale heroes and heroines, and models are disproportionately fair-haired. Blonde waitresses have been shown to get bigger tips.[6] And for those not lucky enough to have been born with the requisite A (adenine) in place of a G (guanine) in chromosome 12, there is always hair dye.[7] As the coiffed lady from Clairol's 1960s hair advertisements said, "If I have only one life, let me live it as a blonde."

Lead-tin yellow

There are many art world mysteries: the identity of
Vermeer's *Girl with the Pearl Earring*; the whereabouts
of Caravaggio's *Nativity with St. Francis and St. Lawrence*
[page 250]; who pulled off the 1990 Isabella Stewart
Gardner Museum heist, to name but a few. One that
has attracted little popular attention, and has yet to be
completely solved, is the curious case of the yellow that
vanished.

Peter Paul Rubens and Isabella Brant were married
in St. Michael's Abbey in Antwerp on October 3, 1609.
Isabella was the daughter of Jan Brant, an important
citizen; Rubens had just returned from a fruitful eight-year
stay in Italy, honing his skill as an artist. He had a large
workshop in Antwerp, and had just been appointed as
a court painter. The double portrait Rubens painted of
himself and his new wife brims with love and confidence.
Isabella wears a dashing straw hat, a large ruff, and a long
stomacher embroidered with yellow flowers; Rubens—
his right hand clasping his wife's, his left fingering the hilt
of a sword—wears a rich doublet with sleeves of yellow
and blue shot silk, and a slightly whimsical pair of
grapefruit-colored hose. The pigment Rubens used for all
these symbolic golden-yellow touches was lead-tin yellow.[1]

He was far from alone in his reliance on this color:
it was the key yellow from the fifteenth to the mid-
eighteenth century. It first crops up around 1300, later
appearing in Florence in paintings ascribed to Giotto, and
then in the works of Titian, Tintoretto, and Rembrandt.[2]
From around 1750, however, and for no obvious reason,
use of the pigment began to peter out, and it doesn't
appear at all in nineteenth- or twentieth-century works.
More intriguing still, before 1941 no one even knew that
it existed.[3]

Part of the reason for this is that the pigment we now

Lead-tin yellow, continued.

call lead-tin yellow wasn't known by any one name.
To Italians, it was usually known as *giallorino* or *giallolino*;
in northern European sources it was at times known as
massicot, at others *genuli* or *plygal*.[4] Perplexingly, these
terms were also sometimes used for other pigments, like
Naples yellow [page 76]. To add to the confusion, another
lead-based yellow, lead oxide (PbO), was also known as
massicot.[5] Another reason it slipped beneath art historians'
radars for so long is that, until the twentieth century, the
tests available to restorers and researchers did not allow
them to identify all the ingredients in a paint. If they found
lead in a yellow paint they assumed it was Naples yellow.

We owe our knowledge of lead-tin yellow's existence
to Richard Jacobi, a researcher in the Doerner-Institute
in Munich. While doing some research in around 1940,
he repeatedly found tin in yellow samples from various
paintings.[6] Intrigued, he began experimenting to see if
he could create this mysterious yellow pigment himself.
He found that by heating three parts of lead monoxide
with one part tin dioxide a yellow began to form.[7] If the
mixture was heated between 1,202 and 1,292°F the
compound produced was more ruddy; between 1,328
and 1,472°F it was more lemony. The end product was
a heavy yellow powder, very opaque in oils and stable,
unaffected by exposure to light. As an added bonus it was,
like lead white [page 43], both cheap to produce and
accelerated the drying of oil paint.[8] When Jacobi published
his findings in 1941 the art world was dumbfounded.
As with all good riddles, however, many questions remain.
How and why was the secret of its manufacture lost?
Why did artists begin using Naples yellow instead, which
even its admirers admitted had many flaws? Answers
remain elusive, but that this was the yellow of the Old
Masters is beyond doubt.

Indian yellow

For all its sunny brightness, Indian yellow has an obscure history. Although many Indian painters, particularly from the Rajasthani and Pahari traditions, used this pigment in the seventeenth and eighteenth centuries, no one is quite sure where it came from or why its use died out.[1] For Westerners, this pigment, like gamboge [page 80], which it closely resembled, was a product of trade and empire.[2] It began making its way to Europe from the East in the late 1700s, in the form of powdery balls of a rotten mustard color, with yolk-bright centers and a distinctive telltale reek of ammonia. So strong was its scent that recipients—colormen like George Field and Messrs. Winsor and Newton—would have been able to guess the contents of the packages the moment they began unwrapping them.

While the French colorman Jean François Léonor Mérimée admitted that the odor was very much like that of urine, he stopped short of making a definitive connection.[3] Others were less delicate. *The New Pocket Cyclopædia* of 1813 ventured that it "[is] said to be an animal secretion."[4] An acquaintance of the English artist Roger Dewhurst told him in the 1780s that Indian yellow was possibly made from animals' piss and strongly advised that the pigment be diligently washed before use.[5] George Field was less circumspect: "[It] is produced from the urine of the camel." But even he wasn't completely sure: "It has also been ascribed, in like manner, to the buffalo, or Indian cow."[6] In the 1880s Sir Joseph Hooker, the great peppery Victorian explorer and botanist, decided he needed a more definite answer to the riddle of Indian yellow and its peculiar smell. Busily engaged as he was in his role as director of Kew Gardens, Hooker decided to make inquiries.

On January 31, 1883, he dispatched a letter to the India

Office. Nine and a half months later, by which time
Hooker had no doubt forgotten all about the obscure
pigment, he received a reply.[7] Half a world away
Trailokyanath Mukharji, a 36-year-old civil servant,
had seen Hooker's letter and taken decisive action.
"Indian yellow" or *piuri*, Mr. Mukharji informed Hooker,
was used in India to paint walls, houses, and railings and,
very occasionally, to dye clothes (although the smell
prevented this latter use from catching on).[8] He tracked
the mysterious yellow balls to what he said was their sole
point of origin: Mirzapur, a tiny suburb of Monghyr,
a town in Bengal. There, a small group of *gwalas*
(milkmen) tended a herd of ill-nourished cows they fed
only on mango leaves and water. On this diet the cows
produced extraordinarily luminous yellow urine—about
three quarts per day per cow—which the *gwalas*
collected in small earthen pots. Each night they boiled
this down, strained it, and rolled the sediment into balls
that were gently toasted over a fire and then left to dry
out in the sun.[9]

Hooker forwarded Mr. Mukharji's letter to the Royal
Society of Arts, who published it in their journal the very
same month—but the mystery refused to remain solved.
Shortly afterward, the pigment vanished altogether, and,
while it was believed that the practice had been outlawed,
no record of such laws could be found. Stranger still,
contemporary surveys of the region by British officials,
detailed enough to note the number of adult cows and
the havoc wreaked by syphilis in the nearby town of
Shaikpoora, made no mention of these valuable cows or
the yellow balls made from the contents of their bladders.[10]
Victoria Finlay, a British writer, decided to retrace Mr.
Mukharji's footsteps in 2002 only to draw another blank.
None of Mirzapur's modern denizens—including the

local *gwalas*—had the slightest clue what *piuri* was. Perhaps, Finlay mused, Mukharji had been a nationalist, wanting to gently poke fun at the gullible Brits.[11]

This seems unlikely. Mr. Mukharji worked for the Department of Revenue and Agriculture, which, despite its stuffy name, was comparatively progressive in relying on and promoting local Indian professionals. A few months before writing his letter to Hooker he had produced the catalog for the 1883 Amsterdam Exhibition, and he was to do the same for the 1886 Colonial and Indian Exhibition and another held two years later in Glasgow.[12] He also became the assistant curator in the Art and Economics section of London's Indian Museum and, in 1887, donated a collection of nearly one thousand different minerals and botanical samples to the National Museum of Victoria in Australia. He even presented a copy of his book, *A Visit to Europe*, to Queen Victoria in 1889—hardly the actions of a hardened nationalist. It may be that even as he wrote up his account of the poor cows and the brilliant yellow pigment made from their urine, he had an inkling that he might not be believed. Perhaps this is why he sent his report off to Sir Joseph with some corroborating evidence: some balls of pigment he had bought from the *gwalas*, an earthen pot, some mango leaves, and a sample of the urine itself, all of which arrived on November 22, 1883. While the urine, pot, and leaves have vanished, the pigment, still faintly malodorous, remains in Kew's archive to this day.

Acid yellow

In 2015 the *Oxford English Dictionary* announced that its word of the year was not, in fact, a word, but an emoji: "face with tears of joy." The same year Unicode, an organization that ensures texts (and emojis) are represented consistently across different platforms, announced that people had been using many of these little yellow faces incorrectly for years. The one with a double jet of steam coming out of its nose, for example, commonly used to express fury, was intended to appear triumphant. And Unicode 1F633 ("Flushed Face") was used differently depending on the system: Apple users used it to signal alarm, while the Microsoft version looked "happy go lucky, but with sheepish eyes."[1]

One that seemingly needed no clarification, though, was the original smiley. The origins of the crude design—a perfect bright yellow circle outlined with black, two small lines for eyes, and a semicircular mouth—are contested. A crude smiley appeared in an American television program in 1963; two brothers based in Philadelphia printed a similar design on badges, some 50 million of which had been sold by 1972. But during the political upheavals of the 1970s, the childlike smiley was co-opted as a symbol of subversion. By 1988 it was a pop-culture phenomenon, inextricably linked with music and the new club scene. A yellow smiley was used on the UK cover for the Talking Heads' song "Psycho Killer," on "Beat Dis" by Bomb the Bass, on an iconic flyer for London's Shroom club, and later—with crosses for eyes and a squirming mouth—as an informal logo for the band Nirvana.[2] A blood-spattered version was also the primary visual motif of *Watchmen*, the 1985 dystopian graphic novel by Alan Moore and Dave Gibbons.

Soon the acid yellow of the smiley seeped out to become the signature color of the dance-happy youth, euphoric one moment, insidious, chemical, and rebellious the next. Rave culture—or rather the drugs that were believed to fuel it—began to cause moral panic. "Acid" could refer both to the subgenre of house music and to LSD, while this bright yellow also evoked the laser light shows of nightclubs.

Although rave culture has come down from its pre-millennial high, its informal mascot, the seemingly benign acid yellow smiley face, beams on. For a new generation it signals something very different. It is believed that the first emoticon smiley appeared in a bone-dry email about humor from Scott E. Fahlman, a research professor at Carnegie Mellon, sent in 1982: "I propose . . . the following character sequence for joke markers :-)."[3] From such inauspicious beginnings the emoticon smiley has become intrinsic to modern communication, its subversive traces, for the moment, forgotten.

Naples yellow

Sometime in the early 1970s a collection of 90 small
bottles was discovered in an old German pharmacy near
Darmstadt. Some were as round and plain as jam jars,
others looked like inkwells, and some resembled tiny,
stoppered perfume bottles. Each had its own carefully
written calligraphy label, but even so it was hard to identify
what each contained. The powders, liquids, and resins
were labeled with words as unfamiliar and outlandish
as "Virid aëris," "Cudbeard Persia," and "Gummi gutta."[1]
When examined in a laboratory in Amsterdam, it was
discovered that this was in fact a cache of pigments
from the nineteenth century. One, bearing the cramped
legend "Neapelgelb Neopolitanische Gelb Verbidung dis
Spießglaz, Bleies," was Naples yellow.[2]

The pigment's owner did not yet know it, but at the
time that it had been stashed, Naples yellow's days as
an essential part of the artist's palette were numbered.
The name properly applies to a synthetic preparation
of lead antimonate,[3] which is usually pale yellow with
just a suggestion of warm red undertones. The earliest
use of the term is thought to be in a Latin fresco treatise
written between 1693 and 1700 by Andrea Pozzo, an
Italian Jesuit brother and baroque painter. He mentions
a yellow pigment, "*luteolum Napolitanum*," and either the
name stuck or it was already in common use. References
to *giollolino di Napoli* appear more frequently from the
beginning of the eighteenth century and the term soon
made its way into English.[4]

Although beloved for its color, and better behaved
than chrome yellow [page 78], Naples yellow was far from
being the most stable pigment. George Field approvingly
mentioned its "considerable reputation," opacity, and
"pleasing, light, warm, yellow tint," but was forced to
admit that it had major drawbacks. Not only was it "liable

to change even to blackness by damp and impure air" if incorrectly glazed; care also needed to be taken to ensure that no iron or steel implements came into contact with it. Field suggested using a spatula of ivory or horn instead.[5]

Part of the pigment's appeal was that, like the bottles discovered in the German pharmacy, no one was quite sure where it came from. Many—including Field, writing in 1835, and Salvador Dalí, writing in 1948—suggested that it was mined from Mount Vesuvius. In fact lead antimonate is one of the oldest synthetic pigments. (The ancient Egyptians manufactured it, a process that required a good deal of skill and specialized knowledge, since the principal ingredients—lead oxide and antimony oxide—also had to be chemically produced.)[6] Another, more practical reason for its popularity was that, with the exception of the yellow iron ochers, which even at their best tended to be a little dull and brownish, there were no yellow pigments that were completely reliable until the twentieth century. Naples yellow was one of the best of a bad bunch and, notwithstanding its drawbacks, remained indispensable for many artists. In 1904 the post-impressionist Paul Cézanne, upon seeing a fellow artist's palette bereft of this pigment, was thunderstruck. "You paint with just these?" he cried. "Where is your Naples yellow?"[7]

Chrome yellow

The baking late summer of 1888 was the happiest of
Vincent Van Gogh's life. He was in the "Yellow House"
in Arles in the south of France, eagerly awaiting the arrival
of his hero, Paul Gauguin. Van Gogh hoped that together
they would found an artists' commune in Arles and he was,
for once, optimistic about the future.[1]

He wrote to his brother Theo on Tuesday, August 21,
to say that he had received a note from Gauguin to the
effect that he was "ready to come to the south as soon as
chance permits," and Van Gogh wanted everything to be
perfect. He began working on a series of sunflower
paintings, with which he planned to cover his whole studio.
He told Theo he was painting them "with the gusto of a
Marseillais eating bouillabaisse," and he hoped they would
be a symphony of "harsh or broken yellows" and blues,
"from the palest Veronese to royal blue, framed with thin
lathes painted in orange lead." The only thing slowing him
down, it seemed, was nature itself. He found he could
only work in the early morning, "[b]ecause the flowers
wilt quickly and it's a matter of doing the whole thing in
one go."[2]

While the avant-garde artists of the day had access
to wonderfully saturated reds and blues, they were lacking
an equivalent for the third primary: yellow. Without this,
they believed, they would be unable to create balanced
compositions, or create sufficiently bright pairings of
complementary colors, which impressionist art relied
upon for its drama. Chrome yellow arrived none too soon
and Van Gogh was one of many to fall hard for it. It owed
its genesis to the discovery in 1762 of a scarlet-orange
crystal in the Beresof gold mine in deepest Siberia.[3] The
mineral, called crocoite (from the Greek word for saffron,
krokos [page 98]) by the scientists who discovered it and
plomb rouge de Sibérie (Siberian red lead) by the French,

wasn't much use as a pigment—the supply was too
irregular and the price too high. However, the French
chemist Nicolas Louis Vauquelin began working on
crocoite and soon discovered that the orange stone
contained a new element.[4] It was a metal, which he named
chrome or chromium, after another Greek word meaning
"color," because its salts seemed to come in an
extraordinary variety of hues. Basic lead chromate, for
example, could range from lemon yellow to "a yellowish-red
or sometimes a beautiful deep red," depending on the
method used to make it.[5] In 1804 Vauquelin suggested
that these might make useful pigments; by 1809 they were
already on artists' palettes.

Sadly for artists and art lovers alike, chrome yellow
has a nasty habit of browning as it ages. Research carried
out on Van Gogh's paintings in Amsterdam over the past
few years has shown that some of the chrome yellow in the
flowers' petals has darkened significantly, due to the
reaction of chrome yellow with other pigments in sunlight.[6]
Van Gogh's sunflowers, it seems, are wilting, just as their
real-life counterparts did.

Gamboge

When William Winsor and Henry C. Newton first started
selling artists' pigments from a small shop at 38 Rathbone
Place in London in 1832, gamboge, one of their principal
pigments, would have arrived in regular packages from
the offices of the East India Company. Each package
contained a few thin cylinders, about the circumference
of a quarter and the color of old earwax, wrapped in
leaves.[1] Winsor & Newton's workers would have broken
up these pipelike lumps using a metal anvil and a hammer.
Once crushed, the pigment would be made up into small,
brownish cakes. Experienced artists, though, would have
been in on the secret: when touched with a drop of water,
these toffee-brown blocks yielded a yellow paint so bright
and luminous it almost seemed fluorescent.

Although by this time gamboge had been a fixture
on palettes for two centuries—the East India Company first
imported it in 1615—little was known of its origins.[2]
In his 1835 treatise on pigments, George Field waxed
evasive: "[It] is brought principally, it is said, from Cambaja
in India, and is, we are told, the produce of several trees."[3]
He was right about the trees. Gamboge is the solidified sap
of *Garcinia* trees, and comes principally from Cambodia—
or Camboja, as it was once known, which is how Gamboge
got its name.[4] Milking the trees requires patience. When
they are at least a decade old, deep gouges can be cut
into their trunks. Hollow lengths of bamboo are used to
catch the sap as it trickles out. It takes over a year for the
bamboo to fill up and the sap to harden. When some
unprocessed resinous clots were broken open during the rule
of the Khmer Rouge, it was discovered that they contained
stray bullets, trapped like ancient insects in amber.

Artists in Japan, China, and India had used it on scroll
paintings, illustrated capitals, and ancient miniatures for
centuries, but when the pigment first made its way into

Europe—in the hull of a Dutch trading galley in 1603—
color-starved Western painters fell hungrily on the
new sun-bright yellow.[5] Rembrandt favored it in oils,
where it took on the golden hue that often haloes the
figures in his paintings.[6] It has also been found in the
work and palettes of J. M. W. Turner and Sir Joshua
Reynolds.[7] William Hooker, the Royal Horticultural
Society's botanical artist, mixed it with a little Prussian
blue to produce Hooker's green: the perfect color for
painting leaves.[8]

Like many early pigments, gamboge was as at home
on the shelves of the apothecary as on an artist's palette.
In a lecture given on March 7, 1836, Dr. Robert Christison,
MD, described it as "an excellent and powerful purgative."
Just a small amount could produce "profuse watery
discharges"; larger doses could be fatal.[9] Workers who
crushed gamboge at Winsor & Newton would have to
rush to the toilet once an hour while working with it. It is
hardly an illustrious side effect for a pigment, yet perhaps it
was the scientific community's familiarity with gamboge
that led French physicist Jean Perrin to use it in 1908 in
his experiments to prove the theory of Brownian motion,[10]
an idea Einstein posited three years earlier. Using tiny
puddles of gamboge solution, just 0.005 in. deep, Perrin
showed that, even days after being left untouched, the little
yellow particles still jiggled around as if they were alive.
He was awarded the Nobel Prize in Physics in 1926.[11]
By this time gamboge had mostly been replaced in artists'
palettes by aureolin, an artificial yellow that, though
slightly less bright and translucent, was less prone to fading.
Winsor & Newton continued to receive packages of raw
gamboge until 2005, when the company finally stopped
selling it; a great relief, no doubt, for the workers, if not
for the artists.

Orpiment

In his *Il Libro dell'arte*, Cennino Cennini writes that
orpiment is "made by alchemy."[1] It is true that by the early
Renaissance most of the pigment that artists were using
was manufactured, but orpiment is actually a naturally
occurring mineral: a canary-yellow sulfide of arsenic
(As_2S_3) that is around 60 percent arsenic.[2]

In its glittering natural form, which was thought to
resemble gold, it was one of the mineral pigments (like
azurite and the green copper ore malachite) and one of
two yellows, along with ocher, used in ancient Egyptian
art. It appears on papyrus scrolls and decorates the walls
of Tutankhamen's tomb, where a small bag of it was
discovered on the floor.[3] The intense yellow can also be
found illuminating the ninth-century *Book of Kells*, the
walls of the Taj Mahal, and the medieval text the *Mappae
clavicula*. The Romans, who called it *auripigmentum*,
"golden," were much enamored with it too. As well as
using orpiment as a pigment, they believed gold could
be extracted from it using a mysterious method. Pliny
recounts a story about the emperor Caligula, who, greedy
for riches, smelted a vast quantity of raw orpiment, with
little success. Not only were such experiments futile—
orpiment does not really contain any trace of the precious
metal—it could also prove fatal for the slaves who mined it.

Cennini warned his readers: "Beware of soiling your
mouth with it, lest you suffer personal injury."[4] In fact,
orpiment is deadly. Although it was occasionally taken
in minute amounts as a purgative in Java, Bali, and China,
where it occurs naturally and was popular as a pigment
until the nineteenth century, the risks of abusing it were
well known.[5] A delightfully named German merchant
called Georg Eberhard Rumphius recalled seeing a woman
who had taken too much in Batavia (now Jakarta), in 1660,
in his book *The Ambonese Curiosity Cabinet*.

She had become mad, "and climbed up the walls like a cat."[6]

Even as a paint orpiment was not without its drawbacks. It dried badly in oils and could not be used in frescoes. It also reacted with a host of other pigments, particularly those that contained copper or lead. Prudent artists could make use of it, as the Venice-based Renaissance colorist Paolo Veronese did in his *The Dream of St. Helena* (c. 1570), only if they made sure it was carefully removed from other pigments it might discolor.[7] Orpiment really had only one thing going for it: its color. It was, in the words of Cennini, "a handsome yellow more closely resembling gold than any other color."[8] And that, it seems, was enough.

Imperial yellow

Katharine Augusta Carl probably thought of herself as imperturbable: she was born in New Orleans two months before the end of the Civil War, and unrest had seasoned her childhood. Thereafter she had been a wanderer, first leaving America to study art in Paris and later traveling through Europe and the Middle East. It was on a visit to China, though, that a life-defining opportunity presented itself when she was asked to paint the portrait of the empress dowager Cixi, the feared former concubine who had ruled China for over 40 years. This was how Katharine found herself, just before 11 a.m. on August 5, 1903, standing in the throne room in the heart of the Forbidden City, contemplating the world's most powerful woman.[1]

Heightening the sense of intimidation was the liberal use of the red-gold yellow fiercely reserved for royalty. While most Chinese roof tiles, for example, were gray, those of the royal palaces were golden.[2] Cixi's gown was of imperial yellow silk. Stiffly brocaded with wisteria and decorated with strings of pear-shaped pearls and tassels, it seemed more to encase than clothe her. Her right hand, with its clawlike two-inch nail protectors, lay in her lap. At precisely 11 a.m., the time the royal augurs had prescribed as the most auspicious for portrait painting, each of the 85 clocks in the throne room began to chime simultaneously; shakily, Katharine reached forward and began to sketch the empress's likeness.[3]

In China even regular yellow had been special for over a thousand years. Together with red, blue-green, black, and white, it was one of the five colors of the five-element theory. Each color corresponded with a season, direction, element, planet, and animal. Yellow was allied with the element of earth—an ancient Chinese saying is "The sky is blackish blue and the earth is yellow"—the center, Saturn, late or long summer, and the dragon.

The *Chur Qiu Fan Lu* (*Rich Dew of the Spring and Autumn Annals*), written sometime in the second century B.C., describes yellow as "the color of rulers." They soon began to jealously guard its use, particularly this one shade: the first law that mentions it was passed in A.D. 618 at the very beginning of the Tang dynasty. "Common people and officials," it read, "are forbidden to wear clothes or accessories in reddish yellow."[4]

Even by ancient standards, the dyeing method was labor-intensive. The key ingredient was the *Rehmannia glutinosa*, or Chinese foxglove, a plant with trumpet-shaped flowers and roots that look like elongated golden beetroot. To achieve the precise color desired, the tubers were harvested at the end of the eighth lunar month, and then pounded by hand into a smooth paste. It took around 1.7 quarts of root paste to dye a 50-square-foot piece of silk.[5] The mordant, a substance that helps a color bite into a fabric so it doesn't wash away, had to be made from the ashes of oak, mulberry, or beach wormwood; the cauldron had to be rustproof; each piece of silk went through two slightly different dyeing vats.

Although neither woman in the throne room knew it, imperial yellow's days were numbered. Its prestige had begun to wane during the previous decades. Initially reserved for royals, it was first granted to household bodyguards and, in a few instances, as an honor to commoners. In one scandalous instance, the empress herself had rewarded a humble train driver with an imperial yellow jacket. Just a few short years after Katharine painted China's last empress, the Xinhai Revolution would topple the Qing dynasty, China's last. With the fall of imperial power, the talismanic color was shorn of the symbolic significance it had possessed for a millennium.

Gold

Anyone who requires proof that gold is the color of desire
need only see the portrait of Adele Bloch-Bauer,
immortalized by Gustav Klimt in 1907. It is so ardent and
adoring that when it first arrived at the Belvedere Palace
gallery in Vienna, people speculated that subject and
painter were having an affair. While proof of a liaison has
never emerged, there is no doubt that the painting is an
expression of reverence. In the work, the last of Klimt's
"Golden Phase," Adele sits in a field of the precious metal,
some of it plain and flat, some worked into a pattern of
symbols and tessellations. Her dress is also a complex swirl
of gold. Only the hands, hair, and face—lips slightly
parted, eyes intense—portray a living, breathing woman;
the setting and clothing are those of a goddess.

Gold has always been both the color of reverence and
revered itself. Part of its allure lies in the mineral's scarcity
and uneven distribution. Although mines have been
discovered all over the world, gold rushes mean that they
are quickly exhausted and abandoned in favor of those
that have been newly uncovered. Europe has relatively
few gold deposits and has historically relied on gold traded
from Africa and the East.[1] The Carthaginians, whose
empire ringed the Mediterranean in the millennia before
the birth of Christ, were for many years the principal
conduit for African gold into Europe, a right that they
defended vigorously.[2] (Even their supplies, though, were
limited. After a serious military defeat in 202 B.C. they
were unable to pay reparations in gold. Instead they paid
in silver—a little under 360 tons over the next 50 years.)[3]

Gold has also been used to inspire awe. When the pious
Mansa Musa, the emperor of Mali, traveled through Cairo
on his pilgrimage to Mecca in 1324, European and Arabic
traders saw for themselves the glittering wealth of the
African continent. The emperor traveled with a caravan of

60,000 men; 500 slaves walked before him, each carrying
a gold staff weighing four pounds; his baggage train of 80
camels carried another 300 pounds of gold. His legendary
journey and generosity left the price of gold in the region
artificially low for over a decade.[4]

Cloth of gold—fabric woven from threads with a core
of silk or linen wrapped in gold—had been around since
Roman times and was beloved by European royalty.
The famous meeting in 1520 of Europe's two youngest,
lustiest, and most glittering monarchs, Kings Henry VIII
of England and Francis I of France, is known as the Field
of the Cloth of Gold, after the pair vied to outdo each other
with the splendor of their retinues. Henry arguably won:
his marquee was made entirely from golden cloth.

Like its sister metals iron, copper, and silver, gold has
a structure that contains mobile electrons that strongly
reflect light. It is this that gives these metals their
distinctive sheen.[5] Gold's rich glimmer, coupled with its
resistance to tarnishing, makes it an easy emblem for
divinity. The medieval Christian Church binged on the
metal. The Uffizi Gallery in Florence, for example, has a
room dedicated to three vast altarpieces, all depicting the
Virgin and Child. The last of the three, created by Giotto
around 1310, was painted for the Ognissanti Chapel, a few
blocks upriver from the gallery. Just as in the other
altarpieces, Giotto's figures are not shown in a room or
landscape but lie on a smooth golden ground. The frame
too is gold, as are the saints' halos (the halos of the saints
in front obscure the faces of those behind them, a great
scandal at the time because it was thought to be impious)
and the decorative border on the Virgin's deep blue robe.

Gilding such panels was painstaking work. The gold
came in gossamer-thin sheets, each about 11.5 inches square,
which had been hammered from coins; a good goldbeater

Gold, continued.

could pound as many as a hundred leaves from a single ducat. Each leaf would be taken up with tweezers and pressed onto the panel, molding, or frame. The sheets were so thin that almost any glue could be used—honey, gum arabic, and glair, made from egg white, were all popular. At this point the gold would still be a bit dull, its sheen unfocused by imperfections underneath; to really shine it had to be burnished. Cennini recommends using either hematite [page 150] (probably because of the medieval association between red and gold), a precious stone like a sapphire or an emerald ("the choicer the stone, the better it is"), or the tooth of a lion, wolf, dog, or "any animal which feeds decently upon flesh."[6]

Objects, when rendered in flat gold leaf, do not look real; the light falls across them evenly rather than glinting white off the highlights and falling blackly into the shadowed areas as it would do naturally. Artists used gold not for realistic effect, but because of its intrinsic value, and even once Renaissance artists began placing their figures in more natural settings and mastering perspective, they still liked to make use of rich gold paint.[7] It could indicate wealth if used to pick out decorative trimmings in rich fabrics, or it could represent divinity. In *The Birth of Venus* (c. 1484–6), Botticelli wove it through Venus's hair.

The natural counterpoint to our desire for and devotion to gold is its tendency to bring out our baser instincts: greed, envy, and avarice. This ambivalence is evident in the myth of King Midas, who is granted his foolish wish of being able to turn anything into solid gold just by touching it, only to find that this means he kills anything he touches, and cannot eat. Disgust at the human preoccupation with gold can be found in Pliny's *Natural History*: "We probe her [Mother Earth's] entrails, digging into veins of gold and silver . . . we drag out her entrails . . . to be worn upon a finger."[8] Today, those who binge on gold are looked down upon as tacky and tasteless. Klimt's golden painting was seized by the Nazis during the annexation of Austria and later spent half a century in a gallery there, despite the wishes expressed in the will of its last owner that it should pass to his heirs. After a prolonged legal battle with the Austrian government it was returned to Adele's niece. Bloch-Bauer now gazes out from her precious golden shroud at visitors to the Neue Galerie in Manhattan.

Dutch orange
Saffron
Amber
Ginger
Minium
Nude

Orange

Those who have ever wondered which *orange* referred
to first, the color or the fruit, need wonder no longer.
The fruit was probably first cultivated in China, and then
gradually spread west, leaving its name scattered in its
wake like a carelessly discarded whorl of peel: from *nārang*
in Persian to *nāranj* in Arabic; then *nāranga* (Sanskrit),
naranja (Spanish), *orenge* (French), and finally *orange* in
English. Orange as a name for a color only emerged during
the sixteenth century; before that English speakers had
used the cumbersome portmanteau *giolureade* or yellow-
red.[1] One of the word's first-recorded adjectival outings
was in 1502, when Elizabeth of York bought "slevys of
orenge color sarsenet" for Margaret Tudor.[2]

In his book *Concerning the Spiritual in Art* (1912),
Wassily Kandinsky, the Russian abstract artist, wrote,
"Orange is like a man, convinced of his own powers."[3]
There is no doubt that orange has a confidence to it.
If blue is a stand-in for the hazy unknown, its color-wheel
opposite has urgency. It's used to draw attention to
potential danger.[4] It is the color of Guantánamo Bay
jumpsuits, Agent Orange, and, since 9/11, the second-highest
terror-threat level in the United States. Orange is used in
traffic signage and warning symbols on roads, in part
because it forms a high contrast against the blue-gray
asphalt, even in low light.[5] And the black boxes on aircraft,
which record flight information, are, in fact, orange, in
the hope this will make them easier to find in the event of
a crash.

Thanks to the influence of the House of Orange on
early modern Europe, its heraldic color [page 96] has
had a wide geographical reach. Its most obvious association
is with the Netherlands: Dutch teams play in *oranje*, and
a Boer-controlled region in South Africa was known as
the Orange Free State—with a flag to match, naturally.

The color is also linked with Protestantism and protest, particularly in Ireland, where Protestants are known as Orangemen.[6]

When the architect Irving Morrow was deciding in 1935 what color to paint the Golden Gate Bridge that spans from San Francisco to Marin County, he settled on a rusty shade, now called GGB international orange, which would blend in with the hills but pop against the sea and sky.[7] Occasionally, orange also pops in fashion too. The wonderfully flamboyant art deco cover illustrations for *Vogue* by Helen Dryden show orange as a permanent fixture of 1920s fashion, and it also had a moment in the late 1960s and '70s.[8] It was expedience, though, that helped it become the signature color of one of the world's most successful luxury brands, Hermès. Prior to the Second World War the company's packaging was cream; it was wartime shortages that forced them to switch to mustard until, finally, they had no choice but to use the last paperboard color available: orange.[9]

Kandinsky also described orange as "red brought nearer to humanity by yellow."[10] And indeed it does seem to be forever in danger of sliding into another color category: red and yellow on either side, brown below. This was even true of the shades featured in this book. Several destined for orange—chrome and ocher to take just two—ended up elsewhere upon further research. In part this is because orange wasn't seen as a separate color in its own right until relatively recently and so even colors that now seem obviously orange—minium [page 107] is a good example— were once thought of as red or yellow.

It was the impressionists who convincingly illustrated orange's power. The painting that gave the movement its name, Claude Monet's *Impression, Sunrise*, has, at its center, a bright orange sun. This new school of artists, fired

up on new optical theories of color contrasts, made
extensive use of orange. Paired with blues (its opposite
on the color wheel) the super-bright chrome and
cadmium pigments produced zinging contrasts that
were deployed again and again by artists including
Toulouse-Lautrec, Munch, Gauguin, and Van Gogh.

Whatever the medium, there is no denying orange's
air of braggadocio. *Godey's Lady's Book* pronounced it
"too brilliant to be elegant" in 1855.[11] Anthony Burgess
might have been thinking the same thing when he named
his dystopian novel *A Clockwork Orange* in 1962.
(He gave several different explanations for the title during
his lifetime: once saying he had overheard the phrase
"as queer as a clockwork orange" in an East End pub;
on another occasion implying it was a metaphor of his
own making.) Neon-lit signs, invented in 1912 and
originally orange, are still perhaps the loudest and brightest
form of advertising, and the color remains popular for
billboards and storefronts. Many brands, including
Nickelodeon, easyJet, and Hooters, have made use of
its vibrancy and visibility. With apologies to Kandinsky,
perhaps a better summation of the color would be: "Orange
is like a man, desperately seeking to convince others of his
powers."

Dutch orange

Balthasar Gérard was the Lee Harvey Oswald of his day.
On July 10, 1584, he entered the Prinsenhof, the royal
residence of the Dutch rulers, and fired his pistol three
times into the chest of William I, Prince of Orange, who
prayed for mercy for the Dutch people and then died.

To the Dutch, William I (William the Silent) is the
father of their nation—and it was an exceedingly tricky
birth. In the middle of the sixteenth century the northern
Low Countries were not independent, but a largely
Protestant region under the rule of the fanatically Catholic
King Philip II of Spain. William I, a Catholic himself
but a strong believer in religious freedom, led the rebellion
against Spain. The House of Orange continued to exert
huge influence on European politics for several centuries,
and William's descendants remain the Dutch royal family
to this day.[1] Centuries of turbulence have left their mark,
however: the Dutch have fierce pride in their history,
their nation, and the signature color of their ruling family.

The House of Orange is proof that personal branding
isn't new. In portrait after portrait, its members are gilded
in shades of orange. It begins subtly enough: in a study
by Adriaen Thomasz Key painted in 1579, William I
wears a fine brocade suit in a fashionable shade of black,
trimmed with fine embroidery in orange and gold.[2]
A portrait of King William III of England and Dutch
Stadtholder (the honorific the Oranges were given in the
Low Countries), attributed to Thomas Murray, is less
subtle. Here, backed by a swathe of rust brocade, the king
wears a voluminous cloak in flame-colored velvet
trimmed with ermine and secured at the front with two
vast silk tassels in an eye-catching shade of pumpkin.

The Dutch, in gratitude to William I, took to the color
with gusto. (The exact shade favored by the Dutch has
shifted over the years. In contemporary paintings, the

orange worn by the members of the House of Orange
is almost a burnt amber shade; the one favored today
is a sunny mandarin.) Take the humble carrot, for example.
Originally a tough and rather bitter tuber from South
America, prior to the seventeenth century it was usually
purple or yellow. Over the next 100 years, however,
Dutch famers selectively bred carrots to produce orange
varieties.[3] The Dutch flag—today blue, white, and red—
was originally striped in blue, white, and orange to match
the livery of William I, but, try as they might, no one
could find a dye sufficiently colorfast: the orange stripe
would either fade to yellow or deepen to red. By the 1660s
the Dutch gave up and began using red instead.[4]

Perhaps the best, if most short-lived, instance of the
Netherlanders' affinity with this fiery hue occurred on
July 20, 1673. On that day Dutch soldiers captured the
city of New York, marching up Broadway to take it back
from the British.[5] In triumph they immediately
rechristened the city New Orange, a name it bore for less
than 12 months. The Dutch, who were fighting several
wars simultaneously, had neither the cash nor the stomach
to begin another one on yet another front. In 1674 a treaty
was signed ceding the city—and its name—to the British.
(The New York flag, unlike that of the Netherlands, still
bears an orange stripe, betraying its Dutch origins.)

The legacy of William I may not have given the
Dutch a permanent foothold in the New World, but it has
given them the gift of visibility. At sporting events, they
are unmistakable: a heaving block of joyous orange.
And each April they gather like a flock of exotic birds to
celebrate Koningsdag (King's Day), many dressed from
head to heels in luminous tangerine, and singing *Oranje
boven! Orange boven!* ("Orange on top! Orange on top!")
at the top of their lungs.

Saffron

Imagine a field in the predawn blue haze of an autumn
morning. The field is small, and probably in Iran, although
it could also be in Spain, Macedonia, Kashmir, France,
or Morocco. As the sun rises it shows that the field, which
had been bare earth the night before, is carpeted with
small violet blooms: thousands of *Crocus sativus*. At the
center of each, lasciviously prominent against the purple
of the petals, are three crimson stigmas, part of the flower's
female sex organs, better known (once removed and dried)
as the spice saffron. Before becoming saffron, however, the
crocuses need to be harvested, and there isn't much time:
by the heat of the day the blooms will have begun to wilt;
by the evening they will have withered completely.

No one knows quite when or where *C. sativus* was first
cultivated—the flowers are actually sterile and so can't
grow in the wild—but there are a few tantalizing hints.
Some cave paintings in Iraq made 50,000 years ago were
found to contain traces of saffron. The ancient Greeks used
it to dye their clothes, and we know it was traded across
the Red Sea, from Egypt to southern Arabia, during the
first century A.D.[1] It was being grown in Spain from at least
A.D. 961[2] and was even grown in England for centuries.
Tradition has it that a pilgrim returned from the Levant
during the reign of Edward III (1312–77) smuggling
a single bulb hidden either in the brim of his hat or in a
hollow in his staff—the legends differ. This bulb must have
been peculiarly fecund, because several British towns soon
became saffron-producing powerhouses. The most famous
of these changed its name during the sixteenth century
to Saffron Walden, in celebration of its star produce.
(The town changed its coat of arms too, adopting a rather
charming visual pun: three crocuses surrounded by a stout
set of walls, or "saffron walled-in.")[3] The plant, though,
had a rather stormy relationship with its civic namesake.

In 1540 and 1681 demand plummeted and in 1571 the
soil became overworked and the crop sickly. Even in
the good years—such as the bumper harvest of 1556 when
the saffron farmers, or "crokers," crowed that "God did shite
saffron"—*C. sativus* wasn't an unalloyed boon. In 1575
a royal decree stipulated that the crokers could no longer
throw discarded flowers in the river, on pain of two days
and nights in the stocks.[4]

Saffron is, measure for measure, the most expensive
spice in the world. In 2013 one ounce of saffron cost $364,
while the same quantity of vanilla cost $8 and cardamom
a paltry $3.75.[5] This is partly because the flowers are
so demanding: according to one sixteenth-century
account, *C. sativus* prefers "warme nights, sweete dewes,
fat grounde, and misty mornings." As well as the brief
flowering of the individual blooms, the entire crop comes
and goes in a fortnight.[6] The blooms need to be picked
and the stigmas removed entirely by hand; all attempts
to mechanize the process have failed, as the flowers are
too delicate. It takes between 31,800 and 45,500 flowers
to produce one pound of the spice.[7] For those prepared to
bear with saffron's peccadilloes, however, the rewards are
great. It has been used as an aphrodisiac and a cure for
everything from toothache to plague. In food it lends a
beautiful color, and is also prized for its aroma and flavor,
which is unlike anything else: simultaneously sweet, bitter,
and pungent, with a wisp of a taste that at one moment
might be reminiscent of hay, and the next something rather
more bosky, like mushroom.

At the noon of his power, wealth, and influence,
Cardinal Wolsey scattered rushes impregnated with the
spice on the floor of his rooms at Hampton Court to
scent the air.[8] Cleopatra, who has over the centuries been
accused of any number of extravagant follies, was said

Saffron, continued.

to bathe in it. It was so costly that there have been many
reports of forgery and other crimes. In 1374 the hijacking
of 800 pounds of saffron en route to Basel resulted in the
14-month Saffron War. While in Nuremberg in 1444
a man called Jobst Finderlers was burned alive for the
crime of adulterating his saffron with marigold.[9]

As a color, teetering between yellow and orange,
saffron is similarly in demand. Its most famous use is
for Buddhist robes. Buddha himself stipulated that the
robes could only be dyed using vegetable dye, but of
course saffron itself was much too expensive, and either
turmeric or jackfruit are used as a substitute (although
now many are dyed synthetically).[10] When used as a dye,
the spice imparts an intense color to clothes (although
it is not particularly colorfast) and hair—Alexander the
Great reputedly used it to make his locks look like gold.[11]
Zoroastrian priests used saffron to make a sunny ink,
with which they wrote special prayers to ward off evil.
Later it was used by monastic book illuminators as a
cheaper (and presumably unconvincing) alternative to
gold. According to one early seventeenth-century recipe,
it was made into a pigment by being mixed with glair,
an egg-white concoction, and left for a day and a half.[12]

The color saffron is also present in the national
flag of India. Today it is said to stand for "courage, sacrifice,
and the spirit of renunciation." When the flag was adopted
in 1947, however, the meaning was a little different. As Dr.
S. Radhakrishnan explained at the time, "the saffron color
denotes renunciation or disinterestedness. Our leaders must
be indifferent to material gains and dedicate themselves to
their work."[13] Sadly for the idealists of 1947, corruption
scandals continue to plague India. Perhaps, though, that is
not entirely surprising: saffron has seldom brought out the
best in people.

Amber

In June 1941 Hitler's Germany and Stalin's Soviet Union
had been grimly making peace for two years. War, though,
was coming. Operation Barbarossa, the Nazi invasion,
began on June 22, when around 3 million German soldiers
poured into Soviet territory.[1] As ever, the invading army
was keen to seize valuable treasures as it went. One of the
things that the Nazis were keenest to find was holed up in
the palace at Tsarskoye Selo, the Russians having plastered
over it with thin wallpaper in a desperate attempt to prevent
it from being looted. This was the Amber Room, also
known as the "Eighth Wonder of the World."

The room was, properly speaking, a series of intricately
carved panels and mosaics made of glowing honeyed
amber, studded with semiprecious stones and backed
by gold leaf. It had been designed by a German, the
seventeenth-century baroque sculptor Andreas Schlüter,
and made in 1701 by a Danish craftsman, Gottfried
Wolfram. In 1716 Frederick I of Prussia gave the room
to Peter the Great in celebration of the alliance between
Prussia and Russia against Sweden. The panels—carefully
packed into 18 large boxes—were promptly shipped from
Frederick I's seat at the Charlottenburg Palace in Berlin
to St. Petersburg. They were moved again 40 years later,
just a few miles south to Tsarskoye Selo, where they
were reconfigured and expanded to fit a new, larger space.
The panels—now measuring over 180 square feet, weighing
around 6 tons, and costing, it has been estimated, $142
million in today's money—became the pride of Russia's
royalty. Czarina Elizabeth used the Amber Room as a
meditation space; Catherine the Great entertained guests
there; Alexander II used it as a backdrop for his trophies.[2]
In 1941, however, wallpaper proved insufficient cover for
such a famous treasure, and the Amber Room was packed
up in a bare 36 hours and shipped to Königsberg.

Amber, continued.

One of the few organic gemstones, true amber is extremely old. It is made of fossilized tree resin that once oozed from species of cedar and other conifers long since extinct.[3] (Young amber, not yet fully fossilized, is known as copal.) For many, amber conjures up the scene from the film *Jurassic Park*, where a scientist extracts DNA from an insect that has been trapped and preserved in a sticky drop of resin. Insect occlusions in amber aren't all that rare, probably because amber is a wonderful natural preservative. (The ancient Egyptians, noticing this quality, used it in their embalming rituals.) In 2012 researchers discovered a spider entombed in the act of attacking its prey, a miniature dramatic tableau that has remained frozen at the moment of crisis for 100 million years. Earlier the same year scientists photographed the oldest parasitic mite ever discovered, trapped in an amber droplet from northern Italy 230 million years ago.[4]

Amber is most commonly found around the Baltic, where vast forests of conifers once grew; it still washes up on beaches there after storms. Elsewhere, though, amber is rare and consequently treasured. It can be set on fire and used to scent the air with an aroma like burning pinewood. And its clarity and colors—most often palest honey to smoldering ember, but occasionally black, red, or even blue—have made it valuable for jewelry and decoration.

The Etruscans and Romans loved it, despite the belief of one Roman historian that amber, which he called *lyncurius*, was made from dried lynx urine. Pieces of amber, intricately carved to resemble the heads of rams, monkeys, or bees, have been found at many ancient burial sites. A dark hunk that was sculpted in the first century A.D. to resemble the head of Medusa is now part of the J. Paul Getty Collection.[5] The Greeks called the gemstone *elektron*, associating it with light from the sun.

(This is the origin of the English words *electric* and *electron*.) In a famous myth, Phaeton, the bastard son of Helios, god of the sun, borrows the chariot his father uses to pull the sun across the sky and, desperate to prove himself, sets off to do his father's duty for a single day. Phaeton—young, vain, rash, and ambitious—fatally lacks his father's strength and horsemanship. The horses sense his weakness and begin to plunge closer and closer to the earth, scorching it, laying waste to fertile land. Seeing the plumes of black smoke, Zeus strikes down Phaeton with a thunderbolt, and Helios resumes control. Less well known is the fate of Phaeton's sisters, the Heliades, whose grief over the death of their brother is so fierce that they are turned into poplar trees, their cascading tears transfigured into droplets of golden amber.[6]

Some believe that amber, like opal, brings bad luck, and the ultimate fate of the Amber Room remains fittingly murky. The trail goes cold in 1943, when panels were still installed in Königsberg; a year later, the city was bombed by Allied troops and the museum where the room had been held was decimated. Some believe that the panels were moved before the bombing. Optimists argue the room is still hidden somewhere in the city. In a book published in 2004 Adrian Levy and Cathy Scott-Clark claimed that it was the Red Army itself that wrecked the treasured Russian artwork, either through ill-discipline or ignorance, and that the Soviets hushed the matter up out of shame. In the late 1970s the Russians began working on a reconstruction; 25 years and $11 million later, the replica can now be seen at the restored Catherine Palace in St. Petersburg, freezing history in place.

Ginger

The Zingiberaceae plant family is an industrious one.
Among its members are *Curcuma longa* (turmeric),
Elettaria cardamomum (cardamom), and *Zingiber officinale*,
a perennial with long narrow leaves, yellow flowers, and,
hidden from view beneath the soil, a pale dun rhizome
known, simply, as ginger. Originating in the tropical forests
of south Asia, ginger was among the first spices traded
to the West (from around the first century A.D.), and our
appetite for it has yet to wane. It is used to enliven all
manner of foods from stir-fries to sticky loaves of
gingerbread. To taste, it is hot and pungent, insistent
and exotic. And, somewhere along the way, it was these
qualities that led to its association with a particular group
of people: redheads.

Like blondes, redheads are in the minority (which
probably explains the string of evocative if unflattering
names that have been bestowed on them: carrot-top,
copperknob, piss-brindle, ginger, and red). They make
up less than 2 percent of the global population, although
there are a few more—around 6 percent—in northern and
western Europe, and up to 13 percent of the population of
Scotland have red hair.[1] Those with red hair are stereotyped
as fiery and intense—just like the ginger root. Jacky Colliss
Harvey, the author of *Red*, and a redhead herself,
remembers being told by her grandmother that God gave
women red hair for the same reason he gave wasps stripes.

This myth certainly seems to have found expression
in some famous British royals. Dio Cassius described
Boudicca, the ruler who for a short time terrorized the
Roman invaders, as having a flowing mass of red hair.
(Although, as he was writing nearly a hundred years
after her death, he may have been saying this purely
to make her sound even more fearsome and exotic to
his dark-haired Greek and Roman readers.)

King Henry VIII, however, rarely noted for his
sweetness of temper, was definitely redheaded. In 1515,
when the king was 24 years old, the Venetian ambassador
wrote, "His majesty is the handsomest potentate I ever set
eyes on; above the usual height, with an extremely fine calf
to his leg, his complexion very fair and bright, with auburn
hair combed straight and short, in the French fashion."[2]
(Even this, though, is confusing: "auburn" started out
referring to a pale yellow or brown, a kind of off-white,
but during the sixteenth and seventeenth centuries, its
meaning shifted to a deeper ruddy brown.) Henry's
daughter by Anne Boleyn—whose hair color was possibly
also reddish (descriptions vary)—was Queen Elizabeth I,
the redheaded ruler par excellence. The precise shade of
her hair, though, is elusive: strawberry blonde in one
portrait, red-gold in another, coppery auburn in a third.

Away from the British throne, redheads, particularly
women, punch well above their weight in terms of cultural
visibility. Many fictional female characters, including
Annie, Jessica Rabbit, and Wilma Flintstone, are imagined
with red hair. Then there are redheads in art. While Titian
favored rosy caramel tresses, and Modigliani preferred
auburns, Rossetti and his fellow Pre-Raphaelite
brotherhood were not fussy, just so long as their models'
hair was red. Elizabeth Siddal, a copper-headed poet,
was the muse for several of the Pre-Raphaelites: she is
Sir John Everett Millais's "Ophelia," and Rossetti's "Beata
Beatrix." She was also Rossetti's lover and, later, wife.
When she died of a laudanum overdose, Rossetti buried
a book of his poetry with her, but years later he disinterred
her to retrieve it. A witness said that Siddal's flaming hair
had continued to grow, so that it filled the coffin when
they prized it open. Rossetti never quite recovered.

Although the origin and whereabouts of the ur-redhead

Ginger, continued.

are still a mystery, some tantalizing evidence of its history
came to light in 1994. Two jawbones were unearthed
in the El Sidrón cave in northern Spain. At first, because
the bones were in such good condition, it was assumed
they were relatively recent, perhaps dating back to the
Spanish Civil War. As more bones began to surface,
showing marks where knives had sliced muscle from
bone, the scene began to take on the grim character of
a cannibalistic massacre. Police and forensic scientists
were called in. They discovered that a crime had indeed
taken place, but that they were about 50,000 years too
late to catch the culprits.[3]

The cave contained the remains of a family of
Neanderthals: three men, three women, three teenage
boys, two children, and a baby. Enough evidence remained
to show that two of the individuals had bright red hair.[4]
They were the victims, rather than the aggressors.

Minium

In the opening pages of the Gladzor Gospels the text is
pressed beneath a heavily gilded pediment decorated
with a portrait of a tonsured saint. Surrounding him
is an explosion of colorful, curlicued foliage filled with
fantastical creatures. A pair of blue cranelike creatures with
red and green wings face each other, beaks open
in silent screeches. Over the page are a startled peacock
and four birds that resemble lilac partridges, each with
a heart-shaped red leaf clasped in its beak. Some pages
are so choked with gilded greenery and bizarre, peeping
figures that it seems as if the words were an afterthought.

Prior to Johannes Gutenberg's invention of printing
with movable type sometime around 1440, books were
restricted to noblemen, clergy, and a few others, such as
clerks, who needed to be literate in order to do their jobs.
They were also expensive. Manuscripts were created by
hand—in Latin *manu* means hand while *scriptus* means
written—and were usually commissioned by a powerful
patron to reflect his or her piety and status. Each book
represented hundreds of hours of labor and was wholly
unique, from the animal skins that made up the leaves
of parchment, to the pigments used for the illuminations,
to the fists of the scribes.

The Gladzor Gospels were created during the
fourteenth century, in a small region in central Armenia,
halfway between the Black and Caspian Seas. Then, as
now, Armenia was caught both politically and culturally
between the East and the West, the Muslim world and
the Christian one. Under the aptly named Gregory the
Illuminator, it had been the first country in the world to
convert to Christianity, in A.D. 301.[1] Perhaps it was pride
in this fact, coupled with anxiety over the Mongol
occupation, that led those who worked on the Gladzor
Gospels to pour so much frenzied creativity into the

Minium, continued.

manuscript and its illustrations. As in most monastic
endeavors, the production of this manuscript required
a precise division of labor. First, scribes would have copied
the text, carefully leaving space for the paintings, and then
a team of artists would have begun their work.[2]
If the team that worked on the volume was large enough,
it would have been the sole responsibility of one person
to add the capitals, headings, and pilcrows (¶) in a
particular shade of orange-red so bright that they leapt
off the page.

The pigment used was minium. The person who
worked with it was called a miniator, and his work,
an eye-catching symbol or heading in a manuscript,
was called a *miniatura*. (This is the origin of the word
"miniature," which in its original sense did not mean small
at all.)[3] Minium was used extensively in manuscript
illumination during the Middle Ages, and use of it only
gradually died out as vermilion [page 144] became
more readily available from the eleventh century.[4]

Although minium, or lead tetroxide, can be found
in naturally occurring deposits, this is rare, and it has
more commonly been manufactured. The process is
essentially a continuation of the one used to make lead
white [page 43] and was described, in a pleasingly
magical way, in the eleventh-century *Mappae clavicula*:

*[T]ake a pot that has never been used, and put sheets of lead in it.
Fill the pot with very strong vinegar, cover and seal it. Put the pot in
a warm place and leave it for a month. Next . . . shake out the deposits
around the sheets of lead into a ceramic pot, and then place [it] on the
fire. Stir the pigment constantly, and when you see it turn white as
snow use as much of it as you like; this pigment is called basic lead white,
or ceruse. Then take whatever is left on the fire, and stir it constantly
until it becomes red.[5]*

Minium was often used as a cheap alternative to vermilion and cinnabar; in fact, the three pigments were often confused, even though minium is generally much yellower than either (Pliny the Elder described it as "flame colored").[6] Perhaps the confusion was in part due to wishful thinking: although it is cheap, bright, and easy to make, minium is far from an ideal pigment. Even though, like its near relation lead white, it was used as a cosmetic in ancient Greece and China, it is just as poisonous.[7] Another major problem is that it does not mix well with others, including the near-ubiquitous lead white, and has, George Field reported in 1835, a tendency to turn black in impure air.[8] Luckily for historians, the Armenian air proved equal to the challenge. While the stone walls of the Gladzor monastery have long since disappeared, the minium in this particular manuscript is as illuminating as ever.

Nude

The wardrobe choices of women in politics often cause
a stir, but in May 2010 the column inches surrounding
one particular outfit spooled out further than usual.
At a state dinner given at the White House in honor
of the president of India, the first lady (and the first African
American first lady), Michelle Obama, chose
a warm-cream-and-silver gown designed by Naeem Khan.
This was a subtle act of sartorial diplomacy: Mr. Khan
was born in Mumbai.[1] The problem arose, however,
when the story was reported. Associated Press called
the dress "flesh-colored"; others used Khan's own
description: "sterling-silver sequin, abstract floral, nude
strapless gown." The response was immediate. As Dodai
Stewart, a journalist for *Jezebel*, put it: "Nude? For whom?"[2]

The terms for this particular pale shade—"nude"
and "flesh," and even the less common "suntan" and "bare"—
presuppose a Caucasian skin tone and are therefore
problematic. Despite being painfully out of step with
a global fashion market, they are curiously obdurate.
Nude heels are wardrobe staples; nude lipsticks are daubed
on millions of pouts every day. In reference to clothing
the terms persist despite the existence of a plethora of
alternatives: sand, champagne, biscuit, peach, and beige
[page 58]. The color first became popular for women's
underthings—corsets, girdles, pantyhose, and bralettes—
in the 1920s and '30s. Soon the association between
naked flesh and these silky undergarments invested the
color with an erotic charge. Designers have drawn on it
again and again, particularly in the 1990s and early 2000s
with the rise of the "underwear-as-outerwear" trend.[3]

The idea behind such "nude" undergarments was
presumably that they would be less visible through
diaphanous fabrics. Of course, just like their modern
equivalents, they only really matched the skin color

of a very select few, even among Caucasian women.
One person who understands this better than most is
the Brazilian photographer Angélica Dass. Since 2012
Angélica has been working on a "chromatic inventory"
of human skin tone. The ongoing "Humanæ" project is
now composed of over 2,500 portraits of different people
from around the world. The subject of each portrait—
seemingly naked although only the head and shoulders are
visible—is shot with the same clean, bright light.
What makes the portraits special is the backgrounds. Each
is dyed to match the subject's complexion (a sample is
taken from the face), and the matching alphanumeric
Pantone code is printed at the bottom. Angélica is a
Pantone 7522 C.[4] The portraits' power lies in being
viewed as a group, and looking at them makes clear
immediately how feeble and inadequate the labels "white"
and "black" really are. The variety in skin tone is both
staggering and oddly moving.

   It could be argued that "nude" as a color term is
sufficiently divorced from any actual skin color to be
harmless. The problem, though, is not with the color,
or even the word itself, but with the ethnocentrism
behind it. "Those of us with skin darker than 'nude,'"
wrote Ms. Stewart in 2010, "have realized how non-
inclusive the color is—from Band-Aids to pantyhose
to bras—for years." There have been advances of course:
fewer makeup companies pretend that one shade of sandy
pale foundation will "suit all skin tones," and in 2013
Christian Louboutin launched a range of pumps in five
different skin colors, from pale to dark.[5] We all know
that "nude" is a spectrum and not a shade; it is high time
the world around us reflected that too.

Baker-Miller pink
Mountbatten pink
Puce
Fuchsia
Shocking pink
Fluorescent pink
Amaranth

Pink

Pink is for girls and blue is for boys; the evidence is
everywhere. In the "Pink & Blue Project," which began
in 2005, the Korean photographer JeongMee Yoon
captures images of children surrounded by their
possessions. All the little girls sit marooned in
identical pink seas.

Amazingly enough, the strict girl-pink boy-blue
divide only dates from the mid-twentieth century. Just
a few scant generations ago the situation was completely
different. In an article on baby clothes in the *New York
Times* in 1893 the rule stated was that you should "always
give pink to a boy and blue to a girl." Neither the author
nor the woman in the shop whom she was interviewing
were quite sure why, but the author hazarded a
tongue-in-cheek guess. "[T]he boy's outlook is so much
more roseate than the girl's," she wrote, "that it is enough to
make a girl baby blue to think of living a woman's life
in the world."[1] In 1918 a trade publication affirmed that
this was the "generally accepted rule" because pink was
the "more decided and stronger color," while blue was
"more delicate and dainty."[2] This is probably closer to
the real explanation. Pink is, after all, just faded red,
which in the era of scarlet-jacketed soldiers and red-robed
cardinals was the most masculine color, while blue was
the signature hue of the Virgin Mary. At the turn of the
century even the idea of different clothes for children
of different sexes was a little odd. The mortality and birth
rates were so high that all children under the age of two
wore easy-to-bleach white linen dresses.

The word *pink* itself is relatively young too. The first
reference in the *Oxford English Dictionary* of the word
being used to describe pale reds is the late seventeenth
century. Before then *pink* usually referred to a kind of
pigment. Pink pigments were made by binding an organic

colorant, such as buckthorn berries or an extract of the broom shrub, to an inorganic substance like chalk, which gave it body. They came in several colors—you could have green pinks, rose pinks, or brown pinks—but were, more often than not, yellow.[3] It is an odd quirk that while light reds acquired a name of their own, pale greens and yellows did not for the most part (although several languages, including Russian, do have different words for pale and deep blues). Most romance languages made do with a variation of the word *rose*, from the flower. Although it is not certain, it is likely that the English derived their word for the color from another flower, the *Dianthus plumarius*, also known as the pink.

Pink, however, is far more than the color of flowers and princess dresses. Dressed (or not) in salmon-colored silks, the women depicted by the eighteenth-century rococo artists, such as François Boucher and Jean-Honoré Fragonard, while hardly feminist pinups, were certainly shown as being in full control of their allure. Their figurehead was Madame de Pompadour, the mistress of King Louis XV of France and a consummate consumer who helped popularize bright pink Sèvres porcelain. Daring, full-blooded pinks were a hit with strong, characterful women. It was a favorite of magazine editor Diana Vreeland, who liked to call it "the navy blue of India."[4] Elsa Schiaparelli, an Italian fashion designer; Daisy Fellowes, an heiress and magazine editor; and Marilyn Monroe, who needs no introduction, all made shocking pink [page 126] the color of choice for twentieth-century women who wanted to be both seen and heard.

Pink's current image problem is partly due to the feminist backlash against old-fashioned sexism. It is seen as simultaneously infantilizing and, ever since artists first

put mixtures of cochineal, ocher, and white to canvas
to depict naked female flesh, sexualizing. Nudes are still,
overwhelmingly, female. In 1989, while 85 percent of the
Metropolitan Museum's nudes were women, only 5 percent
of the artists represented were. In a recent article, the
Guerrilla Girls, a group pressuring the art world for greater
diversity, said that since then the figures have become
worse still.[5] The case against pink as the color of female
objectification was only helped in the 1970s by a surprising
discovery made about a particular shade [page 118].

Recently it was revealed that products for women,
from clothes to bike helmets to incontinence pads,
routinely cost more than products for men and boys that
are practically identical. In November 2014 French
secretary of state for women's rights Pascale Boistard
demanded to know "*Le rose est-il une couleur de luxe?*"
("Is pink a luxury color?") when it was discovered
Monoprix was selling a pack of five disposable pink razors
at $1.93. A ten-pack of blue disposable razors, meanwhile,
cost $1.85.[6] The phenomenon has come to
be known as the "pink tax." Color preferences may have
reversed over the past century, but it seems in many ways
the boy's outlook remains more roseate.

Baker-Miller pink

In the late 1970s American cities were scourged by wave after wave of drug epidemics and spiking violent crime rates. So when in late 1979 a professor announced that he had found a way of making people less aggressive, the nation pricked up its ears. The secret, Alexander G. Schauss announced in the pages of *Orthomolecular Psychiatry*, was a sickly shade of bright pink.

Over the course of the past year Schauss had conducted numerous tests. First, he had measured the physical strength of 153 young men, half of whom had stared at a deep-blue piece of cardboard for one minute, the other half at a pink piece of cardboard.[1] All but two of the men shown pink were weaker than average. Intrigued, he used a more accurate measure of strength, a dynamometer, to test 38 men: pink did for every one of them what a haircut had done for Samson. Away from the lab the hue seemed just as effective. On March 1, 1979, two commanding officers at the U.S. Naval Correctional Center in Seattle, Washington, Gene Baker and Ron Miller, turned one of their holding cells pink to see if it would have an effect on their prisoners. They carefully added one pint of semigloss red trim paint to a gallon of pure white latex paint to obtain the perfect Pepto-Bismol shade, and set to work coating the walls, ceiling, and ironwork of the cell.[2] Before this, violence had been a "whale of a problem," said Baker, but over the next 156 days there wasn't a single incident.[3] Similar results were reported at the Kuiper Youth Center in San Bernardino; in fact, reported Dr. Paul Boccumini, happily, "it has worked so well that the staff must limit their [delinquents'] exposure because the youngsters become too weak."[4]

Schauss began making public appearances to demonstrate how the newly christened Baker-Miller pink (named after the two officers in Seattle) could sap the strength of even the toughest man. During one memorable television appearance he tried it out on the reigning Mr. California; the poor man could barely complete a single bicep curl. It soon became something of a pop-culture phenomenon in America. It crept over the seats of bus companies, the walls of housing estates, small-town drunk tanks (hence its other nickname, "drunk-tank pink"); and, finally, the visitors' locker rooms at college football stadiums.[5] (This last use led to a ruling that football teams could paint visitors' locker rooms any color they chose, just as long as the home team's locker room was painted to match.)

There was, naturally, an academic backlash. Over the next decade scientists probed the efficacy of Baker-Miller pink on everything from anxiety levels to appetite to coding ability. Results were contradictory. A 1988 study could not find a link between the shade and blood pressure or strength, but did see significant effects on the speed and accuracy of participants in a standard digit-symbol test.[6] A 1991 study found that there were reductions in the systolic and diastolic blood pressures of emotionally disturbed participants who were put in a room painted pink. Another study, carried out on prisoners and male university students pretending to be prisoners, found that both Baker-Miller-painted walls and pink-filtered light could reduce the time it took for those exposed to become calm.[7]

Today, however, Baker-Miller pink is pretty rare, even in prisons. It seems that as crime rates in the United States—the country where the overwhelming majority of the testing had been done—began to fall, priorities shifted. It is also a rather sickly color, so it may be that the guards, nurses, and wardens had no more desire to be surrounded by it than those under their care. For the moment, the world's interest in Baker-Miller pink lies dormant and hundreds of questions remain unanswered—until the next crime wave perhaps.

Mountbatten pink

For the first six decades of the twentieth century, at precisely 4 p.m. each Thursday, the horn of a large cruise liner would sound across Southampton Water and a Union-Castle ship would slip from its berth and steal south, bound for Cape Town. Even if the timing hadn't been as regimented, it would still have been difficult to mistake these ships for any other: they had scarlet funnels trimmed at the top with a stripe of black; their upper decks were gleaming white while their hulls were an indeterminate dull lavender-gray-pink shade. It was a feature their poster advertisements made much of: those proud pinkish hulls slicing through blue waves, with sunlit landscapes visible in the background.

It was probably not such jaunty images, though, that preoccupied the mind of Lord Mountbatten, the British statesman, while he was aboard his ship, the HMS *Kelly*, in 1940.[1] In the first year of the Second World War the Royal Navy had suffered tremendous losses: the Luftwaffe sighted convoys from above while packs of German U-boats closed in from below. The sheer loss of life was terrible enough, but during the war Britain was utterly dependent on the supplies being brought in from abroad. It was all too clear that something needed to be done. Captains began testing different kinds of camouflage in the hope of evading their hunters. Some elaborated on the strident dazzle designs that had been used during the Great War, the aim of which was not to hide the ships but, like the bold stripes on a zebra, to confuse attackers, making it difficult for enemies to estimate the dazzle-painted ships' bearing, speed, and distance. Others tried two-tone grays—dark on the hull, pale on the superstructures—so that the ships' coloring echoed the difference between sea and sky.[2]

Perhaps it was these efforts that were in Mountbatten's

mind when he noticed that a requisitioned Union-Castle
liner, still bearing its civilian livery, disappeared into
the gloaming well before the other ships in the convoy.
He became convinced that the Union-Castle's distinctive
hull color might be the very thing that the navy had
been looking for. While it stood out during the day,
at dawn and dusk—two of the most treacherous times
for attacks on ships—the dull, pucey color seemed to
disappear. Before long all the destroyers in his flotilla
were painted medium gray with a dash of Venetian red,
a tone that quickly became known as Mountbatten pink.

Other captains followed Mountbatten's lead, and
the color might have spread across the entire navy
had it not been for the official camouflage section of the
Admiralty, which began putting different paints and
patterns through their paces. Ships were soon being
painted official camouflage colors: a subdued gray-and-
blue version of the dazzle design.

It is not known whether the Admiralty included
Mountbatten pink in its tests; nor has it been recorded how
sailors felt about the ever-shifting colors of their ships. We
do know, though, that just at the time Mountbatten pink
was being phased out in 1942, many had become
convinced of its effectiveness. One story
in particular is still remembered in favor of Mountbatten
pink's miraculous powers of concealment. In the final
months of 1941 HMS *Kenya*—nicknamed "the Pink
Lady" after her paint job—came under heavy fire just
off Vaagso Island near the Norwegian coast. Although
strafed by two large guns for minutes on end, she escaped
with only cosmetic damage and no casualties. Proof,
or so it seemed to some, that this particular shade of pink
was the very thing the navy had been searching for.

Puce

Prerevolutionary France was awash with evocative color nomenclature. Apple green and white stripes, for example, were called "the lively shepherdess." Other favored individual shades included "indiscreet complaints," "great reputation," "stifled sigh," and "the vapors."[1] Then, as now, indulging in the latest fashions signaled status, wealth, and a sense of tribal belonging in the jeweled echo chamber of the French royal court. It was in this stultifying environment that puce became the color of a season.

In the summer of 1775, 20-year-old Marie Antoinette had been the queen of France for one year, and her reign was not going well. In the spring, a wave of riots over the price of grain—known as the Flour Wars—had convulsed the country, and the foreign-born queen was rapidly becoming an object of loathing. Rumormongers told tales of her wild gambling, her faux-milkmaid exploits at the Petit Trianon on the grounds of Versailles, and her closets stuffed with expensive clothes and hats. To her starving subjects, such profligacy was galling. Alarmed at the reports from France, her mother, the redoubtable Empress Maria Theresa, wrote to scold her daughter for her "extravagances of fashion," telling her that she was "hurtling toward an abyss." "[A] queen," she wrote, "only degrades herself . . . through unthrifty expenditure, especially in such a difficult time."[2] But the young queen would not listen.

Her husband, King Louis XVI, sensing his wife's sartorial indulgences were dangerously unseemly, was less than thrilled when he found her trying on a new lutestring (glossy silk taffeta) gown in a peculiar shade somewhere between brown, pink, and gray. Had he been feeling more chivalrous he might have called it "faded rose" but instead he observed that it resembled the *couleur de puce*—the color of fleas.[3] If it had been the king's intention to shame his wife, though, his words backfired. "The next day," recalled Baronne d'Oberkirch, "every lady at court wore a puce-colored gown, old puce, young puce, *ventre de puce* [flea's belly], *dos de puce* [flea's back]."[4] Writing to her daughter from the French court that summer, Lady Spencer described puce as "the uniform at Fontainebleau and the only color that can be worn."[5]

A few days after the fall of the monarchy 17 years later on August 10, 1792, the Bourbon royal family found themselves in drastically different circumstances. Their new, post-Revolution apartments consisted of a cramped and dirty cell-like suite in the Little Tower at the Temple. Here the royal couple were kept under guard until their executions the following year. Naturally, Marie Antoinette was not allowed many clothes, and those she did have had to suit her new life. They needed to survive the squalor of her new rooms and repeated washings, and to signify her status as a prisoner and "assassin of the people." Her trousseau consisted of several simple white shifts, an embroidered muslin skirt, two capelets, and three dresses: a printed brown toile de Jouy; a simple chemise with an equestrian-style collar, in a color known as "Paris mud"; and a taffeta gown the color of fleas.[6]

Fuchsia

Fuchsia is one of the many colors that owe their name to
a flower,[1] and although the fuchsia's distinctive, double-skirted
flowers actually come in a variety of ballerina hues—including
whites, reds, pinks, and purples—it is an achingly bright
blue-based pink that adopted the name. Today that might
not be considered much of an honor; fuchsia was voted one
of the three least popular colors in Britain in 1998, and the
word has been the bane of spelling-bee entrants for years.[2]
However, the story behind the flower's name is, at its
heart, about love: the love of botany.

Hippocrates, born sometime around 460 B.C. on the
island of Kos, is perhaps the earliest known person to have
shown a considered interest in plant life. His study was
related to the practice of medicine: many plants were used
to treat ailments, or to cause them, and a good doctor
needed to know which was which. Later came another
Greek, Theophrastus (c. 371–c. 287 B.C.), who published
the first treatise on the subject; then Pliny the Elder
(A.D. 23–79), who mentioned over 800 species of flora in
his *Natural History*; and Avicenna, the Persian philosopher,
scientist, and prodigious author—some 240 of his titles
still survive—who was born around A.D. 980.[3] Over 500
years later, however, when Leonhard Fuchs, who was
studying to become a physician in Bavaria, began his
own researches into plants, the field had barely advanced
at all.

To rectify the situation, Fuchs began creating a garden
that he filled with every kind of plant he could lay his
hands on. (All the likenesses of him from that time show
a man with a plant grasped in one hand and a singularly
focused expression.) He applied to friends all over Europe
and those setting off to explore the New World, beseeching
them to send him samples or descriptions of plants that
they came across. The fruit of all his hard work, the finely

illustrated *De historia stirpium commentarii insignes*
(*Notable Commentaries of the History of Plants*), was finally
published in 1542.

"We have devoted the greatest diligence," Fuchs
proudly wrote, "so that every plant should be depicted
with its own roots, stalks, leaves, flowers, seeds, and fruits."[4]
Three artists worked on the book's 512 images. Altogether
it described some 400 wild and 100 cultivated plants,
including descriptions of species from the New World
that few Europeans had ever seen before, such as the
chili pepper—the name he gave it meant "big pod" in
Latin. He also gave evocative names to plants that people
must have seen hundreds of times, like the beautiful
Digitalis purpurea (which means purple fingers) to the
common foxglove.[5]

Strangely, though, Leonhard Fuchs never saw the
plant that now bears his name. Though now common
across much of the world, the first specimen known to
Europeans wasn't found until 1703—some 137 years after
Fuchs's death—growing wild on the island of Hispaniola
in the Caribbean. The man who found it, Père Charles
Plumier, was a botanist and, wanting to honor his hero,
named it in Fuchs's honor.

Shocking pink

Known to Winston and Clementine Churchill as "the Imbroglio," Daisy Fellowes was a very shocking woman indeed.[1] Born in Paris in the dog days of the nineteenth century, she was the only daughter of a French aristocrat and Isabelle-Blanche Singer, the sewing machine heiress. In the 1920s and '30s she was a notorious, transatlantic bad girl: dosing her ballet teacher with cocaine, editing the French *Harper's Bazaar*, carrying on a succession of high-profile affairs, and throwing parties to which she only invited pairs of mortal enemies. She was, according to an artist acquaintance, "the beautiful Madame de Pompadour of the period, dangerous as an albatross"; to Mitchell Owens, a writer for the *New York Times*, she was "a Molotov cocktail in a Mainbocher suit."[2]

One of her numerous vices was shopping, and it was one of her purchases from Cartier that unleashed this scandalous shade of pink onto the world. The bright pink Tête de Bélier ("Ram's Head"), a 17.47-carat diamond, had once belonged to Russian royalty.[3] Fellowes wore it one day when meeting one of her favorite designers, the inventive, surrealist couturier Elsa Schiaparelli (Fellowes was one of the only two women brave enough to wear the infamous high-heel hat designed in collaboration with Salvador Dalí. Schiaparelli herself was the other.) It was love at first sight. "The color flashed in front of my eyes," Schiaparelli later wrote. "Bright, impossible, impudent, becoming, life giving, like all the lights and the birds and the fish in the world together, a color of China and Peru but not of the West—a shocking color, pure and undiluted."[4] She immediately incorporated it into the packaging for her first perfume, released in 1937.[5] The bottle, designed by the surrealist painter Leonor Fini, was modeled after the voluptuous torso of the actress Mae West, and came in a distinctive hot-pink case.

Its name, of course, was "Shocking." The color became
something of a touchstone for the designer, cropping up
again and again in her collections and even in her own
interior decoration: her granddaughter, the model and
actress Marisa Berenson, remembers Schiaparelli's bed
being covered with heart-shaped, shocking pink pillows.[6]

Age has not dimmed the color's appeal. In the brash
1980s Christian Lacroix often paired it with bright red;
most, however, use it only sparingly. A notable exception
can be found in the film *Gentlemen Prefer Blondes*. In 1953
the costume designer William Travilla was urgently called
to the set. The filmmakers were panicking about its star,
Marilyn Monroe, as a nude calendar featuring the actress
had just been released and the press was in a slavering
uproar. The studio decided her assets needed to be more
jealously guarded. "I made a *very covered dress*," Travilla
later wrote, "a very famous pink dress with a big bow in
the back."[7] It is this outfit Monroe wears when singing the
tune that helped seal her place in Hollywood's firmament,
"Diamonds Are a Girl's Best Friend." No doubt Daisy
Fellowes, by then a determinedly soignée 63-year-old,
wholeheartedly agreed.

Fluorescent pink

On April 21, 1978, the British punk band X-Ray Spex
released 15,000 limited-edition copies of their new single,
"The Day the World Turned Day-Glo," on pumpkin-
orange 7-inch vinyl. On the cover a globe, roughly colored
in a mixture of yellow, red, and poison-bright pink, stands
against a lime background. The song's lyrics—almost
incomprehensible in lead singer Poly Styrene's screeching
yowl—bemoan the world's seeping artificiality.

Fluorescent colors were a hot new thing in the 1970s,
amped-up versions of the bright colors beloved by
advertisers and pop artists in the 1960s. In 1972 Crayola
introduced a special-edition box of eight fluorescent
crayons, including the ultra pink and hot magenta colors,
all of which glowed brightly under a black light. The
strident brashness of super-bright colors perfectly suited
the aesthetic of the emerging punk movement too. Highly
saturated fluorescent-style pinks were used to paint
Mohawks and the lettering of many classic punk albums
of the era, like the pink-and-yellow design on the Sex
Pistols' *Never Mind the Bollocks* album designed by Jamie
Reid in 1977.

Most of the colors we think of as fluorescent are
actually just very high-intensity hues. True fluorescents
are so bright not only because the colors are very
saturated but also because the chemical structure of the
dye or material absorbs the very shortwave light in
the ultraviolet portion of the spectrum, which humans
can't see, and re-emits it as longer wavelengths, which we
can.[1] This is what gives them that particular glowing
brightness in daylight, and is also why they shine under
black lights.

A favorite use of this technology worldwide is in the
humble highlighter pen. Created in the 1960s, highlighters
were originally just felt tips with thin, water-based inks

that allowed the original text to show through. A decade
later fluorescent dyes were added to highlighters to
make the portions of text they were brushed over seem
even more attention-grabbing. Stabilo has sold over
2 billion highlighters to date, and although they are
available in an ever proliferating array of colors, two stand
head and shoulders above the rest: 85 percent of sales go to
yellow and pink.[2]

Amaranth

"A rose and an amaranth blossomed side by side in a garden," begins Aesop's fable. The amaranth, a leggy plant with fresh green leaves and dense, catkin-like blooms, speaks to her neighbor. "How I envy your beauty and your sweet scent! No wonder you are such a universal favorite." But the rose replies, a little sadly: "I bloom but for a time: my petals soon wither and fall, and then I die. But your flowers never fade . . . they are everlasting."[1]

Aesop's audience would have known exactly what he meant. Although many of the 50 or so species that make up the genus have some rather unpleasant monikers— "careless weed," "prostrate pigweed," "love-lies-bleeding"— amaranth has long been revered. Its name is homonymic, referring to the plant and also meaning "everlasting." Garlands of amaranth were used to honor heroes like Achilles because they hinted, with their long-lasting blooms, at immortality.[2] This symbolism made it irresistible for writers: in *Paradise Lost* John Milton gave the angelic host crowns woven from amaranth and gold [page 86].

The people with the richest relationship with amaranth, however, were the Aztecs, who called it *huautli*. The earliest archaeological evidence for amaranth comes from what is now Mexico and dates from 4000 B.C. The plant was an important foodstuff: the leaves can be cooked like spinach and the pinhead-sized seeds can be toasted or milled or popped like corn.[3] Some amaranth was grown on special floating gardens, boats filled with soil and set adrift on lakes; the water helped regulate the temperature of the soil and stopped animals from getting at the crop.[4] Farmers delivered some 22,000 tons of seed to Montezuma (1466–1520), the last Aztec ruler, each year.[5]

The Spanish conquerors were highly suspicious of amaranth. The problem was not the role it played in the Aztecs' diet, but in their religion. They considered the plant

sacred and it played a key role in many rituals. The Catholic
Spaniards were particularly disturbed by the practice of
mixing a little blood from human sacrifices into amaranth
dough and baking it into cakes, which were then broken up
and eaten by the faithful. It was all a little too close to a
parody of Holy Communion for them to stomach.[6] Growing,
eating, and even possessing amaranth were outlawed.

What saved the amaranth was its toughness and
fecundity. A single seed head can contain 500,000 seeds,
and it will grow anywhere. Try as they might, the Spaniards
could neither stamp the amaranth out completely, nor erase
its association with the divine. In 1629 a priest complained
that the locals were supplementing their Christian devotions
with little edible figures of Christ baked from amaranth
dough. In the nineteenth century there were reports of
rosaries being made out of the stuff, and popped amaranth,
mixed with honey, is still used to make a sweet called
alegria ("happiness") in Mexico.[7]

As a color, too, amaranth has gone into a decline.
It was well enough known in the eighteenth and nineteenth
centuries to make it into both dictionaries and fashion
reports. In May 1890, for example, *Harper's Bazaar*
recommended it for both silks and woolens, along with
aubergine, prune, and lees-of-wine.[8] It was also the name
given to an artificial raspberry-hued azo dye first created
in the 1880s. This is still used as a food additive—under
the name E123—in Europe, where it gives maraschino
cherries their distinctive color, but has been banned in
America because it is thought to be carcinogenic.

Although the name is still occasionally used, there is now
no consensus on whether it refers to a cherry red, a dusty
grape, or a rich plum. Time, sadly, has given the lie to
Aesop: the rose's beauty is as beloved as ever, while
amaranth's fortunes have withered.

Scarlet
Cochineal
Vermilion
Rosso corsa
Hematite
Madder
Dragon's blood

Red

In 2012 a study was published in the *Journal of Hospitality and Tourism Research*, advising waitresses to wear red. Why? Research found that if they wore this color, the tips they were given by male patrons would be increased by up to 26 percent. (It had no effect on female diners, who were stingier tippers overall anyway.)[1]

Psychologists have long been fascinated by red's influence on the human psyche. A 2007 study, for example, tested the effect of color on intellectual performance. The test subjects were required to solve anagrams. Those whose tests had red covers performed worse than those with green or black; they also chose easier options when given the choice.[2] At the 2004 Olympic Games in Athens, combat-sport competitors who wore red won 55 percent of the time. And in a study of games played since the Second World War, English soccer teams who wear this color are more likely to be champions and on average finish higher in the leagues than teams in any other.[3] Nor are we the only species to be susceptible. Monkeys such as rhesus macaques and mandrills have cherry-colored areas on their rumps, faces, and genitalia that indicate their testosterone levels and aggression.[4] (However, the animal most famously irked by red, the bull, is color-blind. It is the flutter and swish of the matadors' small muleta cape that the bulls react to—tests have shown that they charge at the capote, which is magenta [page 167] on one side and blue on the other, with equal fury.)

It is believed that people first began dyeing cloth sometime between the sixth and fourth millennia B.C. Most of the scraps of dyed cloth that date from this time until the Roman era were colored a shade of red.[5] (So special was this color that for the Romans the words *colored* [*coloratus*] and *red* [*ruber*] were synonyms.)

Ancient Egyptians wrapped mummies in linens dyed
with hematite [page 150]; Osiris, god of the afterlife and
underworld, was also known as the "lord of the red cloth."[6]
It is, along with black, one of the colors the ancient
Chinese associated with death, and the contrasting pair
appear frequently in tombs and graves. Later it formed
part of the influential five-element system, associated
with fire, summer, and the planet Mars.[7] Now, in addition
to its link with the Party, the Chinese see it as the color
of joy and good luck: gifts of money, called *hongbao*, are
given in lacquer-red envelopes at special occasions like
weddings.

As the color of blood, red is also strongly associated
with power. The Inca deity Mama Huaco was said to
have emerged from the Cave of Origin wearing a red dress.[8]
Pliny mentioned that the red dye cochineal was reserved
for Roman generals, and the color, however conspicuous
and impractical, has often been used by warriors since,
including the British redcoats. The Aztecs painstakingly
deposited cochineal [page 141] insect eggs onto cactus
leaves with fox-hair brushes so that their rulers would have
a ready supply of red-fringed headdresses and their priests
could attract the attention of the gods during rituals.[9]
On the other side of the Atlantic, both kings and cardinals
were inordinately fond of luxurious red clothes. In 1999 it
appeared in 74 percent of the world's flags, making it by far
the most popular color to exemplify a nation's identity.

As well as power, red has baser associations with lust
and aggression. The devil is traditionally depicted in red.
The association of red and sex in the West dates back at
least until the Middle Ages. It was frequently the color
assigned to prostitutes in the many sumptuary laws passed
over the course of the period.[10] Small wonder that it has
had a stormy relationship with women. Hester Prynne,

the heroine of *The Scarlet Letter*, has so fascinated readers
since the novel's publication in 1850 because she defies
easy categorization. On the one hand, she flouts the
conventional sexual purity of her age and sex, but on
the other, she accepts the condemnation of her Puritan
neighbors and meekly wears a scarlet A as punishment.
The ambivalent relationship between women and red can
be seen in other works of fiction, including *The Bride Wore
Red*, "Little Red Riding Hood," and *Gone with the Wind*.

This potent brew of power and sexuality make the
color a bold but tricky choice for brands. Virgin is
perhaps the best example of a company that has
successfully harnessed red's innate power, but only by
positioning itself as a bold outsider. Coca-Cola owes its
livery to the red-and-white flag of Peru, which is where
the company sourced the coca leaves and cocaine its
drinks contained until the 1920s.[11] Artists of all stripes
have relied heavily on the shades between oxblood and
persimmon to add drama, eroticism, and depth to their
work. For the Pre-Raphaelites reds—and redheads
[page 105]—were almost talismanic. Rothko, who wrote
that his art's principle concern was "the human element,"
layered tone upon tone of red on his giant canvases.
He identified it, as the art critic Diane Waldman put it,
"with fire and with blood." Anish Kapoor, an avid user
of color, spent the 1980s rendering his pyramidic, phallic,
and vulva-like sculptures in a red so bright it almost
vibrates. His *Svayambh* (2007) was a slow, crimson train
of pigment and wax that squeezed itself back and forth
through the triumphal doorways of the Royal Academy
in 2009, looking, absurdly, like a voluptuously overweight
lipstick. This mobile artwork, just like the red light on
the traffic light, stopped people in their tracks.

Scarlet

On February 8, 1587, Mary Queen of Scots was executed
after 18 years' imprisonment. Contemporary accounts of
her death at Fotheringhay Castle are gruesome: several
report that it took two blows to sever her neck; others say
that when her head was held aloft her wig came off to
reveal the near-bald scalp of a sick old woman. What many
agree on, however, is that before the execution, Mary
carefully removed her somber outer clothes to reveal a
bright scarlet undergown. Sympathetic onlookers would
have had no difficulty unraveling her intended message:
scarlet was closely associated in the Catholic Church
with martyrdom. For those hostile to the Scottish queen
and her faith, however, her bright red dress was a clear link
to the archetypal scarlet woman, the biblical Whore of
Babylon.

This binary reading is typical of scarlet. Although
it has long been prized as a color for the prestigious and
powerful, it has, from the beginning, always been a victim
of unintended meanings. The very name, for example,
did not initially refer to a color at all, but to a kind of
particularly admired woolen cloth. From the fourteenth
century, because fine cloth was so often colored with
kermes, the brightest and most resilient dyestuff then
known, the word came to denote the color instead.

Like cochineal [page 141], kermes dye was made
from the bodies of insects so small that they were often
mistaken for seeds or grains.[1] (Pliny, writing in the
first century A.D., described it as "a berry that becomes
a worm.") Making a single gram of this precious red
required the bodies of up to 80 female kermes beetles
imported from southern Europe, making it very expensive,
and getting precisely the right tone took skill. The finished
product, though, was a dye so bright and colorfast
that cloth dyed with it became the epitome of luxury.

An account book from the reign of King Henry VI, who
ruled England during the fifteenth century, shows that
it took a master mason a month to earn enough to buy
a single yard of the cheapest scarlet cloth; the dearest cost
twice as much.[2]

Charlemagne, the Frankish king who ruled during
the early Middle Ages, is said to have worn scarlet leather
shoes when he was crowned Holy Roman Emperor in A.D.
800. Richard II of England followed sartorial suit 500 years
later. Sumptuary laws passed in León and Castile in the
thirteenth century restricted use of the color to kings.[3]
Red-haired Elizabeth I, who knew a thing or two about
the power of appearances, enjoyed wearing scarlet as a
princess. It would not do, though, as a color for the virgin
queen, and so after her coronation in 1558 she took to
wearing neutral or broken tones like tawny, gold, and ash.
However, this emblem of majesty was too useful to cast
aside completely: Elizabeth hit upon the ruse of dressing
her ladies-in-waiting and retainers in scarlet instead,
presumably so that they could act as a dramatically
symbolic backdrop. William Shakespeare, in his role
as a royal actor, was given four and a half yards of cloth
with which to fashion himself scarlet livery to wear at the
coronation of Elizabeth's successor, James I.[4] And where
wealth goes, power soon follows. Pope Paul II decreed
in 1464 that his cardinals were to wear robes of rich
scarlet instead of purple, the poor Tyrian-purple mollusks
[page 162] being all but extinct by this time.[5] The habit
stuck and scarlet became inextricably linked with insignia,
particularly in the Church and academia, a heritage
Mary was drawing on at her execution.

Although many associate the British with the idea
of red military uniforms, scarlet's dalliance with men
in uniform dates back much further. The highest orders

Scarlet, continued.

of Roman generals wore bright red *paludamenta*—cloaks signaling leadership, which fastened over one shoulder.[6] It was taken up by the English under Oliver Cromwell, who specified that officers' coats should be dyed scarlet in Gloucestershire using a newly discovered recipe.[7]

In 1606 Cornelis Drebbel, a Dutch scientist and the first man to build a working submarine, was making a thermometer in his lab in London. As the (likely apocryphal) story goes, he boiled up a solution of purple-red cochineal and left it under his windowsill to cool. Somehow a phial of *acqua regia*, a strong acid mixture, broke and spilled across the tin window frame, splashing into the cooling cochineal and instantly turning the liquid bright scarlet.[8] One dyer's manual called the result "[f]lame-colored scarlet." "The finest and brightest color," the author wrote, "on the orange, full of fire, and of a brightness which dazzles the eye."[9]

Naturally, this brilliant red has had plenty of detractors too. It was a favorite of the Wife of Bath, Chaucer's morally ambivalent character in *The Canterbury Tales*. Shakespeare used it in conjunction with hypocrites, indignation, and "sinne."[10] A purple passage from the book of Revelation in the King James Bible—"I saw a woman sit upon a scarlet colored beast"—led Puritans to argue that the entire Catholic Church, now known for its red-robed cardinals, was evil. It was this heritage that Aleister Crowley, the twentieth-century occultist, drew on when he created the Scarlet Woman, the Thelemic deity of female desire and sexuality. And while the hue has been almost continually in fashion since the fourteenth century, not everyone has approved. Scarlet "is a charming color," *Arthur's* magazine conceded in February 1885, "in spite of its being a favorite with Indians and barbarians generally."[11]

Cochineal

Viewed with the naked eye, the female *Dactylopius coccus*
could be mistaken for a seed or a piece of grit; scarcely
bigger than a pinhead, it is a gray, slightly ridged oval.
It was only when one was examined under a microscope
at the very end of the seventeenth century that lingering
doubts were put to rest: *Dactylopius coccus* is, in fact,
an insect. And, while it may look inconsequential, this
insect has made and felled kings and empires, and helped
shape history.

Today the cocci are most likely to be encountered in
Mexico or South America, huddled in a snowy white
cluster on the sunny side of a prickly pear cactus leaf,
on which they feed exclusively and voraciously.[1] If you
were to pluck one off and squeeze hard enough to crush
it, your guilty fingers would be stained bright crimson.
Turning this bright red bug juice into a dye, often called
carmine, is relatively easy. One needs only the insects and
a mordant, usually alum, to help the color adhere to the
cloth; by using other additives, such as acids or metals
like tin, the color of the dye can be shifted from pale
pink to a red so dark it is almost black.[2] It requires a lot
of insects—around 70,000 dried bugs for a pound of raw
cochineal—but the end result is one of the strongest and
brightest the world has ever known. The colorant (mostly
carminic acid), from a pound of "domesticated" or farmed
cocci, is said to be equivalent to around 10 or 12 pounds of
kermes [page 138].[3]

Civilizations have been aware of cochineal's colorful
secret for quite some time. It was used as a dye in Central
and South America from at least the second century B.C.
and became intrinsic to the Aztec and Inca Empires. A list
written around 1520 recorded the tributes the Aztecs
required from their subjects: the Mixtec people were
to give 40 sacks of cochineal per year; the Zapotecs,

Cochineal, continued.

20 bags every 80 days.[4] It was also used to signal personal
power in the region. Captain Baltasar de Ocampo, who in
1572 witnessed the execution of Túpac Amaru, the last
of the royal Inca line, carefully described the king's outfit
in a moving eyewitness account of his death.

*[Dressed in a] mantle and doublet of crimson velvet. His shoes were
made of the wool of the country, of several colors. The crown or
headdress, called mascapaychu, was on his head, with fringe over
his forehead, this being the royal insignia of the Inca.*[5]

When his head fell, the Inca ruler was clothed in a
symphony of cochineal.

It was in part for the sake of cochineal that this Inca
king—and many other South American rulers—died.
The Spanish were desperate to exploit the region's natural
resources, and they were not slow to capitalize on them
once they gained control. Along with gold [page 86] and
silver [page 49], cochineal provided the financial sinew
on which the Spanish Empire depended. One observer
wrote that in the year 1587 alone, around 144,000 pounds
or 72 tons of cochineal were shipped from Lima to Spain.[6]
(That is roughly 10,080,000,000 insects.)

Once the shipments arrived in Spain—they were
legally required to land in Seville or Cádiz until the
eighteenth century—cochineal was exported to paint the
towns and people of the world red. It dyed the famous
Venetian velvets from the mid-sixteenth century, funded
the Dutch dye industry, clothed Roman Catholic cardinals,
gave women's cheeks a rosy flush, and was also used as
medicine. King Philip II of Spain was dosed with a
revolting mixture of crushed bugs and vinegar when he
felt under the weather.[7] Later it was traded to Cambodia
and Siam, and by 1700 the Chinese Kangxi emperor

referred to a foreign dyestuff called *ko-tcha-ni-la*, later
renamed *yang hong*, or "foreign red."[8] Americans, desperate
for the bright dyestuff but furious that, because it could
only be traded to them via Spain, it cost so much, would
pore over the contents of shipwrecks in case they contained
cochineal. The *Nuevo Constante*, which sank off the
coast of Louisiana in 1766, was found to contain over
10,000 pounds of the dye in leather sacks.[9] It was deemed
so valuable that there were several attempts to bug-nap
cochineal in order to break the Spanish monopoly.
A foolhardy attempt in 1777 by Nicolas-Joseph Thiéry
de Menonville, a botanist from Lorraine, was covertly
financed by the French government.[10]

Beetles are still being harvested today to produce
the cochineal used by the cosmetics and food industries.
It is found in everything from M&M's to sausages, red
velvet cupcakes to Cherry Coke (to soothe the squeamish
it is usually hidden under the far more innocuous label
E120). There are signs, however, that humanity's appetite
for cochineal may finally be waning: in 2012 Starbucks
abandoned it as the principal red food coloring in
strawberry Frappuccinos and cake pops after an outcry
from vegetarians and Muslims. Excellent news for
Dactylopius coccus, but perhaps less so for the world's
prickly pears.

Vermilion

By the beginning of the twentieth century, Pompeii had been the site of an archaeological dig for over 150 years. What had begun as a scramble to strip away ancient trophies for the private collection of the Bourbon king Charles III had evolved into an effort to preserve the wonders of the city that had been simultaneously destroyed and preserved by the eruption of Vesuvius in A.D. 79. In April 1909, when it seemed as if Pompeii might have disgorged most of its secrets, archaeologists discovered a luxurious home with large windows, overlooking the sea. Within a week of the first excavation, a red mural was uncovered that was so well conserved, elaborate, and unfathomable that ever since the site has been known as the Villa dei Misteri—"Villa of Mysteries."

The walls of the room are covered with expressive images of people on an intense ground of deep red vermilion. In one corner a winged figure raises a whip to strike the back of a naked woman kneeling with her face buried in the lap of another. Near the entrance a small boy is lost in the contents of a scroll he is reading; at the center a drunken man lolls against the skirts of a seated figure. Guesses as to what it all means are boundless, but the extravagant use of vermilion tells us that whatever its purpose, this room was intended to induce awe: vermilion was the most coveted red pigment available at the time.

A natural supply of vermilion (mercury sulfide) comes from the mineral cinnabar. This wine-red stone is the principal ore of the metal mercury—the Roman architect Vitruvius picturesquely described the dark red rocks sweating droplets of quicksilver. To become a useful pigment it need only be finely ground. The Romans adored it. A jar of ready-ground cinnabar of the kind used in the villa was unearthed in a pigment shop in the town

below the Villa dei Misteri. Pliny wrote that it was used
during the religious holidays, smeared on the face of statues
of Jupiter, and on the bodies of worshippers.[1] Vermilion,
though, was scarce. Much of the Roman supply came,
under guard, from Sisapu in Spain, and cost 70 sesterces
a pound, ten times the price of red ocher.[2]

It was when people discovered how to manufacture
vermilion artificially, however, using a reaction that
resembled magic, that desire for the pigment really
intensified. No one is quite sure who made the discovery,
or when: alchemists were fond of using elaborate codes
for ingredients and hinting that they possessed special
knowledge, without revealing precisely what this
knowledge might be. The Greek alchemist Zosimus
of Panopolis insinuated that he knew the secret sometime
around A.D. 300, but the first clear description is in
Compositiones ad tingenda ("Recipes for Coloring"),
a Latin manuscript from the eighth century.[3]

The reason for all this subterfuge lies in alchemists'
obsession with creating gold [page 86], which to them
was red, rather than yellow, and which they therefore
linked with this new red pigment. Even more significant
was the fact that making vermilion required the
combination and transformation of two key alchemical
ingredients: mercury and sulfur. The alchemists forging
vermilion were convinced the secret to producing
unlimited supplies of gold could not be far away.

The most evocative description of what became
known as dry-method vermilion was written by the
twelfth-century Benedictine monk Theophilus.
He described mixing one part ground sulfur with two
parts mercury, which was then carefully sealed in a jar:

Vermilion, continued.

Then bury [the jar] in blazing coals and as soon as it begins to get hot,
you will hear a crashing inside, as the mercury unites with the
blazing sulfur.

If conducted carelessly, the reaction could be even more
dramatic than intended. The mercury fumes released if
the jars weren't sealed properly were so poisonous that
the process was banned in Venice in 1294.[4]

Vermilion was once as costly and precious as gold.[5]
It reigned supreme as medieval artists' red and was used,
reverently, alongside gold leaf and ultramarine for
manuscript capitals and on tempera panels. It was glazed
with a revolting mixture of egg yolk and earwax.[6]

But this prince of reds was too profitable for recipes
and manufacturers to remain scarce. In 1760 Amsterdam,
the principal source of Dutch dry-method vermilion during
the seventeenth and eighteenth centuries, exported just
under 32,000 pounds to England.[7] A wet method of
manufacture, discovered by the German chemist Gottfried
Schulz in 1687, made it more common still. Even as early
as the fifteenth century artists had been all but profligate
with its use; Leonardo da Vinci occasionally used it as a
grounding layer for his paintings.[8] Not only was vermilion
becoming more common, it was also adversely affected
by the rise of oils as the painting medium of choice in the
West from the fifteenth century onward: vermilion was
less opaque in oils, and so worked better either as a base
layer on which to apply other red glazes, or as a glazing
layer itself.

In tempera and lacquerwork, though, its color is
breathtaking, and it has seduced artists the world over.
A Chinese handscroll painting, *Tribute Horse and Groom*
by Chao Yung, shows a man wearing a fire-red coat with
an indigo collar, and a strange, rust-colored pointy hat,

leading a beautiful dappled gray horse. Although it was painted in 1347, the vermilion-painted coat still strikes the eye like a hammer. The same effect was used three centuries later by Peter Paul Rubens in the central panel of his triptych *The Descent from the Cross* (1612–4), although its use declined thereafter.[9] In 1912, just a few years after the Villa of Mysteries was uncovered, Wassily Kandinsky described vermilion's color as "a feeling of sharpness, like glowing steel which can be cooled by water".[10]

Rosso corsa

In September 1907 a neatly built man with a deep widow's
peak and a large nose sat at his desk in his neo-Gothic
palace on the Isola del Garda. Although a month had
elapsed since his return to the island, he was still sunburnt
and travel sore and, although he knew it was unbecoming
to show it, rather pleased with himself. "There are people
who say that our journey has proved one thing above
all others," wrote the man the society pages knew as
Prince Scipione Luigi Marcantonio Francesco Rodolfo
Borghese. "Namely, that it is impossible to go by motorcar
from Peking to Paris."[1] He was being facetious, of course,
because that is precisely what he had just done.

It had all begun some months earlier, when the French
newspaper *Le Matin* had printed a challenge on the front
page of the January 31, 1907, edition: "Will anyone agree
to go, this summer, from Peking to Paris by motorcar?"[2]
Prince Borghese, who had already traveled through Persia
and had acquired a taste for adventure, promptly accepted,
along with four other teams, three of them French and one
Dutch. The only prize was a case of Mumm champagne—
and national honor. Naturally Borghese, as a proud Italian
aristocrat, insisted that his vehicle be a product of his
native country. The technology was still in its infancy—the
first car ever built was only then celebrating its twenty-first
year—and choices were few. Borghese chose a "powerful
but heavy" 40-HP Itala model from Turin, which was
painted a strident poppy red.[3]

The race took the contestants some 12,000 miles, past
the Great Wall of China and through the Gobi Desert and
Ural Mountains. So confident was Borghese of winning
that he strayed several hundred miles from the route so that
he and his passengers could attend a banquet held in their
honor in St. Petersburg. As they suffered on the long
journey, so the car suffered too. Before its departure Luigi

Barzini, a journalist and one of Borghese's companions, wrote of the Itala: "It conveyed an immediate impression of purpose and go." At Irkutsk, a city in southeast Russia, it was looking rather more forlorn. Even after a "careful external toilette" by Ettore, Borghese's mechanic, "It was weather-beaten and, like ourselves, had taken on a darker shade." By the time they reached Moscow it was "the color of the earth."[4]

None of this mattered, however—to either the contestants or their adoring Italian fans—when the team roared victorious through the Parisian boulevards. In honor of their victory their car's original hue became Italy's national racing color and later the one adopted by Enzo Ferrari for his cars: *rosso corsa*, racing red.[5]

Hematite

When Wah, an ancient Egyptian storehouse manager, was mummified in around 1975 B.C., he was first wrapped with undyed linen. Amulets and trinkets were secreted between the layers and then, as the finishing touch, he was swathed in a hematite-red cloth that had the words "Temple linen to protect" along one edge. Osiris, the ancient Egyptian god of the afterlife, was, after all, referred to as "lord of the red cloth" in the Book of the Dead, and it never hurts to show up to a big event appropriately dressed.[1]

The use of hematite in Wah's preparation for the afterlife is just one example of the central role it has played in a whole host of spiritual duties. For the sake of simplicity, *hematite*, which is, strictly speaking, the mineral form of iron oxide, here also includes other kinds of red iron oxides and ochers. All owe their coloring to the same compound: Fe_2O_3, anhydrous iron oxide, or, more simply, rust.[2] This incestuous family of pigments occurs naturally and widely across the earth's crust. They come in many different shades of red, from pink through to cayenne; when heated, yellow ocher can even be turned red.

Objects stained deep red have accompanied human habitation since the Upper Paleolithic era, some 50,000 years ago.[3] Although not ubiquitous, hematite's use is so widespread that in an article from 1980, the anthropologist Ernst E. Wreschner went so far as to call its collection and use one of the "two meaningful regularities in human evolution," the other being toolmaking.[4] Tools, shells, bones, and other small objects stained with hematite have been found at Paleolithic sites in Gönnersdorf in Germany, North Africa, Mesoamerica, and China.[5] Perhaps because it resembles blood, it was also widely used in ancient burial rituals. Sometimes it seems as if it has just been sprinkled over or on the body, but in other cases its use is more elaborate. In China it is often found paired with black.[6]

In Egypt, linens stained with hematite, such as those used to wrap Wah's body, have been found dating back to the second millennium B.C.

Natural sources of hematite were much prized. In the fourth century B.C. a law was passed granting Athenians a monopoly over a particularly rich variety on the island of Kea, which they used in everything from shipbuilding to medicine to ink.[7] (The ink was so popular for titles and subtitles that the word *rubric*—from the Latin *rubrica* or *red ocher*—evolved from this practice.)

So why all the prehistoric fuss? The answer seems to lie in the human affinity for the color red. Most anthropologists and archaeologists believe that, as the color of blood, red is associated with life—celebration, sex, joy—danger, and death. As a conduit to so many useful symbolic meanings, hematite was prized. The fate of the mineral as a pigment provides compelling proof for two theories: if the first is that the color red holds a special place in the human psyche, the second is surely that people are shamelessly attracted to bright colors. Hematite—which, though red, is not bright—was demoted the moment a more vivid alternative became available. It seems that humanity, or at least its taste in reds, has rather ungratefully evolved past it.

Madder

"The flower is very small, and of a greenish yellow color,"
the man said. "The root is cylindrical and fleshy, and of
a reddish yellow color."[1] The audience did not know it yet,
but the lecture being delivered to the Royal Society
of the Arts in London on the evening of May 8, 1879,
was going to be a long one. Though the speaker was
distinguished, with an imposingly full set of whiskers,
he was neither naturally entertaining, nor brief. Over
several hours William Henry Perkin, the scientist and
businessman who had discovered mauve [page 169]
and revolutionized the dye industry, told the assembled
listeners, in rich, exact detail, about another breakthrough:
the synthesis of alizarin. By the end, only the most
determined of his listeners would have grasped the
significance of his achievement. Alizarin was the red
colorant in the roots of *Rubia tinctorum*, *Rubia peregrina*,
and *Rubia cordifolia*, better known as madder. Perkin
had been able to create in a lab something hitherto
produced only by nature.

As he went on to explain to his increasingly inattentive
listeners, madder is an ancient dyestuff. Although madder
plants are unprepossessing, their pinkish roots, when
dried and crushed, pounded and sifted, relinquish a fluffy,
orange-brown powdery pigment that has been a long-serving
source of red. It was used in Egypt from about 1500 B.C.,
and fabric stained with the plant's root was found in
Tutankhamen's tomb.[2] Pliny wrote of its importance
in the classical world, and it was discovered among the
wares of a paint-maker's shop in the fossilized city of
Pompeii.[3] Once the use of mordants that made madder
more colorfast spread, its influence grew still further.
India's chintz fabrics were printed with it; it dyed medieval
wedding clothes an appropriately celebratory shade; and it
was used as a cheaper alternative to cochineal [page 141]

for British redcoats.[4] It could also be used to make rose
madder paint, a bright pinky-red artists' pigment, which
George Field waxed passionate about in *Chromatography*
in 1835.[5]

It was as a dye, however, that the big money could
be made from madder. For a long time the Turkish had
a monopoly on a special method of using madder to obtain
a red so bright it could almost trump its more expensive
rivals. In the eighteenth century, first the Dutch, then the
French, and finally the British uncovered the malodorous
secret of Turkey red—it was a tortuous process involving
rancid castor oil, ox blood, and dung.[6] The trade must
have seemed unassailable. By 1860 imports to Britain
were worth over £1 million annually but were often of
poor quality. The French were accused of adulterating
their madder with everything from brick dust to oats.[7] The
cost soared too: by 1868 a hundredweight (approximately
112 pounds) cost 30 shillings, a week's wages for a laborer.
A year later the same amount would cost just 8 shillings.[8]
This, of course, was due to the simultaneous discovery by
Mr. Perkin in Britain, and three German scientists in
Berlin, of the process for synthesizing alizarin. For the first
time in history, clothes could be dyed madder red without
a single *Rubia tinctorum* being uprooted.

Dragon's blood

On the morning of May 27, 1668, a gentleman was riding
through a remote corner of Essex in southeast England
when he stumbled across a dragon. It had been sunning
itself at the edge of a birch wood but suddenly reared up
at his approach. It was vast: nine feet from hissing tongue
to tail, about as thick as a man's thigh, with a pair of
leathery wings that appeared far too small to get its
enormous bulk airborne. The man spurred his horse and
"with winged speed hafted away, glad that they had
escaped such an eminent danger."

But the tale of the beast was not quite over yet. Men
from the nearby village of Saffron Walden, perhaps worried
that the dragon might become peckish and begin making
inroads into their cattle herds, or perhaps bored and
skeptical, set out in pursuit. To their surprise they found
it in almost exactly the same place. Again it lifted the front
of its body into the air and, hissing loudly, disappeared
into the underbrush. The villagers saw it again and again
over the next few months, until one day, without
explanation, they found the birch wood to be dragon-free
once more. The whole saga was written down in a
pamphlet, *The Flying Serpent, or Strange News out of Essex*,
a copy of which is still on view at the local library.[1]

It is odd to think that, at the same moment villagers
were scouring the local countryside trying to see off a
dragon, some 40 miles away in London Isaac Newton was
beginning to foment the Scientific Revolution. Perhaps the
dragon's appearance was a last-gasp display from a creature
that was on the cusp of being driven forever into the realm
of myth by the advance of the Enlightenment. And with
the dragon, of course, went its blood, which had been an
exclusive pigment since before the birth of Christ. When
Pliny, deploring an ever-expanding palette distracting
artists from the serious business of art, wrote that "India

contributes the ooze of her rivers and the blood of dragons and elephants," he was referring to dragon's blood.[2] The belief was that elephants had cooling blood and dragons, during the dry season, craved something cool to slake their thirst. The dragons would hide in trees, waiting to ambush any elephants that might wander underneath, and then pounce. Sometimes they killed the elephants outright and drank their blood, but sometimes the elephant would crush the dragon and they would die together, their two bloods mixing to form a red resinous substance called dragon's blood.[3]

As with most myths, this one contains a nub of truth overlaid with a great deal of embellishment. For a start, no animals of any kind, even mythological, are harmed in the production of dragon's blood. But this pigment does exist, it does come from the East, and trees do play a part in its production. It is in fact a wound-red resin, drawn often, though not exclusively, from the *Dracaena* genus of trees.[4] George Field, writing in 1835, wasn't enthusiastic. Not only was the pigment "deepened by impure air, and darkened by light," but it also reacted with the ubiquitous white lead and took forever to dry in oils. "It does not," Mr. Field concluded sternly, "merit the attention of the artist."[5]

He was, by this time, preaching to a choir of disenchanted artists: they had little use for yet another red, particularly one with such obvious limitations. Without widespread belief in dragons to sustain it, dragon's blood followed Saffron Walden's winged serpent into obscurity.

Tyrian purple
Archil
Magenta
Mauve
Heliotrope
Violet

Purple

In *The Color Purple*, the Pulitzer Prize–winning novel by
Alice Walker, the character Shug Avery seems at first like a
superficial siren. She is, we are told, "so stylish it like the
trees all round the house draw themself up tall for a better
look." Later, though, she reveals unexpected insightfulness,
and it is Shug that supplies the novel's title. "I think it
pisses God off," Shug says, "if you walk by the color purple
in a field somewhere and don't notice it." For Shug purple
is evidence of God's glory and generosity.

The belief that purple is special, and signifies power,
is surprisingly widespread. Now it is seen as a secondary
color, sandwiched in artists' color wheels between the
primaries red and blue. Linguistically, too, it has often
been subordinate to larger color categories—red, blue, or
even black. Nor is purple, per se, part of the visible color
spectrum (although violet, the very shortest spectral
wavelength humans can see, is).

The story of purple is bookended by two great dyes.
The first of these, Tyrian [page 162], a symbol of the
wealthy and the elite, helped to establish the link with
the divine. The second, mauve [page 169], a man-made
chemical wonder, ushered in the democratization of
color in the nineteenth century. The precise shade
of the ancient world's wonder dye remains something
of a mystery. In fact *purple* itself was a somewhat
fluid term. The ancient Greek and Latin words for the
color, *porphyra* and *purpura* respectively, were also used to
refer to deep crimson shades, like the color of blood.
Ulpian, a third-century Roman jurist, defined *purpura* as
anything red other than things dyed with coccus or carmine
dyes.[1] Pliny the Elder (A.D. 23–79) wrote that the best
Tyrian cloth was tinged with black.[2]

Even if no one is quite sure precisely what Tyrian
purple looked like, though, the sources all agree it was the

color of power. While he griped about its odor, which
hovered somewhere between rotting shellfish and garlic,
Pliny had no doubt about its authority:

This is the purple for which the Roman fasces and axes clear a way.
It is the badge of noble youth; it distinguishes the senator from the knight;
it is called in to appease the gods. It brightens every garment, and shares
with gold the glory of the triumph. For these reasons we must pardon the
mad desire for purple.[3]

Because of this mad desire, and the expense of creating
Tyrian, purple became the symbolic color of opulence,
excess, and rulers. To be born into the purple was to be
born into royalty, after the Byzantine custom of bedecking
the royal birthing chambers with porphyry and Tyrian
cloth so that it would be the first thing the new princelings
saw. The Roman poet Horace, in his *The Art of Poetry*
written in 18 B.C., minted the phrase "purple prose": "Your
opening shows great promise, / And yet flashy purple
patches; as when / Describing a sacred grove, or the altar
of Diana."[4]

Purple's special status wasn't confined to the West.
In Japan a deep purple, *murasaki*, was *kin-jiki*, or a
forbidden color, off-limits to ordinary people.[5] In the 1980s
the Mexican government allowed a Japanese company,
Purpura Imperial, to collect the local *caracol* sea snail for
kimono dyeing. (Unsurprisingly, a similar Japanese species,
Rapana bezoar, is vanishingly rare.) While the local Mixtec
people, who had been using the *caracol* for centuries,
milked the snails of their purple, leaving them alive,
Purpura Imperial's method was rather more fatal for the
snails, and the population went into freefall. After years of
lobbying the contract was revoked.[6]

Like many special things, purple has always been

a greedy consumer of resources. Not only have billions
of shellfish paid dearly to clothe the wealthy; sources of
slow-growing lichens like *Roccella tinctoria*, used to make
archil [page 165], have been overexploited, forcing people
to look further afield or do without. Even mauve required
vast quantities of raw produce: in the early stages it was so
demanding of scarce raw material that its creator, William
Perkin, later admitted that the whole enterprise was close
to being abandoned.[7]

Luckily for Perkin, his new dye became immensely
fashionable, and the prospect of the fortunes to be made
meant that an explosion of other aniline colors followed
swiftly on mauve's heels. Whether this was also good for
purple is another matter. Suddenly everyone had access
to purple at a reasonable price, but they also had access to
thousands of other colors too. Familiarity bred contempt,
and purple became a color much like any other.

Tyrian purple

One of the most notorious seductions in history took place
in late 48 B.C. Shortly before, on August 9, Julius Caesar
had defeated the far larger army of his rival and son-in-law
Pompey at the Battle of Pharsalus. Now he was in Egypt,
and the most famous woman in the world, less than half
his age, had smuggled herself past his guards and into his
apartment rolled in a rug. When, nine months later,
Cleopatra gave birth to a son called Caesarion, "Little
Caesar," the proud father returned to Rome and promptly
introduced a new toga, which only he was allowed to wear,
in his paramour's favorite color: Tyrian purple.[1]

This rich tone—ideally the color of clotted blood,
according to Pliny—was the product of two varieties of
shellfish native to the Mediterranean, *Thais haemastoma*
and *Murex brandaris*. Were one to crack open the shell
of one of these spiky, carnivorous gastropods, one would
see a pale hypobranchial gland or "bloom" transecting its
body. If this were squeezed, a single drop of clear liquid,
smelling of garlic, would be released. Within moments,
the sunlight would turn the liquid first pale yellow, then sea
green, then blue, and finally a dark purple-red. The best
color, so deep it was tinged with blackness, was obtained
by mixing the fluids from both kinds of shellfish.[2] Getting
the color to adhere and permeate cloth involved a long and
foul-smelling process. The liquid harvested from the
shellfish glands was placed in a vat of stale urine (for the
ammonia) and allowed to ferment for 10 days before
the cloth was added; some accounts recommended treating
cloth to two separate baths.[3]

The earliest evidence of Tyrian dyeing comes from
the fifteenth century B.C.[4] The odor of rotting sea snails,
aging urine, and the fermenting mixture must have been
overpowering—archaeologists have tended to find ancient
dyeworks relegated to the outskirts of towns and cities.

The dye was particularly associated with the Phoenicians, from Tyre, who gave it fame and made a fortune trading it across the region. Tyrian-dyed cloth is mentioned in Homer's *Iliad* (c. 1260–1180 B.C.) and Virgil's *Aeneid* (c. 29–19 B.C.) and depictions of it have also been found in ancient Egypt.

The color's popularity was terrible news for the *Murex* and *Thais*. Since each specimen contained a single drop, it took around 250,000 to make an ounce of dye.[5] The piles of shells discarded millennia ago are so large they have become geographical features littered along the eastern coast of the Mediterranean. The huge labor involved— each snail, for example, had to be caught by hand—had two, interrelated effects. The first was to make Tyrian purple eye-wateringly expensive. In the mid-fourth century B.C. it cost as much as silver; soon enough, Tyrian-dipped cloth was literally worth its weight in gold. By the third century, one Roman emperor told his wife he could not afford to buy her a Tyrian dress.[6]

The second was to associate the color with power and royalty. In republican Rome it was a tightly constrained badge of status. Triumphant generals could wear a purple-and-gold robe; those in the field, plain purple. Senators, consuls, and praetors (a kind of magistrate) wore a broad Tyrian band on their togas; knights, a narrow band.[7] This visual hierarchy changed upon Caesar's return to Rome, when the rules became even more draconian. By the fourth century A.D. only the emperor was allowed to wear Tyrian purple; anyone else caught wearing it could face death.[8] Once, the emperor Nero saw a woman in mollusk-mauve at a recital. He had her dragged from the room, stripped naked, and relieved of her property, so seriously did he equate the color with imperial power. Diocletian, a Roman ruler who was more pragmatic (or perhaps just

Tyrian purple, continued.

greedier) than the others, said that anyone could wear the color, just so long as they could afford the exorbitant fee and all the profit went to him.[9] Farther east, Byzantine queens gave birth in wine-dark rooms so that the royal offspring were said to be born "in the purple," thus cementing their right to rule.

Fortunately for the poor snails, international politics and fate granted them a reprieve before they could be wiped out completely. In 1453 Constantinople, the capital of the Roman and Byzantine Empire, fell to the Turks and with it was lost the secret of the manufacture of the world's finest purple. It was another four centuries before an obscure French marine biologist called Henri de Lacaze-Duthiers stumbled across the murex and its purple.[10] The year, though, was 1856: the very same year in which another shade of purple, mauve [page 169], went into production.

Archil

Color can be found in the most unpromising of places.
Archil (alias: orchil, orchell, tournesol, orcein, and cudbear)
is a dark red-purple dye, made from lichens. Most people
know lichen when they see it growing flatly on bricks
or the bark of trees, but few take much notice. On closer
inspection, lichen proves more intriguing. It is not a single
organism but usually two, typically a fungus and an alga,
living in a symbiotic relationship so close that it takes
a microscope to distinguish one from the other.[1]

Several lichens can be used to make dye. Early modern
Dutch dyers produced one called lac or litmus, which they
sold in the form of small, dark blue cakes. (Lichens are
very sensitive to differing pH levels; and doctors could
grind up various species and use them to test the acidity
of a patient's urine, hence "litmus test.") The one
principally used for archil is called *Roccella tinctoria*.
Seen clinging to a rock, it does not look very promising
at all. Like most of the archil-producing lichens, it is
a nasty buff-gray color, and it grows in small clumps
that resemble pallid seaweed. Lichens such as this grow
in many places, including the Canary and Cape Verde
Islands, Scotland, and various small sites in Africa, the
Levant, and South America.[2]

The secret of archil production seems to have been
lost to the West until the fourteenth century, when an
Italian merchant called Federigo traveled to the Levant
and discovered the tinting properties of the local lichens.[3]
On his return to Florence, he began using the lichens to
dye wools and silks the much-loved, rich purple color that
had previously been associated only with the (much more
expensive) *Murex* pigments. Federigo's enterprise made
him rich. His family, sensing a branding opportunity,
changed their name to Ruccellis.[4] Gradually knowledge of
the dye spread, first to other Italian dyers—a fifteenth-century

Archil, continued.

Venetian dyers' manual devotes four chapters to it—and then to other European countries.

Making archil was arduous. First a source had to be discovered, and because lichen populations proved so fragile, each site was quickly exhausted.[5] To feed the market, lichens were imported at great expense from increasingly far-flung locations as trade routes and empires blossomed.[6] The lichens had to be carefully harvested by hand—in May and June for some varieties, August for others—and ground to a fine powder. The following stages were even more finicky. The two essential ingredients are ammonia and time. For much of the period that archil was produced, the most readily available source of ammonia was putrid human urine. A Venetian recipe from 1540 calls for 100 pounds of powdered archil and 10 pounds of an alum such as potash to be mixed with urine until it was the consistency of dough. This had to be kneaded frequently, up to three times a day—adding wine when it got too dry— and kept in a warm place for up to 70 days. After which time, "it will have become so thick that it will be good to use."[7] Even modern recipes require up to 28 days to produce the right color.[8]

Some lichens were said to smell wonderful—like violets— as they developed into a dye, but even so it must often have been unpleasant, stinky, and labor-intensive work. The rewards, though, were the colors produced at the end. One was a full-blooded purple fit for royalty; another was much redder. In one telling story, when the Napoleonic army landed in Fishguard, Pembrokeshire, in February 1797, the invading army was spooked by the sight of a group of Welsh women wearing rosy lichen-dyed cloaks. Mistaking them for a crack troop of redcoats, the invaders scattered without having fired so much as a single shot.

Magenta

During the latter half of the nineteenth century, while waves
of settlers were busy colonizing one frontier in America,
another Wild West–style struggle was surreptitiously
being waged across Europe. The spoils at stake in this
European contest, though, were not territories, but colors.

The colors in question were the aniline dyes, a family
of synthetic colorants produced from sticky, black coal tar.
The name *aniline* came from *anil*, Spanish for
indigo [page 189], coined in 1826 by Otto Unverdorben,
a German chemist who had been working on isolating
the indigo plant's colorant in his lab. The first synthetic
aniline to be created was the startlingly purple mauve
[page 169], which was accidentally discovered by a
London teenager in 1853. This, though, was only the
beginning. It was immediately obvious that aniline had
a good deal more to offer the world of color. Across
the world, scientists began feverishly testing the new
compound with anything and everything they could get
their hands on.

One of the first to strike it lucky was François-Emmanuel
Verguin. He had been the director of a factory that
produced yellow from picric acid, but in 1858 he joined a
rival firm, Renard Frères & Franc, and, almost
immediately, created a rich color on the cusp between
red and purple by mixing aniline with tin chloride.[1]
He called his new creation fuchsine, after the flower
[page 124]. Almost simultaneously, the British firm
Simpson, Maule & Nicholson hit upon aniline red.
This eye-searing color was an immediate success.
The first customers, intriguingly, were several European
armies, who used it to dye their uniforms. The names
though—"fuchsia" in France and "roseine" in Britain—
would not do for so dashing and assertive a hue. Instead
it became known as "magenta," in honor of the small

Magenta, continued.

Italian town near Milan where, on June 4, 1859, the
Franco-Piedmontese army had won a decisive victory
against the Austrians.

Soon magenta was pouring out of rival factories in
Mulhouse, Basel, London, Coventry, and Glasgow, and
onto the backs of a public hungering for bright, affordable
new clothing. Within the space of a few years a slew of
other anilines—a yellow, two shades of violet, aldehyde
green, bleu de Lyon, bleu de Paris, Nicholson's blue,
dahlia (somewhere between mauve and magenta), and
a black—had flooded the market. Regulars at the Black
Horse pub, an establishment a stone's throw from Perkin's
dyeworks at Greenford Green, were fond of saying that
their stretch of the Grand Junction Canal turned a different
color each week.[2]

All this experimentation, sadly, contained the seeds
for magenta's decline in fashion. For the next decade the
industry was paralyzed by a succession of lawsuits, as firms
began trying to enforce their patents and guard their
intellectual property. Verguin himself profited little from
his creation: his contract at Renard Frères & Franc had
signed over the rights to any color he created in return
for one-fifth of the profits.[3] In the early twentieth century
it was discovered that a number of these miraculous new
colors contained dangerous levels of arsenic, up to 6.5 percent
in some samples of magenta. More subtly, so much choice
led to consumer neophilia; magenta was now one option
among thousands. Its survival is largely thanks to color
printing. The color is associated almost exclusively
with the (decidedly pink) process ink used in CMYK color
printing.

Mauve

Malaria was rife in Europe during the eighteenth and
nineteenth centuries. In the 1740s Horace Walpole wrote,
with the preoccupation typical of a beleaguered tourist,
of "a horrid thing called the *mal'aria* that comes to Rome
every summer and kills one." (The word *malaria* is a
corruption of the Italian for "bad air," as it was believed
the disease was airborne; the connection with mosquitoes
wasn't established until later.) Half of all the patients
admitted to St. Thomas's Hospital in London in 1853
were diagnosed with ague, or malarial fevers.[1]

Quinine, the only known treatment, was extracted
from the bark of a particular South American tree and cost
a fortune: the East India Company spent around $123,000
on it annually.[2] The financial incentives for synthesizing
quinine were obvious. It was partly these, and partly a love
of chemistry for its own sake, that drove an 18-year-old
scientist to spend his holidays holed up in a makeshift
laboratory in his father's East London attic, trying to
synthesize quinine from coal tar. Today, William Perkin
is celebrated as one of the heroes of modern science.
It is not because of quinine, which he never did manage
to produce, but because of a rich seam of chemistry that
opened up when he accidentally happened upon a
particular shade of purple: mauve.

In the first few months of 1856 Perkin's experiments
with coal tar, the abundant, oily black by-product of gas
lighting, resulted in a reddish powder, which, when further
experimented on, produced not colorless quinine, but a
bright purple liquid.[3] Most chemists would have thrown
this errant slop away. Perkin, who had once dreamed of
being an artist, dipped a piece of silk into his beaker, and
realized that he had made a light- and washproof dye.
Sensing its commercial possibilities, he initially named his
creation after the exclusive color that had been extracted

Mauve, continued.

from mollusks by the ancient Greeks and Byzantines [page 162]. Soon after, however, he adopted instead the French name for the mallow plant, *mauve*, whose blooms are a similar hue.[4]

It was not an immediate success. Dyers, used to working with plant and animal extracts, were dubious of the newfangled chemical. It was also expensive to make. It took 100 pounds of coal to produce just 10 ounces of coal tar, which in turn yielded only a quarter ounce of mauve.[5] Thankfully for Perkin and for us (without his perseverance, it is possible that coal tar might have been abandoned before the discovery of modern commonplaces, including hair dyes, chemotherapy, saccharin and artificial musk), the spoiled, extravagant wife of Napoleon III, Empress Eugénie, decided that the color mauve precisely matched her eyes. The *Illustrated London News* notified its readers of the world's most fashionable woman's preference for Perkin's purple in 1857. Queen Victoria took note, and chose to wear "a rich mauve velvet [dress], trimmed with three rows of lace" with a matching petticoat—"mauve and silver moiré antique, trimmed with a deep flounce of Honiton lace"—to her daughter's marriage to Prince Frederick William in January 1858.[6] By August 1859 *Punch* declared that London was "in the grip of the Mauve Measles" and 21-year-old Perkin had become a rich and well-respected man.[7]

Soon enough, however, mauve went into that most Victorian of things: a decline. Overconsumption, as well as the continuing loyalty of an older generation, meant that the color soon became shorthand for a particular kind of aging lady. "Never trust a woman who wears mauve," Oscar Wilde declared in *The Portrait of Dorian Gray*, published in 1891. "It always means they have a history."

Our current queen, perhaps bearing this stigma in mind, vetoed blooms of this color in palace flower arrangements. More carefree characters, though, have refused to be put off. Neil Munro Roger, the dandy couturier, who invented capri pants and was known to everyone by his childhood nickname of Bunny, was partial to what he liked to call "menopausal mauve." It had become such a signature that at the Amethyst Ball he threw to celebrate his 70th birthday, he wore it from egret-feathered top to glimmering catsuited toe.

Heliotrope

Some colors loom larger in the popular imagination than in real life. Take heliotrope: a plant whose name was forged from two Greek components, *helios*, "sun," and *tropaios*, "to turn," because its purple flowers were supposed to turn and follow the sun as it moved across the sky. The color, in turn, takes its name from the plant's blooms. Really, however, this shrub doesn't follow the light much more than any other, and the most distinctive thing about *Heliotropium* is its sweet, cherry-pie scent. An early ancestor of the plant was used as a perfume ingredient in ancient Egypt and traded with Greece and Rome.[1]

The color's apogee came toward the end of the nineteenth century, the boom time for many shades of purple. Part of the color's appeal was novelty. Before William Perkin's mauve [page 169], purple had been difficult to produce, and still retained the imperial glamour of its ancient status, so perhaps the Victorians should be forgiven for the increasingly lurid combinations heliotrope appeared in over the next decade. In 1880 it was paired with light green or apricot; later it was partnered with canary yellow, eucalyptus green, art bronze, and peacock blue. "No colors seem too bright," as one commentator put it. "The combinations of them are sometimes quite startling."[2]

In the Victorian language of flowers, heliotrope often signified devotion, which is partly why it was one of the few colors women were allowed to wear after the death of a loved one. The cult of mourning reached its zenith during the nineteenth century, with ever more elaborate social rules governing what people, particularly women, could wear in the months and years following the death of a relative or monarch. Heliotrope, and other soft shades of purple, were required wearing during half-mourning. For widows, who endured the most serious degree of grief, half-mourning was reached only after two years of wearing plain, matte black dresses; for remoter relations, mourning was less severe and subdued colors were allowed from the beginning. A serious outbreak of influenza over the winter of 1890 resulted in a rash of black, gray, and heliotrope being worn the following year.[3]

While this hue's fortunes have suffered something of a collapse in the real world, it has had a distinguished literary afterlife. Badly behaved characters are often described as wearing the color. The deliciously immoral antiheroine of Oscar Wilde's *An Ideal Husband*, Mrs. Cheveley, makes her entrance in heliotrope and diamonds, before swashbuckling her way through the remainder of the play and commandeering all the best lines.[4] Allusions to heliotrope also crop up in the works of J. K. Rowling, D. H. Lawrence, P. G. Wodehouse, James Joyce, and Joseph Conrad. The word is pleasurable to say, filling the mouth like a rich, buttery sauce. Added to which, the color itself is intriguing: antiquated, unusual, and just a little bit brassy.

Violet

In Paris in 1874 a group of artists founded the Anonymous
Society of Painters, Sculptors, Printmakers, &c. and began
organizing their first show. They wanted the exhibition
to act as mission statement, rallying call, and, most
importantly, a snub to the Académie des Beaux-Arts,
which had just rejected their work for the prestigious
annual Salon. The founder-members of the new group,
Edgar Degas, Claude Monet, Paul Cézanne, Camille
Pissarro, and others, thought the old, academic style of
art was too dull, too staid, and too coated in a unifying
layer of honey-colored varnish to capture the world
as it really was and, therefore, to have any value at all.
The establishment was equally scathing about the
impressionists. In a biting review for *Le Charivari*
newspaper, Louis Leroy accused Monet's *Impression,
Sunrise*, of not being a finished painting at all but a mere
preparatory sketch. Many more such criticisms were
aimed at the fledgling movement over the following years,
but one constant theme concerned their preoccupation
with a single color: violet.

Edmond Duranty, an early admirer of the
impressionists, wrote that their works "*procédent presque
toujours d'une gamme violette et bleuâtre*" ("almost always
proceed from a violet and bluish range").[1] For others,
this violet tinting was more troubling. Many concluded
that the artists were, to a man, completely mad, or at the
very least suffering from a hitherto unknown disease,
which they dubbed "violettomania." It would be as difficult
to persuade Pissarro that the trees were not violet, joked
one, as to persuade the inmate of a lunatic asylum that
he wasn't the pope in the Vatican. Another wondered
if the artists' fascination with the color was a result of
the impressionists spending too much time *en plein air*:
the violet tint could be the result of a permanent negative

afterimage caused by looking at sunny yellow landscapes
for too long. Alfred de Lostalot, in a review of one of
Monet's solo shows, hypothesized that the artist might
be among that rare number of people who could see into
the ultraviolet part of the spectrum. "He and his friends
see purple," wrote Lostalot. "[T]he crowd sees otherwise;
hence the disagreement."[2]

Their preference for violet was the result of two
new-minted theories. One was the impressionists'
conviction that shadows were never really black or gray,
but colored; the second concerned complementary colors.
Since the complementary color to the yellow
of sunlight was violet, it made sense that this would be
the color of the shade. Soon enough, though, this shade
had transcended its role in the shadows. In 1881 Édouard
Manet announced to his friends that he had finally
discovered the true color of the atmosphere. "It is violet,"
he said. "Fresh air is violet. Three years from now, the
whole world will work in violet."[3]

Ultramarine
Cobalt
Indigo
Prussian blue
Egyptian blue
Woad
Electric blue
Cerulean

Blue

During the 1920s the Catalan artist Joan Miró produced
a group of paintings that were radically different from
anything he had done before. One of his "*peinture-poésie,*"
a large canvas created in 1925, remains almost completely
blank. In the top left-hand corner the word "Photo" is
rendered in elegant, swirling calligraphy; over on the right
there is a popcorn-shaped daub of forget-me-not-colored
paint and underneath, the words, in neat, unassuming
letters, "*ceci est la coleur de mes rêves*" ("this is the color
of my dreams").

Just two years previously, Clyde Keeler, an American
geneticist studying the eyes of blind mice, had made
discoveries that indicated Miró might be on to something.
Inexplicably, although the mice completely lacked the
photoreceptors that enable mammals to perceive light,
their pupils still contracted in response to it. It would be
three-quarters of a century before the link was definitively
proven: everyone, even the nonsighted, possesses a special
receptor that senses blue light. This is crucial because it
is our response to this portion of the spectrum, naturally
present in the highest concentrations in early daylight,
which sets our circadian rhythm, the inner clock that
helps us sleep at night and remain alert during the day.[1]
One problem is our modern world, filled as it is with
spot-lit rooms and backlit smartphones, overloads us
with blue light at odd hours of the day, which has negative
effects on our sleep patterns. In 2015 American adults
reported getting an average 6.9 hours of sleep on a work
night; 150 years ago it was between 8 and 9 hours.[2]

Westerners have a history of undervaluing all things
blue. During the Paleolithic and Neolithic periods, reds,
blacks, and browns reigned supreme; the ancient Greeks
and Romans admired the simple triumvirate of black, white,
and red. For the Romans, in particular, blue was associated

with barbarism: writers from the period mentioned that
Celtic soldiers dyed their bodies blue, and Pliny accused
women of doing the same before participating in orgies.
In Rome wearing blue was associated with mourning and
misfortune.[3] (Exceptions to this ancient aversion to blue
are more common outside Europe; the ancient Egyptians,
for example, were evidently very fond of it [page 196].)
It was largely absent too from early Christian writings.
A nineteenth-century survey of color terms used by
Christian authors before the thirteenth century reveals
that blue was the least used, at a mere 1 percent of the total.[4]

It was during the twelfth century that a sea change
occurred. Abbot Suger, a prominent figure in the French
court and an early champion of Gothic architecture,
fervently believed colors—particularly blues—to be divine.
He oversaw the reconstruction of Saint-Denis Abbey in
Paris in the 1130s and '40s. It was here that craftsmen
perfected the technique of coloring glass with cobalt
[page 187] to create the famous ink-blue windows that
they took with them to the cathedrals at Chartres and
Le Mans.[5] At around the same time, the Virgin was
increasingly depicted wearing bright blue robes—
previously she had usually been shown in dark colors that
conveyed her mourning for the death of her son. As the
status of Mary and Marian-centered devotion waxed in
the Middle Ages, so too did the fortunes of her adopted
color.

From the Middle Ages the pigment most commonly
associated with Mary was the precious pigment
ultramarine [page 182], which remained the most coveted,
bar none, for centuries. This was not the only substance
to have a huge impact on the history of blue, however:
indigo [page 189] was also decisive. Although the first is
a pigment made from a stone and the second a dye wrung

from fermented plant leaves, they share far more than
you might imagine. Both required care, patience, and
even reverence in their extraction and creation. While
colormen and painters were laboriously grinding
and kneading the one, dyers would be stripped to the
waist beating air into nauseating vats of the other.
The pigments' expense helped stoke desire and demand
in a dizzying cycle that ended only with the creation
of synthetic alternatives in the nineteenth century.

Although it was traditionally the color of sadness, many
cultures, including the ancient Egyptians, Hindus, and the
North African Tuareg tribe, have included a special place
for blue and blue things in their lives. A large number
of businesses and organizations use a dark shade for its
anonymous trustworthiness in their logos and uniforms,
perhaps little considering that its history of brisk
respectability began with the armed forces, particularly
the navies (hence navy blue), who needed to dye their
clothes with a color that would best resist the action
of sun and sea.

At the end of the twelfth century the French royal
family adopted a new coat of arms—a gold fleur-de-lis
on an azure ground—as a tribute to the Virgin, and
Europe's nobility fell gauntlet over greaves in their rush
to follow suit.[6] In 1200 only 5 percent of European coats of
arms contained azure; by 1250 this had risen to 15 percent;
in 1300, one-quarter; and by 1400 it was just under
one-third.[7] A recent survey conducted across 10 different
countries on four continents found that blue was people's
favorite color by a considerable margin.[8] Similar
surveys conducted since the First World War returned
similar results. It seems blue, once considered the
color of degenerates and barbarians, has conquered
the world.

Ultramarine

In April A.D. 630, Xuanzang, a Buddhist monk on a journey to India, made a 1,000-mile detour into Afghanistan. He had been lured far out of his way by two immense carvings of the Buddha hewn just over a century earlier directly into the side of a mountain in the Bamiyan Valley. Both were decorated with precious ornaments. The larger one—174 feet from heel to crown—was painted with carmine; the smaller, older one was draped in robes painted with the region's most famous export: ultramarine. In March 2001, nearly 1,400 years after Xuanzang's pilgrimage, the Bamiyan statues were declared false idols by the Taliban government, surrounded with dynamite, and destroyed.[1]

Although now so remote, the site of the Bamiyan Buddhas was once on one of the busiest and most influential trade routes ever known. The Silk Road, which runs through the mountains of the Hindu Kush, was used by the caravans that shuttled goods between East and West. Ultramarine was first bumped along the Silk Road by donkey and camel in the form of lumps of lapis lazuli. When these reached the Mediterranean coast in Syria they were loaded onto ships bound for Venice, and thence traded throughout Europe. Even the word *ultramarine*, from the Latin for "beyond"—*ultra*—and "sea"—*mare*—indicates that this was a color worth going the extra mile for. Cennino Cennini, the Renaissance Italian painter and author of *Il libro dell'arte*, called it "illustrious, beautiful and most perfect, beyond all other colors; one could not say anything about it, or do anything with it, that its quality would not surpass."[2]

The story of this blue begins deep in the ground. Lapis lazuli ("the blue stone" in Latin) is now mined from countries including China and Chile, but the overwhelming majority of the intense, night-colored rock that was used for ultramarine pigment in the West prior to the eighteenth century came from a single source: the Sar-e-Sang mines, tucked in the mountainous folds of Afghanistan, some 400 miles northeast of Bamiyan. Like the Buddha statues, the mines were famous; Marco Polo, who visited in 1271, wrote of a "high mountain, out of which the best and finest blue is mined."[3]

Although lapis lazuli is thought of as a semiprecious stone, it is really a mixture of minerals. Its deep blue color is thanks to lazurite, while the delicate traceries of white and gold are silicates (including calcite) and fool's gold (iron pyrite) respectively. Nuggets of the stone were used for decorative purposes in ancient Egypt and Sumeria, but no one seems to have used it as a pigment until much later. Not only is it difficult to grind, but because lapis contains so many impurities, the result can be disappointingly grayish. Turning it into a usable pigment is an exercise in extracting the blue lazurite. To do this, the finely milled stone is mixed with pitch, mastic, turpentine, and linseed oil or wax, and then heated together to form a paste. This is then kneaded in an alkaline lye solution—"just as," wrote Cennini, "you would work over bread dough."[4] The blue gradually washes out into the lye and sinks to the bottom. It takes a few successive kneadings, each drawing out progressively grayer solutions, to remove all the color; the final extraction will produce only a pallid color known as ultramarine ashes.

The oldest examples of lapis being used as a pigment are found in a small number of fifth-century wall paintings in Chinese Turkmenistan and some seventh-century images from a cave temple at Bamiyan. The earliest known European use is in the San Saba Church in Rome, dating from the first half of the eighth century, where ultramarine was mixed with Egyptian blue [page 196]. (At this time Egyptian blue was the ancient world's preeminent blue,

Ultramarine, continued.

though it was soon to be superseded by ultramarine.)[5]

Not only did the long journey from the mines increase
the pigment's price, it also affected how—and even if—
ultramarine was used. Italian artists, particularly Venetians,
who were first in the European supply chain and could
procure the pigment at its cheapest, were relatively
profligate with this precious pigment. This is evident, for
example, in the vast swathe of star-strewn sky in Titian's
Bacchus and Ariadne, painted with ultramarine in the early
1520s. Northern European artists had to be thriftier.
Albrecht Dürer, the foremost printmaker and painter of
the German Renaissance, used it occasionally, but never
without complaining bitterly of the cost. When buying
pigments in Antwerp in 1521 he paid almost 100 times for
ultramarine what he paid for some earth pigments.[6] The
difference in price and quality meant it made more sense
for artists to buy pigments from Venice if they were
working on prestigious commissions. Filippino Lippi's
1487 contract for the frescoes in the Strozzi Chapel at
Santa Maria Novella in Florence included a provision that
a portion of the fee be set aside for when "he wants to go to
Venice." There was a similar clause in Pinturicchio's 1502
contract for the frescoes in the Piccolomini Library
in Siena: 200 ducats were reserved for a Venetian pigment
expedition.[7]

The reasons for all this fuss were both practical and
emotional. While many other blue pigments are tinged
with green, ultramarine is a true blue, occasionally
bordering on violet, and is extraordinarily long-lasting.
It was also prized because of the esteem in which the raw
lapis lazuli was held. The color's rise in the West also
coincided with the Renaissance's increasing preoccupation
with the Virgin Mary. From around 1400, artists
increasingly depicted the Madonna wearing ultramarine-

blue cloaks or gowns, a material sign of their esteem
and her divinity.[8] Giovanni Battista Salvi da Sassoferrato's
The Virgin at Prayer (1640–50) seems as much a tribute
to ultramarine in all its intensely midnight beauty as to
Mary. While she sits, head modestly bent so her eyes find
the floor, it is the thick, creamy folds of her blue cloak that
capture the viewer's gaze.

The precise use of this pigment was a key point in
many surviving contracts drawn up between artists and
their patrons. The 1515 contract for Andrea del Sarto's
Madonna of the Harpies stipulated that the Virgin's robe
be painted with ultramarine "at least five broad florins the
ounce." Some patrons purchased the pigment themselves
to control its use; a 1459 document suggests that while
Sano di Pietro was working on a fresco on a gateway in
Siena, the town authorities kept hold of his supplies of
gold and ultramarine. They weren't always wrong to be
suspicious. Almost four centuries later, when Dante
Gabriel Rossetti, William Morris, and Edward Burne-Jones
were painting a set of murals in the library of the Oxford
Union in 1857, a potful of ultramarine was upset amid the
"jollity, noise, cork-popping, paint-sloshing, and general
larking about." Their patrons were horrified.[9]

To add salt to the wound, there was, by this time,
a good alternative. In 1824 the Société d'Encouragement
pour l'Industrie Nationale in France offered 6,000 francs
to anyone who could create an affordable synthetic
ultramarine.[10] Four years later the prize was awarded to
Jean-Baptiste Guimet, a French chemist. (Although
Christian Gmelin, a German rival, announced he had
happened on a similar recipe the previous year, the prize
money remained with Monsieur Guimet, and the new
formula was known thereafter as French ultramarine.)[11]
To create the synthetic, china clay, soda, charcoal, quartz,

Ultramarine, continued.

and sulfur are heated together; the result, a green,
glassy substance, is pulverized, washed, and reheated
once more to create a rich blue powder.

French ultramarine was exponentially cheaper.
In some instances the real thing could, ounce for ounce,
sell for 2,500 times more than the synthetic.[12] In the early
1830s the original cost 8 guineas an ounce (equivalent to
just over 11 weeks' wages for a male laborer), while French
ultramarine cost between 1 and 25 shillings per pound. By
the 1870s French ultramarine had become the standard.
Despite this, the interloper still faced initial resistance.
Artists complained that it was too one-dimensional.
Because the particles were all the same size and reflected
light in the same way, it lacked the depth, variety, and
visual interest of the real thing.

The French postwar artist Yves Klein agreed.
He patented International Klein Blue in 1960 and used it
to create his hallmark: the lustrous, textured blue canvases
known as the "IKB series" after the color. (It was these
seemingly simple monochromes that Klein later proudly
called his "pure idea.") While he loved the intensity of the
raw powdered ultramarine, he was disappointed with the
dullness of the paint made from it. He worked with
a chemist for over a year to develop a special resin medium.
This, when mixed with the synthetic to form IKB,
allowed the pigment to approach the clarity and luster
of the original.

Cobalt

On May 29, 1945, shortly after the liberation of Holland,
Han van Meegeren, an artist and art dealer, was arrested
for collaborating. Not only had he amassed a suspicious
fortune during the Nazi occupation, he had sold *Christ
and the Adulteress*, an early work by Vermeer, to Hermann
Göring. If found guilty, he could be hanged.[1]

Van Meegeren not only vigorously denied the
accusation, but countered with a claim of his own.
The "Vermeer," he said, wasn't really a Vermeer at all:
he had painted it himself. At worst, he said, he was guilty
only of forgery, and, since he had completely fooled the
Reichsmarschall, should he not in fact be celebrated as
a Dutch hero? Some of the paintings that he alleged to
have passed off during his career as a forger—several more
Vermeers and a couple of Pieter de Hoochs, among others—
were on display in museums and had been hailed by
critics as long-lost masterpieces. Van Meegeren claimed
to have made 8 million guilders (around $33 million
today). When prominent museum directors and critics
refused to believe him, Van Meegeren found himself in the
unusual position of having to persuade people of his guilt.

He had, he told the court, specialized in Vermeers
because of the huge gap in that artist's oeuvre—most of his
known paintings are from when he was an older man—and
the dissonance between his style as a young man and that
of his later years. Van Meegeren had used a composition
from a Caravaggio for one forgery—*Christ and the Pilgrims
at Emmaus*—knowing that art historians were desperately
looking for proof of the theory that Vermeer's style had
an Italian origin. He had also paid attention to the technical
details. Rather than using the traditional linseed oil as his
paint medium he had used Bakelite, a plastic that sets solid
when heated. This let him fool the standard X-ray and
solvent tests used to determine the age of oil paintings,

Cobalt, continued.

which take much longer to harden. He had painted on old canvases that had authentic craquelure (the network of tiny fissures that develop in old paintings) and had only used pigments that would have been available in the seventeenth century [2]—in every case, that is, except one. The giveaway was a particular shade that was found, upon closer examination, to contain a pigment that wasn't created until 130 years after Vermeer's death: cobalt blue. [3]

It is not surprising that Van Meegeren had missed the switch. Cobalt blue was, after all, one of the blues created specifically as a synthetic substitute for ultramarine. [4] A French chemist, Louis-Jacques Thénard, decided the key would lie in cobalt, the element Sèvres potters used in their blue glazes, just as it had been used to make the sky-colored tiles on the roofs of Persian mosques. It was also present in the famous medieval iris-blue glass at Chartres and Saint Denis in Paris, and in the cheap artists' pigment smalt. In 1802 Thénard made his breakthrough: a mixture of cobalt arsenate or cobalt phosphate and alumina, roasted at high temperatures, produced a fine, deep blue. [5] The chemist and author George Field, writing in 1835, described it as "the modern improved blue . . . neither tending to green nor purple, and approaching in brilliancy the finest ultramarine." [6]

The presence of cobalt blue in Van Meegeren's work, though, had unmasked him, and his works were quietly taken down from museum walls and discreetly stashed away. In November 1947, two years after his arrest, he was finally found guilty. Not of collaboration with the Nazi regime—although a book of his drawings had been found in Hitler's personal library, bearing the inscription "To my beloved Führer in grateful tribute"—but of forgery. [7] He was sentenced to a year in prison, but he died—some said of a broken heart—the following month.

Indigo

In 1882 the British Museum acquired an object it would take
11 decades to understand. The artifact is a tiny clay tablet,
around 2.75 in. square and 0.8 in. thick, covered in minute
text written in Babylon sometime between 600 and 500 B.C.
In the early 1990s, when academics finally cracked the
translation, they discovered that what had been inscribed
in the still-damp clay thousands of years before was a set
of instructions for dyeing wool dark blue. Although it isn't
mentioned, the description of the process—with all its
repeated dipping—indicates that the dye was indigo.

For a long time it was presumed that both the seeds
for the indigo-bearing plants and the knowledge of how to
turn them into a dye the color of the night sky had blown
west with the winds of trade: from India to the Middle
East and Africa. (An imprint of this assumption survives
in the word itself. Its etymological root is the Greek
indikon, which means "a substance from India.") Now,
though, this seems unlikely. Instead, people seem to have
discovered the process independently, and at different
times, across the world. There are many different species
of plant that produce indigo—woad [page 198] is one—
but the one most coveted for its colorant is *Indigofera
tinctoria*.[1] For a dye-producing workhorse it is a pretty
shrub, with small, slightly dusty green leaves, pink blooms
that look like miniature sweetpeas, and dangling seedpods.[2]

Although, unlike woad, *I. tinctoria* is a "nitrogen fixer"
and therefore good for the soil, it is still temperamental and
prone to mishap.[3] Farmers in Central and South America,
for example, not only had to deal with the usual risks—
fluctuating prices and rainfall, sinking trade ships—but also
with a host of others of biblical proportions, including
earthquakes, and plagues of caterpillars and locusts.[4] Even
once the crop was harvested the poor, nerve-shredded
farmers couldn't sleep easy.

Indigo, continued.

Even today, with more chemicals and equipment at our disposal, the process for extracting the dye from the leaves is cumbersome; the traditional process, done entirely by hand, was far worse. First, the greenery was fermented in an alkaline solution. The liquid was then drawn off and vigorously beaten to aerate it. This caused a blue sediment to form, which was then dried into cakes or blocks to be sent off to market.[5]

The result is worth the effort. In addition to the vivid color, indigo ages beautifully, as any denim aficionado worth her Japanese selvage will confirm. It is also the most colorfast of the natural dyes. Where it has been used in combination with others to create colors like green or black, it is often only the indigo that remains. The phenomenon is so common that the now sky-colored foliage in Renaissance tapestries is said to suffer from "blue disease."[6] Unlike most dyes, indigo doesn't need a mordant to fix it to fabric. While the relatively weak indigo content in woad could color absorbent fibers like wool, the dye from other indigo-bearing plants could be up to 10 times stronger, more than powerful enough to saturate less accommodating vegetable fibers like silk, cotton, flax, and linen.[7] Fabric dipped into the chartreuse-hued dye vat changes color upon coming into contact with the air, turning from yellowish green to sea green before settling on a deep, stolid blue.

Indigo is woven into the burial customs of many different cultures globally, from Peru to Indonesia, Mali to Palestine. Ancient Egyptian dyers began threading thin lines of blue fabric into the edges of their linen mummy cloths from around 2400 B.C.; a state robe found in the extensive funerary wardrobe of Tutankhamen, who reigned around 1333–1323 B.C., was almost entirely indigo.[8] The dye has made inroads into other cultural spheres too.

Males of the Tuareg tribe in northern Africa are given *tagelmusts*, or headscarves, at a special ceremony that marks their transition from boy to man. The most prestigious in a community wear the glossiest indigo *tagelmusts*, whose gloriously resonant hue is developed through multiple rounds of dyeing and beating.[9]

Because it has always been so highly prized, indigo has, from as far back as records and educated guesswork allow, been a bedrock of global trade. The wealthiest Romans could import indigo at 20 denarii a pound, around 15 times the average daily wage (prices were so high that some merchants apparently tried their luck selling a counterfeit made from pigeon dung).[10] Adding to the expense were the restricted trade routes. Before Vasco da Gama nosed his ship around the Cape of Good Hope and opened up another passage to the East, goods traveling westward had to make their way overland through the Middle East or around the Arabian Peninsula. This route was unpredictable and difficult to navigate, and prone to civil unrest, and heavy duties were levied by the various rulers along the way, ratcheting up prices for those at the end of the journey. Obstacles were endless. In 1583 there was a dearth of camels following an extreme dry spell and caravans ground to a halt. After nearly causing a diplomatic incident in Bayana, India, by outbidding the emperor's mother for "twelve carts loaded with *nil* [indigo]," a British merchant lost both his precious cargo and his life in Baghdad on the journey home.[11]

Despite Europe's slow adoption of imported indigo— chiefly due to the resistance from local woad farmers— the rise of colonialism in the sixteenth and seventeenth centuries, and the prospect of the fortunes to be made, overcame lingering resistance; trade became almost frenzied. In just one year, 1631, seven Dutch ships carried

Indigo, continued.

a total of 333,545 pounds of indigo back to Europe, a cargo worth five tons of gold [page 86]. Over in the New World, the Spanish began producing indigo on a commercial scale almost immediately after conquering Guatemala in 1524; it soon became the region's principal export.[12]

New trade routes, combined with ample use of slave and forced labor in the New World and India, drove prices downward. Armies began using indigo for their uniforms. Napoleon's Grande Armée, for example, consumed around 150 tons per year.[13] (French infantrymen still wore madder or alizarin red [page 152] trousers until the First World War; this was replaced with indigo when they realized that it was making them too easy a target.) Naturally, after William Perkin unlocked the secret to aniline dyes in 1856, a man-made version of indigo was only a matter of time. After an initial breakthrough in 1865, it would be another 30 years before the German chemist Adolf von Baeyer, with financial backing from the German pharmaceutical giant BASF to the tune of 20 million gold marks, finally got "Pure Indigo" to market.

From being a luxury on a par with Tyrian purple [page 162], indigo has become the color of the "blue-collar" workforces, not only in Europe but also in Japan and China, where the dusty blue Mao suit became ubiquitous in the twentieth century.[14] It is, strangely enough, this workwear association that has proved this pigment's most enduring legacy, in the form of blue jeans.[15] Although it peaked around 2006, the global denim industry, which is dominated by the classic indigo blue, was worth $54 billion in 2011.[16] Jeans have been a wardrobe staple since the 1960s, and, as Giorgio Armani is often quoted as saying, they "represent democracy in fashion." In them one can be at home, and understood, everywhere.

Prussian blue

Sometime between 1704 and 1706, in a dingy room in
Berlin, a paint manufacturer and alchemist called Johann
Jacob Diesbach was making up a batch of his signature
cochineal red lake (a kind of paint made using an organic
colorant and an inert binder or mordant) [page 141].
The chemical process was a relatively simple one using
iron sulfate and potash. On this day, though, when it came
to the crucial stage, Diesbach realized he had run
out of potash. He bought some more from the nearest
supplier and carried on, but something wasn't right.
When he added the potash, the mixture did not turn a
strong red, as it ought to; instead it was pale and pinkish.
Perplexed, he began trying to concentrate it. His "red lake"
solution turned first purple, then a deep blue.

Diesbach found the man who had sold him the potash,
a disreputable fellow alchemist and pharmacist called
Johann Konrad Dippel, and demanded an explanation.
Dippel deduced that the iron sulfate had reacted strangely
with potash because the latter was adulterated with animal
oil. The reaction had created potassium ferrocyanide (a
compound still known in German as *Blutlaugensalz*,
literally "blood alkali salts"), which had combined with the
iron sulfate to produce iron ferrocyanide, a compound we
now know as Prussian blue.[1]

This was a very auspicious time for a new blue.
Ultramarine [page 182] remained the ideal, but it was
still fiendishly expensive and supply was inconstant.
There was also smalt, blue verditer, azurite, and even indigo
[page 189], but these were all slightly greenish, with poor
coverage and not particularly reliable once on the canvas.[2]
Prussian blue was a revelation. A deep, rather cool color
with tremendous tinting strength and the ability to create
subtle tones, it also behaved well with lead white [page 43]
and combined with yellow pigments like orpiment

Prussian blue, continued.

[page 82] and gamboge [page 80] to make stable greens. In his pigment compendium of 1835, George Field called this "rather modern pigment," "deep and powerful . . . of vast body and considerable transparency."[3]

Dippel, who may have been dishonest but clearly did not lack business acumen, began selling it around 1710. The formula remained a secret until 1724, when an English chemist called John Woodwood published the method for making Prussian blue in the *Philosophical Transactions of the Royal Society*.[4] By 1750 it was being manufactured across Europe. Unlike many other pigments of the time (and despite the "cyanide" in its chemical name), it isn't toxic; it was also a tenth of the price of ultramarine. It did have drawbacks, though, becoming discolored by strong light and alkalis. W. Linton, author of *Ancient and Modern Colors* (1852), while conceding that it was "a rich and fascinating pigment to the colorist," said it was "not to be depended upon," and yet fretted it was difficult to avoid.[5]

The color is seen in the works of artists as diverse as William Hogarth, John Constable, Van Gogh and Monet. Japanese painters and woodblock craftsmen were delighted with it. It was also the blue Picasso favored during his blue period in the first years of the twentieth century after the death of a friend, its transparency giving cool depths to his melancholic settings. It is still very much in use: Anish Kapoor's flattened topographical sculpture *A Wing at the Heart of Things*, created in 1990, is made from slate coated in Prussian blue.

The pigment has been busy colonizing other industries too: it has long been used in wallpapers, house paints, and textile dyes. John Herschel, a nineteenth-century British chemist, astrologer, and photographer, worked out how to use it in combination with photosensitive paper to make a kind of proto-photocopy. The results, which showed up as white marks on a blue ground, became known as "blueprints," a word that has come to denote any technical drawing.[6] It is also used to treat people with thallium and radioactive cesium poisoning, as it prevents the body from absorbing them. The only side effect is alarmingly blue feces.[7]

Remarkably, for most of its history no one was quite sure exactly what Prussian blue was; they knew the steps to take to make it, but were unclear on exactly what was reacting with what. Perhaps, though, that isn't so remarkable: iron ferrocyanide, a crystalline blue solid, is a complicated compound with a dizzying lattice structure at a molecular level. That such a thing was created by happy accident seems almost miraculous. As the French chemist Jean Hellot remarked in 1762:

Nothing is perhaps more peculiar than the process by which one obtains Prussian blue, and it must be owned that, if chance had not taken a hand, a profound theory would be necessary to invent it.[8]

Egyptian blue

William, a small ceramic statuette of a hippopotamus, can now be found in the Metropolitan Museum of Art, around 6,000 miles and some 3,500 years away from his point of origin: the banks of the Nile in Egypt. Although to our eyes he cuts rather a beautiful figure, with his blue-green glazed skin decorated with flowers, to his creators he would have seemed far less benevolent. Hippos were dangerous creatures, both in real life and in mythology, where they might upset your journey to the underworld. Figurines like this had their legs broken (William's have subsequently been repaired) and were placed in tombs as talismans to protect their occupants on their onward journeys.

The Egyptians were uncommon in valuing blue: most Western cultures didn't even possess a separate word for the slice of spectrum between green and violet. For the ancient Egyptians, though, the color represented the sky, the Nile River, creation, and divinity. Amun-Ra, the empire's principal deity, was often depicted with blue skin or hair, a trait that other gods borrowed from time to time too. The color was thought to dispel evil and bring prosperity, and was much sought after in the form of beads, which in themselves were believed to possess magical protective qualities.[1] Although the Egyptians also used and valued other blues, including turquoise and azurite, both had their disadvantages: the former because it was rare and expensive, the latter because it was hard to carve. So from the time Egyptian blue was first manufactured, sometime around 2500 B.C., it was put to frequent use. Scribes wrote with it on papyri and it has also been found making up hieroglyphics on walls, used as a glaze on funerary objects, and decorating coffins.[2]

It was the Romans who first referred to the pigment as "Egyptian blue"; the originators themselves called it,

simply, *iryt* (artificial) *hsbd* (lapis lazuli).[3] Its chemical
name is calcium copper silicate, and the raw ingredients
used in its manufacture were chalk or limestone; a
copper-containing mineral, such as malachite, which gave
it the blue color; and sand. These were likely fired together
between 1,742 and 1,832°F, to create a brittle, glassy solid
that was ground down and then refired at between 1,562
and 1,742°F to produce an intense blue that was long-
lasting and versatile.[4] Not only was it resistant to alkalis
and acids but it also lasted well in strong light. Depending
on how finely it was ground, it could be as dark as lapis
lazuli or as pale as turquoise; if it was applied over a dark
base layer it could be almost electric. Producing it was an
extraordinary technical challenge. Not only did the
ingredients need to be fired together at precise
temperatures; the oxygen levels needed to be regulated too.

Mysteriously, given the existence of texts describing
it, the manufacture of Egyptian blue petered out.[5]
Examples from the thirteenth century have been found
in Italy, but it is believed this was due to reuse of old
pigment stock—small balls of Egyptian blue are often
found in Roman excavations.[6] Elsewhere, artists began
to favor ultramarine [page 182] from around the ninth
century.[7] One explanation is that a decreasing demand
for blue (before the twelfth-century revival) meant that
people stopped bothering to pass the secret down and
the technical skills were lost. Alternatively, perhaps a shift
in the idea of preciousness is to blame. While modern
chemists marvel at the skill needed to make Egyptian blue,
Western artists and patrons seem to have preferred raw
materials with intrinsic value, like ultramarine.

Woad

Merton Abbey Mills, in Surrey in the south of England, had
been the site of a textile works for over a century when
William Morris purchased it in June 1881. Morris spent
his young adulthood picking up and then discarding
several careers—priest, artist, furniture maker—before
hitting on the one that would make his name and fortune:
reviving Gothic designs for fabric and wallpapers.
He shunned many of the new synthetic dyes available,
preferring vegetable- and mineral-based ones. These
acquired interesting patinas as they aged and were truer to
the intricate medieval patterns he was partial to. One of his
favorite tricks was showing visitors to Merton Abbey skeins
of wool being dipped into the deep vats of woad. They
would emerge an almost grassy color, and then, before the
astonished eyes of his visitors, they would turn first deep
sea green and then a resonant blue.[1]

The plant behind this miraculous transformation was
Isatis tinctoria (often also called pastel), a member of the
mustard family native to clay-rich soils in Europe. It is one
of the 30 or so plant species that produce the colorant
indigo [page 189]. Extracting indigo from woad plants is
long, complicated, and expensive. Once harvested the leaves
are ground to a paste, formed into balls, and left to cure.
After 10 weeks, when the balls have lost three-quarters of
their size and nine-tenths of their weight, water is added
and the mixture is left to ferment again. After a further two
weeks the woad will be very dark and granular, resembling
tar. This mixture contains around 20 times as much indigo
as the same weight of fresh leaves, but must still undergo
a further round of fermentation, this time with wood ash,
before it can be used to dye cloth.

This process was noxious, requiring lots of fresh water,
producing waste that was often emptied directly into the
nearest river, and draining the soil of nutrients, leaving

those in woad-growing areas at risk of starvation. Prior
to the thirteenth century, woad production was very
small-scale. There is evidence that ancient people were
familiar with the process: leaves and seedpods have been
found at a Viking site called Coppergate in the north of
England, and it was purposefully cultivated at various sites
from at least the tenth century.[2] Classical writers described
the Celts making themselves blue, either daubing it on
before battle or tattooing it directly into the skin. (Tattooed
Celtic remains have been found, both in Russia and in
Britain, although it is impossible to say if woad was the dye
used.) It has even been suggested that the word *Briton*
derives from a Celtic one meaning "painted people."

It was sometime around the end of the twelfth century,
though, that woad's fortunes began to change. Innovation
in the production process resulted in a brighter, stronger
color, which attracted the notice of a more luxurious
market.[3] It also helped that blue, a previously overlooked
color, was not part of the sumptuary system that governed
which colors people were allowed to wear, so it could be
worn openly by anyone. Over the next century, demand
for blue clothes began gaining ascendancy over the
preeminent red ones. It was also used as an under- or
over-dye to add to the longevity and to mix other colors,
including the famous British Lincoln green and even some
scarlets [page 138]. One Elizabethan wrote: "No color
in broadcloth or kersey [woven fabrics, usually woolen] will
well be made to endure without woad."[4]

From around 1230 woad was grown, like madder
[page 152], in near-industrial quantities.[5] This created
fierce rivalries between woad and madder merchants.
In Magdeburg, the center of Germany's madder trade,
religious frescoes began to depict hell as blue; and in
Thuringia, the madder merchants persuaded the

Woad, continued.

stained-glass craftsmen to make the devils in the new church windows blue, rather than the traditional red or black, all in an effort to discredit the upstart hue.[6]

Such tactics proved futile. Areas that grew the "blue gold"—like Thuringia, Alsace, Normandy—became rich. Woad, wrote one contemporary in Languedoc, "hath made that country the happiest and richest in Europe."[7] When Emperor Charles V captured the French king at the Battle of Pavia in 1525, it was an enormously wealthy woad merchant from Toulouse, Pierre de Berny, who was the guarantor for the eye-watering ransom.[8]

Woad's demise was by this time in sight, as other indigo-producing plants were discovered, first in India and then in the New World. On April 25, 1577, representatives of the merchants and dyers of the City of London sent a memorandum to the Privy Council, requesting permission to use indigo imported from India to make a cheaper, "oryent" blue. "[F]ortie shillings bestowed in the same, yeldeth as much color as fiftie shillings in woade."[9]

Just as the madder farmers had done before them, those involved in the woad trade tried to stave off the inevitable. Protectionist laws were passed year after year. Emperor Ferdinand III of Germany declared that indigo was the devil's color in 1654; French dyers could not touch it, on pain of death, until 1737; while in Nuremberg, dyers were still swearing an annual oath not to use it until the end of the eighteenth century. There was even a smear campaign against imported indigo: in 1650 officials in Dresden announced that the newcomer "readily loses its color" and "corrodes cloths."[10] It was all in vain. Often produced using slave labor, indigo could undercut woad on price every time, and had far better tinting strength. The European woad trade collapsed, leaving only empty fields and ruined merchants in its wake.

Electric blue

The sound that Alexander "Sasha" Yuvchenko, a 24-year-old
nuclear engineer, heard at 1:23 a.m. on April 26, 1986, was
not an explosion but a thud, a shaking. It was only two or
three seconds later, as radiation from the nuclear core of
reactor 4 ripped through the nuclear complex in Chernobyl
where he worked, that he heard the almighty boom of the
greatest man-made disaster ever known.[1]

Yuvchenko had taken the position because Chernobyl
was one of the best nuclear stations in the Soviet Union,
the money was good, and the job was interesting. On that
night, though, it was all supposed to be routine: he was
overseeing the cooling of the reactor, which had been
manually powered down earlier for a planned safety test.
He was in his office, chatting to a colleague, as the nuclear
rods were lowered into water to cool them. This
inadvertently caused a power surge so powerful that
the 1,000-ton plate covering the nuclear core blew off,
triggering a series of other detonations and spewing
radioactive uranium, burning graphite, and bits of building
into the sky.[2] Speaking to *New Scientist* in 2004, he
remembered steam, shaking, the lights being extinguished,
concrete walls buckling as if they were made of rubber,
and things falling around him; his first thought was that
a war had begun. He stumbled through the ruined
building, scrabbling past blackened bodies,[3] before
stumbling out into the hole where the reactor building
had been moments before. It was only then that he
noticed the glow:

*I could see a huge beam of projected light flooding up into infinity from
the reactor. It was like a laser light, caused by ionization of the air.
It was light bluish, and it was very beautiful.*[4]

Electric blue, continued.

It is not that surprising that a pale, bright blue has come to be the shade of electricity in the popular imagination. After all, the eerie aureole seen haloing very radioactive material after nuclear tests, and at Chernobyl, is blue. Other electrical discharge phenomena observed and puzzled over from the earliest days, such as sparks and lightning, produce similar effects—St. Elmo's fire, for example, which dances on ships' masts and across the windows in airplanes during storms, is bright blue, sometimes tinted with violet [page 174]. The effect is caused by the air becoming ionized: nitrogen and oxygen molecules become violently excited, releasing photons visible to the naked eye.

The color blue and electricity came together rather earlier than might be imagined, though. A dusty periwinkle shade named "electric blue" came into vogue in the late nineteenth century, just as Joseph Swan and Thomas Edison were groping toward harnessing electricity for producing light. A British drapers' association trade publication mentions "dark electric blue faille and velvet" in its January 1874 issue; while the *Young Ladies' Journal* notes the fashion for a walking dress "of electric blue double nun's cloth" in November 1883.[5]

The idea of electric blue has always been shorthand for modernity. For the Victorians, witnessing the latest electrical innovations creep from the lab and factories into smart hotels and then individual homes, it must have seemed as if the future and the present were coalescing. This shade has—apart from a brief spell in the 1980s and 1990s—dominated our imaginings of a technologically controlled destiny. While the film *The Matrix*, released in 1999, is suffused with the ghostly greenish light emitted from monochrome computer screens (which in reality were mostly phased out in the 1980s, but are still portrayed as futuristic), the technology in *Minority Report*, released just three years later, is powered by electric blue. Similar light can be seen in both the 1982 and 2010 *Tron* films, in publicity stills for *Inception* (2010), and in the disturbing dystopian fate humanity suffers in *WALL-E* (2008).

Although we see it as the color of the future, we are clearly more than a little unnerved by electric blue; perhaps we don't trust ourselves with the forces at our disposal. As Sasha Yuvchenko knows all too well, the cost of mistakes can be devastating.

Cerulean

On February 17, 1901, Carlos Casagemas, a Spanish poet
and artist, was having drinks with friends in the smart
new Parisian cafe l'Hippodrome, near Montmartre, when
he pulled out a gun and shot himself in the right temple.
His friends were distraught, none more so than Pablo
Picasso, who had never quite recovered from watching his
sister die of diphtheria six years previously. His grief cast
a pall over his works for several years. He abandoned
almost the entire palette, except for the one color that
could adequately express his grief and loss: blue.

This isn't the first time blue has helped people express
matters of the spirit. When, at the end of the Second
World War, the UN was formed to maintain global peace,
they chose for their symbol a map of the world cupped by a
pair of olive branches on a slightly grayish cerulean ground.
Oliver Lundquist, the architect and designer who created
the insignia, chose this shade because it is "the opposite
of red, the war color."[1]

It is spiritual as well as peaceful. Many Hindu gods,
including Krishna, Shiva, and Rama, are depicted with
skin the color of the sky, symbolizing their affinity with the
infinite. The French call it *bleu céleste*, heavenly blue.
It is also, confusingly, the color many of the buildings
at the Church of Scientology's Gold Base in California—
including the mansion awaiting the reincarnation of the
religion's founder, L. Ron Hubbard. (The man himself,
when founding Scientology, is reported to have told a
colleague, "Let's sell these people a piece of sky blue.")
Pantone named its paler, forget-me-not shade as the
color of the millennium, guessing that consumers would
"be seeking inner peace and spiritual fulfillment in the
new millennium."[2]

A true cerulean pigment—one of the cobalt family
[page 187]—was not available to artists until the 1860s,

and then only as a watercolor.[3] Made from a mixture
of cobalt and tin oxides known as cobalt stannate, it did
not make much headway until the 1870s, when it was
finally released as an oil paint; in this medium it lost the
slight chalkiness it had in watercolors and seduced
a generation of painters. While Van Gogh preferred to
create his own approximation of the tint using a subtle
mixture of cobalt blue, a little cadmium yellow, and white,
others were less cautious. Paul Signac, known for his airy
pointillism, squeezed countless tubes dry, as did many
of his fellows, including Monet.[4] When the photographer
and writer Brassaï ran into Picasso's Parisian paint
supplier in November 1943, the man handed him a piece
of white paper filled with Picasso's handwriting. "At first
glance it looks like a poem," wrote Brassaï, but, he realized,
it was actually Picasso's last paint order. Third on the list,
just below "White, permanent—" and "White, silver—,"
is "Blue, cerulean."[5]

Verdigris
Absinthe
Emerald
Kelly green
Scheele's green
Terre verte
Avocado
Celadon

Green

There is a Buddhist fable about the color green. In the
tale a deity appears to a small boy in a dream one night and
tells him that to obtain everything he could ever desire
all he need do is close his eyes and not picture sea green.
The story has two possible endings. In one the boy
eventually succeeds and finds enlightenment; in the other
he is so consumed by his continued failure that life and
sanity gradually slip away.[1]

Today green tends to conjure up comforting images of
countryside and environmentally friendly politics. Despite
its association with envy, it is generally seen as a peaceful
color and is often associated with luxury and style. A glaucous
shade was the darling of the art deco movement; emerald
was Pantone's "Color of the Year" in 2013, while greenery,
a tangier, leafy shade, has taken up this mantle for 2017.

The ancient Egyptian hieroglyph for the color was
the papyrus stalk, a plant that the Egyptians held in high
regard. In Latin the word for green is *viridis*, which is
related to a large group of words that suggest growth and
even life itself: *virere*, to be green or vigorous; *vis*, strength;
vir, man; and so on.[2] Many cultures associate the color
positively with gardens and spring. For Muslims, for whom
"paradise" is almost synonymous with "garden," green
became prominent from the twelfth century. It was the
favorite color, along with white, of the Prophet Muhammad.
In the Koran, the robes worn in paradise and silk couches
scattered amidst the trees are both the color of leaves. And
in medieval Islamic poetry Mount Qaf, the celestial mountain;
the sky above it; and the water at its feet are all depicted in
shades of green. This is why the color appears in the flags
of many predominantly Islamic countries including Iran,
Bangladesh, Saudi Arabia, and Pakistan.[3]

In the West green was particularly linked with the
courtly rituals of spring. On May 1, for example, many

courts required members to *s'esmayer* or "wear the May,"
which in practice meant wearing a leafy crown or garland,
or a prominent item of green clothing. Those who were
pris sans verd, or showed themselves without this color,
would be loudly mocked.[4] Possibly because of such rituals,
and the inevitable flirtation and trouble they could cause,
green also became the badge of youth and young love.
The expression "to be green," meaning inexperienced,
was already being used by the Middle Ages. Minne, a
Germanic goddess who, like Cupid, was fond of shooting
people with mischievous arrows of love, habitually wore
a green dress, as did fertile young women—this is one
interpretation, for example, of Jan van Eyck's *Arnolfini
Portrait* (c. 1435) [page 214].

Despite such positive associations green had, in the
West at least, something of an image problem. This was
partially due to an early misunderstanding surrounding
color mixing. Plato, the ancient Greek mathematician
born in the mid-fifth century B.C., stoutly maintained that
prasinon (leek color) was made by mixing *purron* (flame
color) and *melas* (black). Democritus, father of atomic
theory, believed pale green was a product of red and
white.[5] For the ancients green was, like red, one of the
middle colors between white and black, and in fact red
and green were often confused linguistically: the medieval
Latin *sinople* could refer to either until the fifteenth
century.[6] In 1195 the future Pope Innocent III reinterpreted
green's role in the divine order in an influential treatise.
It must, he wrote, "be chosen for holidays and the days
when neither white nor red nor black are suitable, because
it is a middle color between white, red, and black."[7]
This, theoretically, gave it far greater prominence in the
West, but materially it was still rare: it never appeared in
more than 5 percent of heraldic arms.

One reason for this is the long-standing taboo against creating green dyes and pigments by mixing blue and yellow. Not only was this poorly understood for many centuries—see Plato's assertions above—but there was also a deep aversion to mixing different substances together, in a way that is difficult to understand today. Alchemists, who routinely mixed elements together, were mistrusted, and in medieval art colors usually appeared in unmixed blocks with no attempt to show perspective by shading. In the clothing industry this was complicated by guild restrictions and the high degree of specialization: in many countries blue/black dyers were forbidden to work with red and yellow dye substances. In some countries anyone caught dyeing cloth green by dipping it in first woad [page 198] and then weld, a yellow dye, could face severe repercussions, including large fines and exile. Although there were some plants, including foxglove and nettle, that produced a green color without the need for any mixing, these did not produce the kind of rich, saturated color that people of taste and influence wanted to buy. The effect this had is plain from an offhand comment made by the scholar Henri Estienne in 1566: "In France, if one sees a man of quality dressed in green, one might think that his brain was a little off."[8]

Artists had to deal with inferior green pigments. The Dutch artist Samuel van Hoogstraten wrote in the 1670s: "I wish that we had a green pigment as good as a red or yellow. Green earth [page 227] is too weak, Spanish green [page 214] too crude, and ashes [verditer] not sufficiently durable."[9] From the early Renaissance, when the taboo against mixing began to fade, until the late eighteenth century, when new copper greens were discovered by a Swedish chemist called Carl Wilhelm Scheele [page 224], artists had to blend their own green paints.

Even this was tricky. Verdigris was prone to reacting with other pigments and even blackening on its own, and terre verte had poor tinting strength and luminosity. Paolo Veronese, who worked in Venice for most of his career during the sixteenth century and was, like Titian before him, an extremely skilled and resourceful colorist, was famous for being able to coax bright viridescent colors out of recalcitrant pigments. His trick was to apply a precise mixture of three different pigments in two layers and to protect green areas with layers of varnish to stop them reacting. Even he, though, had the occasional green mishap, and as late as the nineteenth century artists were struggling to produce reliable green. The grass in the foreground of Georges Seurat's *Sunday Afternoon on the Island of La Grande Jatte*, for example, appears withered in patches because of misbehaving pigments. This painting, one of the best-known examples of the pointillist technique and the work that launched the neo-impressionist movement, was created in the mid-1880s, which demonstrates just how recently painters were struggling against their materials.

The particular difficulties craftsmen and consumers had with green perhaps contributed to the color's symbolic link with capriciousness, poison, and even evil. The association with poison, at least, had some merit after the development and explosive popularity of the new copper arsenite pigments in the nineteenth century. Scheele's green and its close cousin—variously called vert Paul Véronèse, emerald green, Schweinfurt green, and Brunswick green—were responsible for many deaths, as unsuspecting consumers papered their homes, clothed their offspring, and wrapped their baked goods in an exciting new shade that contained lethal doses of arsenic.

The other charges levied against green, however, were
the result of petty prejudice. In the West green started
becoming visually associated with the devil and demonic
creatures from the twelfth century, possibly as a result
of the Crusades and the increasing antagonism between
Christians and Muslims, for whom the color was sacred. In
Shakespeare's day green costumes were considered
bad luck onstage, a belief that persisted into the nineteenth
century. In 1847, for example, a French author threatened
to withdraw one of his works from the Comédie-Française
because an actress was refusing to wear the green dress that
the author had specified for the character she was to play.[10]
Perhaps the final word on the irrational dislike of green
should go to Wassily Kandinsky. "Absolute green," he
wrote, "is the most anesthetizing color possible . . . similar
to a fat cow, full of good health, lying down, rooted,
capable only of ruminating and contemplating the world
through its stupid, inexpressive eyes."[11]

Verdigris

Ever since the oil dried on the playfully elaborate artist's signature—*Johannes de eyck fuit hic*, "Jan van Eyck was here"—in 1434, the *Arnolfini Portrait* has intrigued and infuriated art lovers in equal measure.[1] In the painting a couple stand, bodies tilted toward the viewer. She wears a bottle-green gown with preposterously long sleeves; he has fishy eyes and looks a little like Vladimir Putin. Is the woman's left hand, loosely clasping her full skirts over the curve of her belly, the protective gesture of an expectant mother or simply an indication of fashionable indolence? Is this a newly married couple or an allegory of abuse? What is the meaning of the little dog? The gargoyles? The discarded clogs?

One thing is for sure: the dress is incontrovertible evidence of the couple's wealth. The trailing bag-sleeves were so decadent that Scottish peasants were expressly forbidden to wear them in the 1430s; the woolen cloth was further lined with the creamy fur of up to 2,000 squirrels.[2] The sap-green color too indicated money. A deep-dyed and even green was a difficult color to achieve. Generally it required two dye baths, first in woad and then in weld, a practice that was actually illegal for much of this period because of the medieval taboo on mixing colors. In January 1386 Hans Töllner, a third-generation dyer from Nuremberg, was denounced for doing precisely this; he was fined, banned from the dyeing profession, and exiled to Augsburg.[3] Van Eyck, using the finest of his brushes to paint the appliquéd Maltese cross decoration on the woman's trailing sleeves, would have felt equally frustrated. Like the dyers striving for the perfect green, artists too struggled to coax this fresh and beautiful color out of lousy raw materials; in this case, verdigris.

Verdigris is a naturally occurring carbonate that forms on copper and its alloy bronze when they are exposed to

oxygen, water, carbon dioxide, or sulfur.[4] It is this green
patina that forms on old copper pipes and roofs, and
which gives the Statue of Liberty the blue-green color of
the misty sea she often faces. It took the elements 30 years
to turn Gustave Eiffel's second most famous structure from
rosy copper to full green, far too long a time for an artist
to wait for his pigment.[5] It is not known exactly when
the technique for speeding the process along was
discovered, but it is thought to have traveled westward
with Arabic alchemy. Traces of this route can be discerned
in the pigment's various names. *Verdigris* is French for
"green from Greece," while its German name is *Grünspan*,
or "Spanish green"—Georgius Agricola, a sixteenth-
century scholar, wrote that it was brought up from Spain.[6]
Similar to the manufacture of lead white [page 43], leaves
of copper were placed in a pot with lye and vinegar or sour
wine. The pots were then sealed and left for two weeks,
after which the sheets were dried, and the green patina was
scraped off, powdered, and formed into cakes with more
sour wine, ready to be sold.[7]

As the green dress in the *Arnolfini Portrait* proves,
verdigris could be used to spectacular effect, but it was
fickle. The acids used to make it often attacked the
surface on which it was used, nibbling through medieval
illuminations of paper and parchment like a caterpillar
munching through leaves. It also had a tendency to
discolor and to react with other pigments. As Cennino
Cennini lamented: "it is beautiful to the eye, but it does
not last."[8] The truth of his words is evident in the works of
everyone from Raphael to Tintoretto, where the greenery
has withered to a shade approaching coffee. Even Paolo
Veronese, a renowned master of the color green, was not
immune.[9] (Perhaps such incidents were why he dreamed
of "green pigments as good in quality as the reds.")[10]

Verdigris, continued.

The problem was exacerbated by the rise of oil paint in the fifteenth century. While verdigris is perfectly opaque in the egg-tempera medium, it becomes glassily transparent in oils, which often led to its being mixed with turpentine resin from pine trees to restore its opacity.[11] This made verdigris even more temperamental, and some began to worry that it should not be used with lead white, rendering it all but useless. Because there were so few alternatives, artists had little choice but to persevere, sandwiching their troublesome green between layers of varnish as a precaution and hoping for the best. For Van Eyck and his wealthy clients, however, it was clearly worth the risk.

Absinthe

In the waning decades of the nineteenth century a green
menace harried Europe's citizens. Absinthe was made
from a combination of plants and aromatics, including
wormwood, aniseed, fennel, and wild marjoram, which
were first bruised and then soaked in alcohol and distilled,
creating a bitter, pear-colored liqueur. It was not an
entirely new concoction: ancient Greeks and Romans had
used similar recipes as an insect repellent and antiseptic.
The modern version was also intended for medicinal use.
Pierre Ordinaire, a well-known French physician living
in Switzerland just after the French Revolution, created
a take on the ancient recipe as a tonic for his patients.[1]
It became commercially available at the turn of the
century, but was still largely considered medicinal:
French soldiers serving in Africa were given it to help
ward off malaria.

Soon enough, though, people began to acquire a taste
for it. At first, it was not so very different from any other
aperitif, a small alcoholic drink taken before dinner,
of which the French were inordinately fond. A measure
would be placed in a glass, and then diluted with ice-cold
water poured through a sugar cube, turning the whole
thing milky pale.[2] The difference was in absinthe's
visibility and, from the 1860s when producers began using
cheaper grain alcohol, its explosive popularity. While at
first it was associated with dissolute bohemians and artists
like Vincent van Gogh, Paul Gauguin, Oscar Wilde, and
Edgar Allan Poe, its appeal soon spread. By the 1870s
a glass cost no more than 10 centimes, considerably less
than wine, and absinthe accounted for 90 percent of
aperitif consumption. In the latter half of the nineteenth
century whole districts of Paris were said to smell faintly
herbal between 5 and 6 p.m., a time that became known as
l'heure verte ("the green hour"). In France consumption

Absinthe, continued.

increased from an average of 0.04 quarts per person in
1875 to 0.6 quarts in 1913.[3]

By this stage, absinthe had become a serious cause for
concern, and not only in France, but also in Switzerland,
where many people drank it, and Britain, where it was
feared many soon would. This strange green drink,
authorities felt, was poisoning the body-social, and a moral
panic swiftly ensued. On May 4, 1868, the *Times* warned
its readers that absinthe was threatening to "become as
widespread in France and as injurious there as opium-eating
is in China." This "emerald-tinted poison" was making
"driveling idiots" out of those who were lucky enough to
drink it and survive addiction and death. Worse still, more
and more respectable people were dallying with it.
"Literary men, professors, artists, actors, musicians,
financiers, speculators, shopkeepers, even"—here one
imagines readers' hands convulsively clutching their
throats—women were becoming absinthe's "ardent lovers."[4]

In France doctors began to suspect that it was really
a poisonous drug. "Absinthomania" was increasingly seen
as a medical complaint quite distinct from mere alcoholism.
People were reporting hallucinations and permanent
insanity. To prove it, two scientists doused an unfortunate
guinea pig with wormwood fumes (wormwood had quickly
become the chief suspect of all absinthe's botanicals),
whereupon he "became heavy and dull, and at last fell on
his side, agitating his limbs convulsively, foaming at the
mouth."[5] Dr. Valentin Magnan, an authority on insanity
and the director of a Parisian asylum, theorized that
madness brought on by absinthe—his experiments had
been conducted on a dog—was responsible for a collapse
in French culture.[6] In Switzerland the final straw came
in 1905, when a man called Jean Lanfray killed his
pregnant wife and two young daughters, Rose and

Blanche, after he had been drinking absinthe. The case was dubbed "the absinthe murder" and the drink was outlawed completely in Switzerland three years later. France followed suit at the outbreak of the First World War in August 1914, in a groundswell of popular patriotic fervor.

Subsequent tests have shown that much of the supposed proof of absinthe's inherently deleterious effects were nonsense. Wormwood does not cause hallucinations and madness. Although the spirit does contain thujone, which is poisonous in large quantities, the doses a person would need to consume mean that they would die of alcohol poisoning long before thujone overdose became a possibility. The real problem with absinthe is that it is very alcoholic, varying between 55 and 75 percent, and in the late nineteenth and early twentieth centuries Europe was experiencing widespread social upheaval of the kind that led many to become alcoholics. Jean Lanfray was typical. While it is true that he had started the day on which he murdered his family with two shots of absinthe, he had gone on to drink wine, brandy, and then more wine— he could not even remember committing his crime.[7] But this didn't matter. Absinthe, with its druglike pouring ritual, working-class and counterculture devotees, and suspicious, poison-green color, was the perfect scapegoat.

Emerald

It was Shakespeare who cemented the relationship
between green and envy. With *The Merchant of Venice*,
written in the late 1590s, he gave us "green-eyed jealousy";
in *Othello* (1603), he has Iago mention "the green-ey'd
monster, which doth mock / The meat it feeds on."
Prior to this, during the Middle Ages, when each deadly
sin had a corresponding color, green had been twinned
with avarice and yellow with envy.[1] Both human failings
were the guiding principles in a recent saga concerning
a vast green stone, the Bahia emerald.

Emeralds are a rare and fragile member of the beryl
family, stained green with small deposits of the elements
chromium or vanadium. The best-known sources are
in Pakistan, India, Zambia, and parts of South America.
Ancient Egyptians mined the gemstones from 1500 B.C.,
setting them in amulets and talismans, and they have been
coveted ever since.

The Romans, believing green to be restful to the eyes
because of its prominence in nature, pulverized emeralds
to make expensive eye balms. The emperor Nero was
particularly enamored with the gem. Not only did he
have an extensive collection, he was also said to use a
particularly large example as proto-sunglasses, watching
gladiator fights through it so that he wouldn't be bothered
by the glare of the sun.[2] When L. Frank Baum wrote
The Wonderful Wizard of Oz in 1900, he used the precious
stone as both the name and the building material for the
city his heroine and her band of misfit friends are trying to
reach. The Emerald City, at least at the beginning of the
book, is a metaphor for the magical fulfillment of dreams:
it lures the characters in because they all want something
from it.

The Bahia was heaved from the beryllium-rich
earth of northeastern Brazil by a prospector in 2001.

Stones from this area are generally not worth much;
they tend to be cloudy and occluded and sell for, on
average, less than $10. This one, however, was gargantuan.
The whole lump weighed 840 pounds (roughly the same
as a male polar bear) and was thought to contain a
Kryptonite-green gem of 180,000 carats. In the years
since its discovery the gemstone's vast size and value
have done little to secure it a stable home. Housed in
a warehouse in New Orleans in 2005, the Bahia narrowly
escaped the flooding caused by Hurricane Katrina. It has
allegedly been used in any number of fraudulent business
dealings—a judge called one such scheme "despicable
and reprehensible." It was listed on eBay in 2007 for a
starting price of $18.9 million and a "buy-it-now" price
of $75 million. Gullible potential buyers were regaled
with a backstory that involved a journey through the
jungle on a stretcher woven from vines and a double
panther mauling.

At the time of writing the Bahia emerald is valued
at around $400 million and is at the center of a California
lawsuit. Around a dozen people claim to have bought
the stone fair and square in the 15 years since it was
discovered, including a dapper Mormon businessman;
a man who says he purchased it for $60,000, only to be
tricked into believing it was stolen; and several of the
people who brought it over to California in the first place.
An international row has been brewing too: Brazil claims
that the stone should be repatriated.[3] The story of the
Bahia emerald is, in short, a parable of avarice worthy
of the Bard himself.

Kelly green

It is well known that the only people more proud of their
Irish heritage than the Irish are the Americans of Irish
descent. New York's St. Patrick's Day Parade, for example,
proudly traces its lineage all the way back to March 17,
1762, 14 years before the Declaration of Independence.
Every year, while the White House dyes the waters
of its fountain the color of mulched leaves, hundreds
of thousands gather to celebrate Ireland by drinking
Guinness, wearing green, and trying out their rusty Irish
accents. By contrast, Kelly green, one name given to the
spring-grass color so many wear on St. Patrick's Day,
is a rather recent invention, emerging only at the beginning
of the twentieth century.[1]

Most people would, if asked, say the connection
between the Irish and Kelly green has to do with St.
Patrick. Everything known about the saint comes from
the man himself: during his lifetime in the fifth century
he wrote his *Confessio*, an account of his life in Latin,
the first text written in Ireland to have survived. It begins
simply: "My name is Patrick. I am a sinner, a simple
country person, and the least of all believers."[2] His first
acquaintance with the country of which he is now patron
saint was not a happy one. He was born to a relatively
wealthy Christian family in a place named Bannavem
Taburniae—which was probably in England, although
no one is quite sure—and was brought to Ireland as a slave
after being captured by Irish raiders. In all he spent six
years as a captive tending sheep, after which he escaped,
returned home, and became a priest. Clearly he did not
bear Ireland any ill will, because he soon returned as
a missionary, converting much of the population, most
famously using a shamrock to explain the idea of the
trinity. He died sometime in the late fifth century,
and was being celebrated as a saint by the seventh.

Strangely, though, the color he was most associated with until the middle of the eighteenth century was a shade of blue.[3]

The shift in Irish loyalty from St. Patrick's blue to green is convoluted. Responding to what they perceived as the anti-Catholic bias of William of Orange and the orange-wearing Protestants [page 96], Catholics wanted a symbolic color of their own. By this time the saint's lesson of the shamrock had become increasingly central to Irish Catholic identity. At the same time green had become associated with revolution when, on July 12, 1789, a young lawyer called Camille Desmoulins picked up a linden leaf in the middle of haranguing a Parisian crowd, stuck it in his hat, and invited patriots to do the same. Soon enough, the linden leaf had become a green cockade, and it might have been adopted as the symbol of the French Revolution had it not been remembered at the last minute that it was the color of the livery of the detested Count of Artois, Louis XVI's younger brother. By July 14, the green cockade had been eclipsed by the tricolor.[4] Nevertheless a green flag, sometimes bearing a golden harp, became the symbol of the fiery Irish Home Rule movement, which sought independence from Britain. In a deliberate snub, when the Prince of Wales visited Ireland in the spring of 1885, a green flag vied for space with the Union Jack.[5] In the end, the Irish decided to follow the French once more in the adoption of a tricolor flag. The green symbolized the Catholic nationalists, orange the Protestants, and white the peace it was hoped would reign between them.

Scheele's green

The island of St. Helena lies like a lost seed in the middle
of the Atlantic, 1,200 miles west of Africa and 2,500 miles
east of South America. It is so remote that it has, for the
majority of its history, been uninhabited, serving only as a
stop-off for ships to collect fresh water and repair their
hulls. It was here that the British decreed that Napoleon
should be sent in October 1815 after his defeat at
Waterloo. And it was here too that he died, six years later.
Although his physician had initially suspected stomach
cancer, when Napoleon's body was exhumed
in 1840 it was found to be curiously well preserved,
a symptom of arsenic poisoning. A sample of his hair,
tested in the twentieth century, was also found to contain
abnormally high levels of the poison. Once it was
discovered in the 1980s that the walls of his damp little
room in St. Helena were papered with a verdant design
containing Scheele's green, the rumor spread that the
British had poisoned their difficult prisoner.

In 1775 Carl Wilhelm Scheele, a Swedish scientist,
was studying the element arsenic when he came across
the compound copper arsenite, a green that, though
a slightly grubby pea shade, he immediately recognized
as having commercial potential in an industry starved
for green pigments and dyes.[1] It went into production
almost immediately and the world fell in love with it.
It was used to print fabrics and wallpapers; to color
artificial flowers, paper, and dress fabrics; as an artists'
pigment; and even for tinting confectionery. J. M. W.
Turner, ever willing to try out the latest innovations,
used it in an oil sketch of Guildford in 1805.[2] After a trip
to Italy in 1845, Charles Dickens returned home seized
with a passion to redecorate his whole house in the newly
fashionable shade. (He was, luckily, dissuaded by his
wife.)[3] By 1858 it was estimated that there were around

100 square miles of wallpaper dyed with copper arsenite greens in British homes, hotels, hospitals, and railway waiting rooms. And by 1863 the *Times* estimated that between 500 and 700 tons of Scheele's green were being made each year in Britain alone to satisfy the ballooning demand.

However, just as it seemed as if the appetite for greens could not be satiated, disturbing rumors and a string of suspicious deaths began to dull consumers' hunger. Over 18 months working as an artificial-flower maker, Matilda Scheurer rapidly sickened—her likely symptoms included nausea, vomiting, diarrhea, rashes, and listlessness— and finally died in November 1861 at age 19. In another case, a little girl had died after sucking the green powder from a bunch of artificial grapes.[4]

As more and more people succumbed after experiencing similar symptoms, doctors and scientists began conducting tests on all green consumables. An article in the *British Medical Journal* in 1871 noted that green wallpaper could be found in all manner of houses, "from the palace down to the navvy's hut"; a six-inch-square sample of such a paper was found to contain enough arsenic to poison two adults.[5] G. Owen Rees, a doctor at Guy's Hospital in London, became suspicious after a patient was apparently poisoned by some calico bed curtains. He did further tests in 1877 and found to his horror that "some muslin of a very beautiful pale green" used for dressmaking contained over 60 grains of an arsenic compound in every square yard. "Imagine, Sir," he wrote to the *Times*, "what the atmosphere of a ballroom must be where the agitation of skirts consequent on dancing must be constantly discharging arsenical poison."[6]

Scheele had known from the beginning that his eponymous pigment was poisonous: he said so in a letter

Scheele's green, continued.

to a friend in 1777, adding that his other principal
concern was that someone else might get the credit for
his discovery.[7] The head of the Zuber & Cie factory
in Mulhouse wrote to a professor in 1870 to say that the
pigment, "so beautiful and so brilliant," was now only
being supplied in small quantities. "To want to prohibit
all trace of arsenic in papers is to go too far," he continued,
"and to hurt business unjustly and needlessly."[8] The public,
it seemed, largely agreed, and no laws were ever passed
banning its use. If this seems strange, it should be
remembered that this was a world where arsenic and its
dangers were accepted with more equanimity. Even after
a mass poisoning in 1858, when a package of powdered
white arsenic was mistaken for powdered sugar and added
to a batch of peppermints in Bradford, it took a long time
for people to come around to the idea of regulations and
warning symbols.[9]

   This more laissez-faire attitude to the poisonous
substance was given some accidental backing by
researchers at Italy's National Institute of Nuclear
Physics in 2008. In order to finally settle the question
of Napoleon's death, they tested other samples of hair
from different stages of his life, and found that the levels
of arsenic had remained relatively stable. They were,
yes, very high by today's standards, but not at all unusual
for his.[10]

Terre verte

Reading treatises and manuals by early artists, it is hard
not to think that they often faced a Sisyphean struggle
to create works of lasting beauty. Pigments were often
mercurial, reacting badly with other pigments or changing
color over time, like verdigris [page 214]; they were
downright lethal, like orpiment [page 82] and lead white
[page 43]; or they were ludicrously expensive and difficult
to acquire, like ultramarine [page 182]. It could be
assumed, then, that if a pigment were found that was
inexpensive, relatively plentiful, completely stable, and
in a color where there were very few other options, that
this pigment would be in high demand. The case of terre
verte shows this is not the case.

Also known as green earth or Verona green, terre
verte is a rather mongrel collection of naturally occurring
pigmented earths of varying hues and mineral makeups.
The green coloring agents are usually glauconite and
celadonite, but can also include many other minerals.[1]
The pigments crop up in great quantities in various
locations throughout Europe, most famously Cyprus and
Verona, and come in a range of colors, from deep forest,
to an almost crocodilian shade, and even a rather beautiful
sea mist. The drawback is their low tinting strength, but
they are all very permanent and stable, rather transparent,
work perfectly in all mediums, give a peculiar, almost
buttery texture to oils, and, crucially, were some of the few
green pigments readily available. And yet, when artists
write about terre verte, their words have the air of a school
report about a child who means well but is totally devoid
of charm. George Field, in his book *Chromatography*,
published in the mid-nineteenth century, is typical in
his indifference:

Terre verte, continued.

[I]t is a very durable pigment, being unaffected by strong light and impure air, and combining with other colors without injury. It has not much body, is semi-transparent, and dries well in oil.[2]

Curiously, prehistoric man seems to have been equally apathetic when it comes to the green earths. In the Lascaux caves in France, where images date back to 15,000 B.C., the pigments that dominate are red and yellow ochers, manganese oxide browns and blacks, and calcite white. At Altamira in Spain, where paintings date from 10,000 B.C., much of the work uses hematite [page 150]. In fact cave art is dominated by browns, whites, blacks, and reds; the use of blues and greens is almost unheard of. With blue, which is very rare in mineral form, this is not surprising, but the absence of green certainly is: terre verte was widely available and easy to process and use.[3] It did get used a lot later on. It can be seen, for instance, in a wonderful naturalistic mural of a tree in Stabiae, a town near Pompeii that was also destroyed by the eruption of Vesuvius in A.D. 79. Terre verte really came into its own, however, when artists discovered that it was perfect for shading the pale pinky-red of European skin. In some European manuscripts, where the top layers have faded, the green underlayer shows through, giving the saints an unsuitably demonic air.

Cennino Cennini, an artist pupil of the Tuscan master Giotto, was undoubtedly a pragmatist. He loved art and also enjoyed showing others how they could replicate it themselves. His *Il libro dell'arte* spent several centuries consigned to oblivion on a dusty Vatican shelf before being rediscovered and republished in the early nineteenth century, and it has remained in print ever since. In this book he explains all manner of processes, from gilding a panel to making glue with the "muzzles, feet, sinews, and

. . . skin" of goats (a practice that should only be attempted in March or January).[4] Terre verte and its uses occur again and again. Cennini notes enthusiastically that the pigment is good for everything from faces to draperies, and works just as well in fresco as it does in secco (dry). To produce good flesh tones in tempera, for example, he tells his readers to lay two coats, mixed with white lead, "over the face, over the hands, over the feet, and over the nudes." He recommends using tempera made with the "yolk of a town hen's egg" for young faces, because their flesh is cooler, while the yolk of a "country or farm" hen is better suited "for tempering flesh colors for aged and swarthy persons." For the flesh of corpses he suggests omitting the pink that was usually layered over the top: "a dead person has no color."[5] It is difficult to know what it was that made him look more favorably upon this rather unlovable pigment. Perhaps the secret lies in his first encounter with it. When he was a boy, Cennino's father, Andrea Cennini, took him to the workings at Colle di Val d'Elsa. "[U]pon reaching a little valley," he wrote, "a very wild steep place, scraping the steep with a spade, I beheld seas of many kinds of color."[6]

Avocado

In February 1969 the beaches of Santa Barbara, California,
turned black. Several days earlier, on the morning of
January 28, an oil well 6 miles off the coast had ruptured.
In all it is estimated that 200,000 gallons of
crude oil escaped, and for 11 days it spewed out from the
seafloor, coating a 35-mile stretch of California coastline
and any marine wildlife in its path. The Santa Barbara
spill marked a turning point in the way the world, and
particularly the United States, perceived the globe and
its fragility.[1] The inaugural Earth Day was celebrated
on April 22 the following year. (It was founded by Senator
Gaylord Nelson, who had seen for himself the damage
at Santa Barbara.) Over the next few years, in response
to popular protests, legal progress against pollution gained
traction in America: the Clean Air, Clean Water, and
National Environmental Policy Acts were passed.

Over the next decade the environmental health
of the world loomed increasingly large in the public
consciousness. A picture of the globe taken on December
7, 1972, by the crew of the Apollo 17, who were bound for
the moon, made the world look, for the first time,
vulnerable. The "Blue Marble" photo became one of
the most iconic and widely shared images of all time.
Artists like Robert Smithson and James Turrell used
the land as a raw material, creating works that frankly
commented on the earth's fragility and challenged
perceptions of the planet as immutable and inexhaustible.[2]
It was during this period that the color green became
the shorthand for nature. The two had always been linked,
of course—the ancient Egyptian hieroglyph for "green"
was a papyrus stalk—but during the 1970s the link became
ubiquitous.[3] A small organization called the Don't Make a
Wave Committee changed its name to Greenpeace in
1972. PEOPLE, the forerunner to the British Green Party,

was founded in 1973; Germany's equivalent, Die Grünen, in 1979; and France's Les Verts were consolidated in the 1980s.

These grand ideas and a burgeoning concern for the natural world were translated into a back-to-nature palette of earthy colors: burnt orange, harvest gold, and, above all, avocado. This shade, which appears so dated now, dominated palettes throughout the 1970s. As shoppers strove to appear sincerely concerned for the welfare of the world, the furthest reaches of consumer goods—clothing, kitchen appliances, baths, even cars—were colonized by this smoky yellow-green tint.

These attempts at environmental redemption through consumption may well seem hopelessly naive, but similar consumer impulses prevail today. And avocado has stealthily been reprising its role since the millennium. Those who doubt this need only check their Instagram feeds. While few advocate for avocado-colored macramé and shag pile, the *Persea americana* has become the poster fruit (technically it's a single-seed berry) for a new kind of luxury consumption underpinned by the concept of natural healthfulness. Lovingly slathered on pieces of toast everywhere from Southern California to Slough, it has become the centerpiece of the eat-clean brand of aspirational lifestyle. And as one of the few heart-healthy, "good" fats that nutritionists consistently agree on, avocado imports have skyrocketed. In 2014, four billion avocados were consumed in America, around four times the number eaten a scant 15 years before. In 2011 alone sales were $2.9 billion, an 11 percent increase on the year before. As Mike Brown, a marketing executive for the Mexican Hass Avocado Importers' Association, told a reporter for the *Wall Street Journal* in 2012: "The stars have aligned."[4]

Celadon

Honoré d'Urfé led a dramatic life. He was imprisoned for his political beliefs, lived much of his life as an exile in Savoy, and married his brother's beautiful widow in order to keep her fortune in the d'Urfé family. It was perhaps this surfeit of intrigue that led him to write the nostalgic, meandering *L'Astrée*. Published between 1607 and 1627, the 5,399-page and 60-book pastoral comedy recounts the futile quest of Céladon, a lovelorn shepherd, to win back his lover Astrée after a misunderstanding.[1] Despite its prodigious length and unwieldy cast of characters, it was a hit with his contemporaries. It was widely translated, circulated throughout Europe, and spawned a stage play and even a fashion for dressing in sylvan green *à la Céladon*.[2]

So firmly linked was Céladon with this particular woodland-fog color that the word *celadon* was soon used to refer to a kind of similarly hued type of ceramics imported from the East. The Chinese had been making celadon objects for centuries before d'Urfé's hero sprang into being. Usually grayish green—although the colors can vary enormously, from blues to grays to ochers and even blacks— these ceramics are characterized by the presence of iron in the clay and iron oxide, manganese oxide, and quartz in the glaze.[3] Pieces are usually fired at just under 2,100°F degrees, and oxygen levels are dramatically reduced midway through. Many have thin networks of fissures in the glazes, as fine as the network of veins in a leaf, which are produced intentionally to make the surface resemble jade.[4] Although the method originated in China, similar ceramics were produced by the Goryeo dynasty on the Korean Peninsula between A.D. 918 and 1392. Even within China, there was a great variance in the style, color, and aesthetic of celadon pieces produced in different regions and eras.[5]

Song-dynasty celadon has been found as far afield as Japan and Cairo, and there is evidence of a healthy trade in celadon with the Middle East. Turkish rulers, who believed celadon was a natural antidote to poison, amassed a vast collection that can still be seen at the Topkapi Palace in Istanbul.[6] A variant, called *mi se* or "mysterious color," was long the most costly and exclusive ceramic made in China, reserved for royal households. Nor was *mi se* a misnomer: few contemporaries outside the courts had ever seen a single piece, so most could only guess at what it looked like. Xu Yin, a tenth-century poet, described the color as "carving light from the moon to dye the mountain stream," which certainly sounds like an artful guess.[7] The true color of *mi se* celadon was only rediscovered by archaeologists in the late 1980s, when a precious cache was discovered in a secret chamber underneath a collapsed temple tower. The mysteriously colored celadon China's rulers had guarded so jealously turned out to be a rather drab olive.[8]

Although "oriental" books and objets d'art had been dribbling west for centuries, Europeans, at the far end of a series of tortuous trade routes, were too distant from the source to understand celadon's myriad classifications. Patterns and colors that, to a trained observer, would have communicated purpose, place, and time of origin, meant nothing to seventeenth-century Europeans. For them, the beautiful, sea-mist ceramics that had traveled so far conjured up only the hapless Céladon in his shabby coat of green.

Khaki
Buff
Fallow
Russet
Sepia
Umber
Mummy
Taupe

Brown

The creation of man from clay is a motif that appears across many cultures and religions, from Babylonian to Islamic. As the Bible has it: "In the sweat of thy face shalt thou eat bread, till thou return unto the ground; for out of it wast thou taken: for dust thou art, and unto dust shalt thou return."[1] It may be symbolic of the rich soil from which we get our food, but we will never show brown our gratitude. After all, it is not only the color of the earth to which we will one day return, but also mud, filth, refuse, and shit.

Brown suffers in part because it is not a hue, but a shade. It is not found in a rainbow or on a simple color wheel; making it requires darkening and graying down yellows, oranges, and some impure reds, or mixing together the three artists' primaries—red, yellow, and blue. That there is no bright or luminous brown led to its being despised by both medieval artists and modernists. For medieval artists, who disliked mixing on principle and saw the glory of God reflected in the use of pure precious materials like ultramarine [page 182] and gold [page 86], brown was inherently corrupt. Centuries later Camille Pissarro boasted that he had expunged all the earth pigments from his own palette (although in actual fact they do crop up occasionally).[2] Where browns were necessary—inevitably, since the impressionists and many who came after them enjoyed painting landscapes *en plein air*—they were made using mixtures of the saturated new synthetics.

This was willfulness on the part of the artists, because iron oxides, known as ochers, are some of the most common compounds on the earth's surface. They were also one of the first pigments used by humankind. The cattle, deer, lions, and handprints found on the walls of prehistoric caves were lent their warm browns and maroons by earth pigments. The ancient Egyptians,

Greeks, and Romans also used ochers. To add to their utility, they were not only plentiful but also found in many different varieties.

Like some blacks, browns have long been used by artists for underdrawings and sketches. Bister, a dark but not particularly colorfast material, usually prepared from the tarry remains of burned beech wood, was popular.[3] Other notable examples include the yellowy sienna from Italy and umber [page 250], which is darker and cooler. A blood-brown earth known as sinopia, after the port it came from, was beloved too. Pedanius Dioscorides, a Greek physician who lived around A.D. 40–90, described it as heavy and dense and the color of liver.[4] In July 1944 an Allied bullet grazed the roof of a building beside the leaning tower in Pisa's famous Piazza dei Miracoli and set it aflame, seriously damaging the Renaissance frescoes within. According to Giuseppe Ramalli, a local lawyer who saw the whole thing, they were left "swollen, dilated, coming off or stained by thick, wide streaks, drawn by the lead dripping down from the molten roof . . . Words fail to convey that ruin."[5] When what remained was ripped off the walls to be repaired, a host of spirited sinopia preparatory drawings were revealed. These can still be seen, in all their fresh and expressive glory, today.

The artistic period most associated with browns, and which valued them most for their own sake, came after the first flush of the Renaissance. The principal figures in the works of artists like Correggio, Caravaggio, and Rembrandt stand out like bright islands in spaces full of capacious shadow. So much shadow demanded an extraordinary array of brown pigments—some translucent, others opaque; some warm, others cool—to prevent the works from looking featureless and flat. Anthony van Dyck, a Dutch artist active in the first half of the seventeenth century, was so skilled with one pigment—cassel earth, a kind of peat—that it later became known as "Vandyke brown."[6]

In an echo of what happened in art, bright, colorfast dyes for cloth, such as scarlet [page 138], were difficult and expensive to come by, and therefore remained the preserve of the wealthy and powerful. This left brown for the poor. Fourteenth-century sumptuary laws reserved russet [page 246]—back then a duller brown-gray shade—for those in the meanest occupations like carters and oxherds. Over time, though, probably in reaction to conspicuous displays of wealth, humbler cloth in humbler colors gained favor. This was helped by both an increased interest among the wealthy in sporting pursuits and soldiers' uniforms. Buff [page 242] leather coats, for example, were worn by cavalry in the sixteenth and seventeenth centuries, and by the mid-1700s buff breeches were an essential part of the well-dressed European gentleman's wardrobe.

Although light tans continued to be a part of military uniform through the nineteenth century, it was usually only as a facing to bolder colors like emerald greens and Prussian blues [page 193]. These helped comrades find each other in battle, and also served to intimidate the enemy. As the nineteenth century drew to a close, however, the limitation of these uniforms began taking its toll. After a series of humiliating military setbacks in its colonies, the British army slowly became more responsive to innovation.[7] One example of this shift was the adoption of khaki [page 240] and, later, camouflage, which helped fighters disappear into their surroundings. By clothing soldiers in brown, thousands were saved from a premature return to the earth.

Khaki

On August 5, 1914, Lord Kitchener became Britain's
secretary of state for war. It must have been a daunting
prospect. The day before, Britain had declared war on
Germany, a country far larger and better equipped;[1] at the
time, Britain's Expeditionary Force consisted of just six
infantry divisions and four cavalry brigades. Over the next
four years much of the government's time and energy was
expended persuading, cajoling, and finally making millions
of British men swap their civvies for khakis in the effort
to provide men for the front.

At the outbreak of the First World War, though,
khaki was only a relatively recent recruit itself. It is said
that when the two sides encountered each other on the
field at the Battle of Mons, some Germans expected their
enemy to be wearing red coats and bearskins; they were
very taken aback to see the new khaki uniforms, which
they thought looked rather like golfing tweeds.[2] The word
is borrowed from Urdu—*khaki* means "dusty"—and was
used to refer to cloth, usually for military clothing, that
was dust-colored. It is thought to have been invented
by Sir Harry Lumsden, who raised a Corps of Guides
at Peshawar, in what is now Pakistan, in 1846. Wanting
to give them a suitable uniform, he bought up yards
of white cotton cloth at a bazaar in Lahore and ordered
it to be soaked and rubbed with mud from the local river,
before being cut into loose tunics and trousers.[3] This
would, he hoped "make them invisible in a land of dust."[4]
It was revolutionary: for the first time in organized military
history, an official uniform had been devised that, rather
than calling attention to itself, blended into the landscape.

It soon caught on, helped in large part by the Indian
Mutiny of 1857, which broke out during the summer,
making the usual kit even more impractical than usual.
Dusty brown uniforms—dyed, when muddy riverbeds

weren't to hand, with coffee, teas, soil, and curry powders—
spread in fits and starts through the Indian army between
1860 and 1870, and then to the rest of the British army
and on to the armed forces of other countries.[5] Changes in
warfare, military tactics, and technology meant that
camouflaged troops had an advantage. For thousands of
years prior to this, warriors had decked themselves
out in eye-catching styles to intimidate opponents. Bright
colors, such as the red cloaks of Roman legions and the
emerald-and-silver jackets of the Russian Imperial Guard,
could make individuals and forces look larger than they
really were, and served as easy identification of friend
or foe on smoke-filled battlefields. At the turn of the
twentieth century, however, increasingly sophisticated use
of planes for reconnaissance, coupled with the invention of
the smokeless gun, meant that the risks of being visible
seriously outweighed the advantages.[6]

By the end of the First World War, four blood- and
mud-stained years later, khaki had become synonymous
with soldiery. Men who had enlisted, or had been
rejected from military service, were given khaki brassards
or armbands with small red crowns sewn onto them.
And when, in the excitement of the first few months
of the war, young working-class women were deemed
too aggressively susceptible to the soldiers' charms, they
were accused of "khaki fever."[7] From posters demanding
"WHY AREN'T YOU IN KHAKI?," to music hall songs and
uniforms,[8] this determinedly inconspicuous color
was continuously pressed into service. On November 11,
1918, four years after Lord Kitchener's first day on the job,
the war ended. At 9.30 a.m., 90 minutes before the silence
of peace rang out at 11 o'clock, private George Edwin
Ellison was shot just outside Mons in Belgium, the Great
War's final khaki-clad victim.

Buff

To do something "in the buff," as everyone knows, is to do
it naked, but this idiom has an unlikely origin. The word
buff is itself slang: a shortened form of *buffalo*. In the
sixteenth and early seventeenth centuries the word was
generally used for a kind of buttery tanned ox leather—
a thicker and more robust form of the kind now known
as chamois.[1] While the material was sometimes used
to make fashionable and decorative jerkins and doublets,
it was most commonly associated with fighting.[2] Long
heavy coats of buff were part of European soldiers'
standard kit during this era, often worn in place of proper
metal armor (although the material was sometimes
worn underneath chain mail for added protection and
padding).[3] Even after fashions and military technology
had moved on, the color—by this time also known
as buff—remained a staple of men's wardrobes and
military uniforms.

Its most memorable turn was during the American
Revolutionary War in the late eighteenth century when
the colonies of North America fought against Britain
and King George III for their independence. George
Washington, later to become the first president of the
United States of America, came to the cause as a veteran
of the Seven Years' War, in which he'd fought for the
British in their traditional scarlet. As a savvy politician,
he knew a change of political allegiance necessitated a
change of colors. When representatives from the fledgling
United States met at the Second Continental Congress
in the summer of 1775, Washington was wearing a new
uniform: the buff and blue of the homegrown Fairfax
Independent Company of Volunteers. It had the desired
effect. John Adams, a Founding Father who later became
the second president of the United States, wrote to his
wife Abigail that "Coll. Washington appears at Congress

in his Uniform, and by his great Experience and Abilities in military Matters, is of much service to Us. Oh that I was a Soldier!"[4] Washington was commissioned there and then as the commander in chief of the Continental Army and thereafter, where possible, clothed his soldiers in buff and blue.[5] In a letter dated April 22, 1777, Washington wrote to Captain Caleb Gibbs to specify the uniform he desired for his personal guard:

Provide for four sergeants, four corporals, a drum and fife, and fifty rank and file. If blue and buff can be had I should prefer that uniform, as it is the one I wear myself. If it can not, Mr. Mease and you may fix on any other color, red excepted.[6]

From its appointment as one of the colors of the new United States of America, buff graduated to a symbol of liberty. On the other side of the Atlantic, the Whig Party, under the influence of Edmund Burke and Charles James Fox, adopted Washington's colors to show their support for American independence. Georgiana, the Duchess of Devonshire and a prominent Foxite, campaigned for the Whigs wearing buff and blue, and chose the combination for the livery of her footmen at Chatsworth. Two centuries later, when Prime Minister Harold Macmillan met John F. Kennedy at a summit in Bermuda in 1961, Macmillan presented Kennedy with a set of silver buttons taken from the Devonshire livery as a token of Britain's enduring friendship with the United States.[7]

Fallow

Sometime in the tenth century, around 90 handwritten
Anglo-Saxon riddles were collected into the back of a book
known as the *Codex exoniensis*. Its origins are murky: we
only know for certain that it was owned by Leofric, the
first bishop of Exeter, who died in 1072, and who donated
the manuscript to his cathedral library.[1] It is also a mystery
why the riddles—which range from the whimsical to the
filthy[2]—are there at all. They are huddled at the back after
pages of serious, Christian content more befitting reading
matter for a man of the cloth. While most of the riddles
have been solved, with answers ranging from an iceberg to
a one-eyed garlic seller, a definitive answer to the fifteenth
still proves elusive.[3] It begins:

Hals is min hwit—heafod fealo
Sidan swa some—swift ic eom on feþe . . .
beadowæpen bere—me on bæce standað . . .
[My neck is white, my head is fallow
And so are my sides. I am swift in my stride . . .
I bear weapons of battle. On my back there is hair . . .][4]

Fallow is a faded, caramel-tawny color, the tint of
withered leaves or grass, and one of the oldest color
names in the English language.[5] From the 1300s the word
has been applied to farmland resting between seasons
of use to replenish the soil—we still speak of fields lying
fallow—but it has also been used to describe animals
with coats that help them melt into their surroundings.
An early debut was in *Beowulf*, where it's used to
describe horses; Shakespeare mentions a "fallow Greyhound"
in *The Merry Wives of Windsor*. The best example, however,
is the coquettishly white-rumped, dapple-bodied fallow
deer, the forebears of which have been common over
Europe and the Middle East for millennia.

Hunting them was a favorite pastime of the Norman nobility after the conquest of England in 1066, and special parks were created to close the deer off from wolves and Britons alike. So seriously did the hunters take their sport that under William the Conqueror the punishment for killing such deer was equal to that for killing a man—even centuries later, if you were caught poaching one you might find yourself being deported.[6]

A deer, however, is not the answer to riddle 15—that would be too easy. This animal, the riddler tells us, walks on her toes on the grass but also burrows, "with both hands and feet . . . through the high hill" to escape the "hateful foe" that means to kill her and her children.[7] Guesses as to the mystery creature's identity have included badger, porcupine, hedgehog, fox, and weasel, with no one animal quite fitting exactly.[8] The answer, it seems, may remain hidden forever, while the hunters keep on hunting.

Russet

Russet is a reminder that a color lives more in the imagination of a generation than bound into a neat color reference. Say the word now and it might call to mind the ruddy color of leaves in autumn, or the hair of a Pre-Raphaelite muse, but this was not the case even as recently as 1930. In A. Maerz and M. R. Paul's influential *Dictionary of Color* it is a more orange- than reddish-brown, and has pronounced ashy gray undertones.[1]

Part of the reason for this is that, like scarlet [page 138], the word *russet* used to denote a type of cloth rather than a color. While scarlet was luxurious to the touch, beloved by the rich, and so usually dyed bright red, russet cloth was for the poor. In 1363—the thirty-seventh year of the reign of Edward III, King of England—Parliament introduced a new statute to regulate the diets and apparel of English subjects. After dealing summarily with lords, knights, clergymen, and merchants, the gaze of the law passed down to the lowest of the low:

Carters, Ploughmen, Drivers of the Plough, Oxherds, Cowherds, Shephards . . . and all other Keepers of Beasts, Threshers of Corn, and all Manner of People of the Estate, and all other People, that have not Forty Shillings of Goods . . . shall not take nor wear no Manner of Cloth, but Blanket, and Russet of Twelve-pence.[2]

To the medieval mind, the closer a cloth was to the color of the raw materials, the cheaper and meaner it was. Russet, a very coarse woolen cloth, was usually just dipped into weak solutions of first blue woad [page 198] and then red madder [page 152] left over from dyeing the clothes of those further up the social scale.[3] Because the end result depended on the qualities of the dyes used and the color of the undyed wool, russet cloth could be any color ranging from dun through to brown or gray.[4]

The skill and honesty of the dyer were other important factors. Surviving records from Blackwell Market in the City of London, where merchants' goods were checked over to ensure they were of acceptable quality, show that there was a good deal of defective material going to market. (Kentish russets were, with 25 entries, second only to whites from Gloucester—50 entries—and Wiltshire—41 entries—in their shoddy quality.) On April 13, 1562, William Dowtheman from Tonbridge, and William Watts and Elizabeth Statie, both from Benenden, were all fined for their inferior russets. Watts, apparently, was not a man to learn from his mistakes: he'd been fined for precisely the same reason on November 17 the previous year.[5]

Just as the precise color of russet has refused to remain stable, shifting significantly over time, so has its symbolism. From being a byword for the poor, after the violent social changes brought about by the Black Death, russet gradually gained a reputation as betokening honesty, humility, and manliness. In *Piers Plowman*, William Langland's fourteenth-century allegorical poem about good and evil, charity "is as gladde of a goune of a graye russet / As of a tunicle of tarse [silk]."[6] It was no doubt this double meaning that Oliver Cromwell was using when he wrote to his Civil War associates in the autumn of 1643: "I had rather have a plain russet-coated captain that knows what he fights for, and loves what he knows, than that which you call a gentleman and is nothing else."[7]

Sepia

If you were to surprise a *Sepia officinalis*, or common
cuttlefish—and finding one would be the first challenge,
as their camouflage is superb—it would respond in one
of two ways. You might find yourself suddenly enveloped
in a dense smokescreen of dark liquid, or confronted with
a host of decoy cuttlefish—dark blobs formed out of a
mixture of the same ink and mucus. The *S. officinalis*,
meanwhile, would have made a dash for it, leaving you
empty-handed.

Almost all cephalopods—a group that includes
octopuses, squid, and cuttlefish—can produce ink. This
burnt coffee-brown liquid is made up almost entirely of
melanin [page 278] and has tremendous tinting strength.[1]
Although now squid ink is most often found lending
seafood risotto the glossy black luster of a raven's wing,
sepia (the ink of the cuttlefish) has long been used as a
pigment for writers and artists. Recipes and methods for
separating cephalopods from their ink abound, but a
common procedure involved removing the sac, drying
and powdering it, and then boiling the extract with a
strong alkali to extract the pigment. Once neutralized,
it could then be washed, dried, ground up, and made into
cakes to be sold.[2]

The Roman writers Cicero and Persius both mention,
and probably used, sepia as ink, and it is likely the poet
Marcus Valerius Martialis did too.[3] Martial was born in
the city of Bilbilis, around 150 miles northeast of where
Madrid now stands, sometime between A.D. 38 and A.D. 41.[4]
His epigrams skewer the pretensions of his fellow city
dwellers in Rome, and satirize stingy patrons and fellow
poets. ("'Write shorter epigrams' is your advice. / Yet you
write nothing, Velox. How concise!," is one such witticism.[5])
Martial's bravado, though, must have been, at least in part,
a ruse to conceal all the usual writer's insecurities.

Once, when sending out his latest collection—probably written in sepia ink—he included a sponge in the package, so that his words could be wiped away if they did not please the recipient.[6] Leonardo da Vinci was fond of using the warm-toned sepia in his sketches, many of which still survive. The colorist George Field described it in 1835 as "a powerful dusky brown color, of a fine texture" and recommended its use as a watercolor.[7]

Today, although artists still value sepia ink for its foxy red undertones, the word is more likely to be used in the context of photography. Originally images were chemically toned to replace the silver in the silver-based prints with a more stable compound, making them longer lasting and a symphony of warm ochers. Now, of course, technology has rendered this unnecessary, but the tones have taken on the mantle of romance and nostalgia. Digital photography tools mean that, with just a few clicks of a button, photographers can disguise their new, fresh images, making them look a century old.

Umber

On October 18, 1969, under cover of a vicious storm, a group of men broke into the Oratory of San Lorenzo in Palermo and stole a priceless Nativity scene by Michelangelo Merisi Caravaggio. Caravaggio was by many accounts a violent, troubled man, but no one who stands before one of his few remaining paintings can doubt his genius. *Nativity with St. Francis and St. Lawrence*, a huge work in oil created 360 years before its theft, shows the birth of Christ as a grim scene of impoverishment and exhaustion. The surviving photos show a very dark composition, just a few figures, heads bowed and disheveled, picked out against a muddy ground. Like many of Caravaggio's other works, this painting probably owed its dark drama to his use of umber.[1]

Although some believe that umber's name is, like sienna's, geographical in origin—one source is Umbria in Italy—it is more likely that the word comes from the Latin *ombra*, meaning "shadow." Like hematite [page 150] and sienna, umber is one of the iron oxide pigments commonly called ochers. But while hematite is red and sienna, when raw or unheated, is a yellow-tinged brown, umber is cooler and darker, perfect as a dark glaze.[2] It is also, like its fellows, a very stable and reliable pigment, and was considered an essential part of every artist's palette up until the twentieth century. However, it is also profoundly unglamorous. George Field, the nineteenth-century chemist and author of *Chromatography*, wrote that "it is a natural ocher, abounding with oxide of manganese . . . of a brown-citrine color, semi-opaque, has all the properties of a good ocher, is perfectly durable both in water and oil."[3] One can almost hear the yawn in his words.

Umber is one of the oldest known pigments used by humans. Ochers were used on cave walls at Altamira in

Spain and at Lascaux, a trove of cave art in southwest
France, which was rediscovered by a dog called Robot
in September 1940.[4] As Robot snuffled around the roots
of a fallen tree, he uncovered a small opening underneath.
His owner, the 18-year-old Marcel Ravidat, returning
with three friends and some lamps, squeezed through
a 40-foot-long shaft and into a vast chamber filled with
Late Stone Age paintings.

Umber really came into its own, however, with the
dramatic tenebrism of the late Renaissance and baroque
artists like Joseph Wright of Derby and Rembrandt van
Rijn. These painters, sometimes called *Caravaggisti*
because of their admiration for their predecessor, gloried
in the drama of strong contrasts between spots of light
and deepest shadow, a technique also known as
chiaroscuro, from the Italian words *chiaro* ("bright")
and *oscuro* ("dark"). Rembrandt, particularly in his
impoverished later years after his bankruptcy in 1656,
used a startlingly small range of pigments to produce the
effect, relying heavily on the cheap, somber ochers,
especially umber.[5] It is there in the backgrounds and
heavy clothing of his late self-portraits, the ones in which
he is so uniquely expressive: sometimes thoughtful, or
wounded, or quizzical, but always catching and holding
the viewer's gaze, his face strongly lit in the pools of
darkness.

In 1996 the fate of Caravaggio's masterpiece painting
was revealed in a spectacular trial. Francesco "Mozzarella"
Marino Mannoia, a Sicilian Mafia specialist in refining
heroin, became a government informer after the death
of his brother. Francesco told the court that he had sawed
the painting from its frame above the altar and bundled it
up to deliver to the man who had commissioned the theft.
Tragically, though, he had no experience with valuable

Umber, continued.

works of art and no idea of the care with which they needed to be handled. When the patron saw the condition of the painting after its rough treatment, he wept. "[I]t was not . . . in a usable condition anymore," Marino Mannoia admitted at his trial 30 years later.[6] Many still refuse to believe it has been destroyed,[7] continually appealing for the painting's safe return, ever hopeful that it will, one day, emerge from the shadows.

Mummy

On July 30, 1904, O'Hara and Hoar placed an unusual
advertisement in the *Daily Mail*. What they wanted—
"at a suitable price"—was an Egyptian mummy. "It may
appear strange to you," the notice read, "but we require
our mummy for making color." Then, to stave off any
pricks of public conscience, they continued: "Surely a
2,000-year-old mummy of an Egyptian monarch may
be used for adorning a noble fresco in Westminster Hall
or elsewhere without giving offense to the ghost of the
departed gentleman or his descendants."[1]

By then such a plea was unusual enough to raise
comment, but mummies had been dug up and reused
in various ways for centuries without much fuss.
Mummification had been common burial practice in
Egypt for over 3,000 years. Internal organs were removed
before the body was washed and embalmed using a
complex mixtures of spices, as well as preservatives,
including beeswax, resins, asphalt, and sawdust.[2] Although
mummies—particularly those of the rich and distinguished,
whose wrappings were likely to contain gold and trinkets[3]—
could be valuable in themselves, those who dug them
up were more often after something else: bitumen.
The Persian word for bitumen was *mum* or *mumiya*, which
had led to the belief (along with the fact that mummified
remains were very dark) that all mummies contained the
substance.[4] Bitumen—and by extension mummies—had
been used as a medicine from the first century A.D. Ground-up
mummy, or "mummia," was applied topically or mixed
into drinks to swallow, and it seemed there was almost
nothing it could not cure. Pliny recommended it as
toothpaste; Francis Bacon for the "stanching of blood";
Robert Boyle for bruises; and John Hall, Shakespeare's
son-in-law, used it on a troubling case of epilepsy.
Catherine de' Medici was a devotee, as was François I

Mummy, continued.

of France, who carried a little pouch of powdered mummy
and rhubarb on him at all times.[5]

Trade was brisk. John Sanderson, an agent for an
importer called the Turkey Company, vividly described
an expedition to a mummy pit in 1586:

*We were let down by ropes, as into a well, with wax candles burning
our hands, and so walked upon the bodies of all sorts and sizes ... they
gave no noisome smell at all ... I broke off all of the parts of the bodies to
see how the flesh was turned to drugge, and brought home divers heads,
hands, armes and feet.*[6]

Mr. Sanderson actually returned to England with one
complete mummy and 600 pounds of sundry parts to
refresh the supplies of the London apothecaries.[7] Demand,
however, outpaced supply, and there are numerous reports
of replacements being hastily made from the bodies of
slaves and criminals. While on a visit to Alexandria in
1564, the physician to the king of Navarre interviewed
one mummy dealer who showed him 40 he claimed
to have manufactured himself in the past four years.[8]

Because apothecaries often dealt in pigments too,
it is not so surprising that the rich brown powder also
found itself on painters' palettes. Mummy, also known
as Egyptian brown and *Caput mortum* ("dead man's head"),
was used as paint—usually mixed with a drying oil and
amber varnish—from the twelfth until the twentieth
centuries.[9] It was well known enough for an artists' shop
in Paris to call itself—tongue, presumably, in cheek—
À la Momie. Eugène Delacroix used it in 1854 when
painting the Salone de la Paix at the Hôtel de Ville in
Paris; his fellow countryman Martin Drölling favored
it too, as did the British portraitist Sir William Beechey.[10]
There was some debate as to which bits of the mummy

to use to get the best and richest browns—recommended for translucent glazing layers for shadows and skin tones. Some suggested using just the muscle and flesh, while others thought that the bones and bandages should also be ground up to get the best out of this "charming pigment."[11]

Gradually though, toward the end of the nineteenth century, fresh supplies of mummies, authentic or otherwise, dwindled. Artists were becoming dissatisfied with the pigment's permanency and finish, not to mention more squeamish about its provenance.[12] The Pre-Raphaelite painter Edward Burne-Jones hadn't realized the connection between "mummy brown" and real mummies until one Sunday lunch in 1881, when a friend related having just seen one ground up at a colorman's warehouse. Burne-Jones was so horrified he rushed to his studio to find his tube of mummy brown, and "insisted on our giving it a decent burial there and then."[13] The scene made a great impression on the teenage Rudyard Kipling, Burne-Jones's nephew by marriage, who was also a guest at lunch. "[T]o this day," he wrote years later, "I could drive a spade within a foot of where that tube lies."[14]

By the beginning of the twentieth century demand was so sluggish that a single mummy might provide a paint manufacturer with pigment for a decade or more. C. Roberson, a London art shop that had first opened its doors in 1810, finally ran out in the 1960s. "We might have a few odd limbs lying around somewhere," the managing director told *Time* magazine in October 1964, "but not enough to make any more paint. We sold our last complete mummy some years ago for, I think, £3. Perhaps we shouldn't have. We certainly can't get any more."[15]

Taupe

Sometime in 1932 the British Color Council (BCC)
began working on a special project. The idea was to
create a standardized catalog for colors, complete with
dyed silk ribbons to show exactly what color was meant
by each term. It would, they hoped, do for color "what
the great *Oxford Dictionary* has done for words."[1] It "will
mark," they wrote, "the greatest achievement of modern
times in assisting British and Empire industries with color
definition," thereby giving Britain trade a competitive edge.

What wasn't mentioned was that Britain was behind
the curve. Albert Henry Munsell, an American artist and
teacher, had been working on a way of three-dimensionally
mapping color since the 1880s; his system was fully
fledged by the first decade of the twentieth century and
has been used with minor tweaks ever since.[2] A. Maerz and
M. R. Paul, who built on Munsell's work but also wished
to incorporate the common names for colors, published
their *Dictionary of Color*—modeled on Samuel Johnson's
idiosyncratic *English Dictionary*—in New York in 1930.
It included pages of color chips, a comprehensive index,
and snippets of information on many common colors.

They all developed a fine appreciation for the difficulty
of the task. Colors were hard to pin down; they could
change name over time, or the shade associated with a
name might morph alarmingly from one decade or country
to the next. Chasing down and collating color terms and
samples had taken the BCC 18 months. Messrs. Maerz
and Paul had labored over the task for years.[3] One color
that vexed both sets of researchers was taupe. It is actually
a French word, meaning "mole." However, while the
color of a mole was, by broad consensus, "a deep gray
on the cold side," taupe was all over the place—the only
thing consistently agreed upon was that it was generally
browner than a mole had a right to be.[4] The BCC's

assumption was that the confusion was due to ignorant English-speakers not realizing that *taupe* and *mole* were different words for the same thing. Maerz and Paul were rather more thorough. They set out on an expedition around the zoological museums of the United States and France to look at foreign specimens from the genus *Talpa*, to determine whether there was a logical reason for using both terms. "[I]ts color certainly varies," they concluded, but what was generally understood by the term *taupe* "represents a considerable departure from any color a mole might possess." The sample they included in their book, therefore, was "a correct match for the average actual color of the French mole."[5]

Despite transatlantic efforts to return this color to something approximating the hue of its parent mammal, taupe has since continued to run wild. Beloved by the makeup and bridal industries, it is roomy enough to contain a plethora of pastel brown-grays while still managing to sound refined and elegant. If only these intrepid color cartographers had taken all the lessons of Samuel Johnson's great enterprise to heart, they might have been spared the wild-mole chase. Johnson, even as he set down definitions next to words in his dictionary in 1755, was realistic enough to appreciate the ultimate futility of his task. This rueful reflection from his preface could just as easily apply to colors: "sounds are too volatile and subtle for legal restraints; to enchain syllables, and to lash the wind, are equally the undertakings of pride."

Kohl

Payne's gray

Obsidian

Ink

Charcoal

Jet

Melanin

Pitch black

Black

What do you think of when you see the color black?
Perhaps a better question would be: what *don't* you think
of when you see black? Few colors are more expansive and
capacious. Like the dark obsidian mirror [page 268] that
once belonged to Dr. Dee, look into black and you never
know what might look back. It is, simultaneously,
the color of fashion and of mourning, and has symbolized
everything from fertility to scholarship and piety. With
black, things are always complicated.

In 1946 Galerie Maeght, an avant-garde Parisian
gallery on rue du Bac on the Left Bank, staged an
exhibition called "Black Is a Color." It was a statement
intended to shock: this was the precise opposite of what
was then taught at art schools.[1] "Nature knows only
colors," Renoir once declared. "White and black are
not colors."[2] In one sense, this is right. Like white,
black is an expression of light, in this case its absence.
A true black would reflect no light whatsoever—the
opposite of white, which reflects all light wavelengths
equally. On an emotional level, this has not affected our
experience or use of blacks as colors; on a practical level,
it has so far proved impossible to find or create a black
that reflects no light at all. Vantablack, a carbon nanotube
technology created in Britain in 2014, traps 99.965 percent
of the spectrum, making it the blackest thing in the
world. In person it is so dark it fools the eyes and brain,
rendering people unable to perceive depth and texture.

A whiff of death has clung to black as far back as
records reach, and humans are fascinated and repelled
by it. Most of the gods associated with death and the
underworld—such as the jackal-headed Egyptian god
Anubis, Christianity's devil, and the Hindu goddess Kali—
are depicted with truly black skin, and the color has
long been associated with both mourning and witchcraft.

However, while black is so often linked with endings, it is present at the start of things too. It reminded the ancient Egyptians of the rich silt that the Nile deposited after the floods each year, making the land fertile. Black's potential for creation is there in the opening passages of Genesis— it is, after all, out of the darkness that God conjures light. Nighttime too has a peculiar fecundity, for all the obvious reasons, and because of dreams that blossom only when we close our eyes to shut out the light. A piece of artists' charcoal [page 274] is a perfect emblem for beginnings. The outline—usually black—was invented over 30,000 years ago. It may be the example *non plus ultra* of artistic artifice, but this has never mattered to artists, and the black line is art's foundation stone. It was to hand when early men and women first began expressing themselves by leaving their marks on the world around them, and it has been used at the inception of nearly all artistic endeavors since.[3] Some 12,600 years after Paleolithic fingers and pads of soft leather daubed fine charcoal powder onto the cave walls at Altamira, Leonardo da Vinci favored fine sticks of the stuff. It was one of these that he used to sketch out a softly blended sfumato—from *fumo*, for smoke— version of what would become his simultaneously mysterious and expressive painting *The Virgin and Child with St. Anne* (1503–19), now in the Louvre.

It was during Leonardo's lifetime, too, that black reached its zenith as the color of fashion. His near contemporary, Baldassare Castiglione, wrote in his *Book of the Courtier* that "black is more pleasing in clothing than any other color," and the Western world agreed.[4] Its rise as the most fashionable of colors had three causes. The first was practical: sometime around 1360, new methods were found for dyeing fabrics true black, rather than dirty brown-grays, which made them more luxurious.

A second reason was the psychological impact of the Black
Death, which decimated the population of Europe, and led
to a desire for greater austerity and collective penitence
and mourning.[5] Philip the Good (1396–1467), who
famously was rarely seen out of black clothing, favored
it to honor the memory of his father, John the Fearless, who
had been assassinated in 1419.[6] The third reason was the
wave of laws that sought to codify social strata through
dress: wealthy merchants were forbidden to wear colors
reserved for the old money, such as scarlet [page 138],
but they could wear black.[7] The obsession lasted until
the first decades of the eighteenth century. Estate
inventories show that in around 1700, 33 percent of nobles'
and 44 percent of officers' clothing was black; it was
popular with domestics too, making up 29 percent of their
wardrobes.[8] At times the streets must have resembled
Rembrandt's paintings. *The Sampling Officials* (1662) and
Anatomy Lesson of Dr. Nicolaes Tulp (1632): crowds of
identical black-clad folk jostling for space.

Despite the ubiquity, black has retained both its
popularity and its fresh, challenging modernity.[9] Kazimir
Malevich's *Black Square*, for example, is believed to be
the first purely abstract painting. Used as we are to abstract
art, the magnitude of this work is difficult to understand.
For Malevich, though, *Black Square* (he created four
different versions between 1915 and 1930) was a statement
of intent. He desperately wanted, as he put it, "to free art
from the dead weight of the real world," and so "took refuge
in the form of the square."[10] This, for the first time, was art
for art's sake, and a revolutionary idea needed a
revolutionary color: black.

Kohl

Lurking in the Egyptology section of the Louvre in Paris
is a curious object. It is a squat, sparkling white statuette
of a bowlegged creature, whose red tongue lolls from
a mouth lined with sharp teeth; it has pendulous, triangular
breasts; a fierce blue V for eyebrows; and a long shaft of
a tail that dangles rudely between its legs. Made between
1400 and 1300 B.C., it depicts the god Bes, who, while he
may look terrifying, was actually rather sweet: a fearsome
fighter, he was popular with ordinary Egyptians because
he was a protector, particularly of homes, women, and
children. What he was protecting in this case, though,
was rather different: hidden in the statuette's hollow head
is a small container intended for kohl eyeliner.

Bes is one of over 50 such kohl pots in the Louvre's
collection. Some, like this one, are decorative and come
in the form of servants or cattle or gods; others are more
functional, just little jars of alabaster or breccia (a kind
of rock).[1] Pots like these turn up in a lot of museum
collections, because everyone in ancient Egypt, from
pharaohs to peasants, male and female, rimmed their eyes
with thick black lines; many were buried with jars of kohl
so that they could continue to do so in the afterlife.
Kohl was believed to have magical protective properties,
and, as it does today, played the visual trick of making
the whites of the eyes stand out, which was then, as now,
considered distinctive and attractive.[2]

The kind of kohl used depended on wealth and social
status. The poor might use mixtures of soot and animal fats,
but, as ever, the wealthy demanded something rather more
special. Theirs would predominantly be made of galena,
the dark metallic mineral form of lead sulfide. This would
be crushed and mixed with powdered pearls, gold, coral,
or emeralds to give sheen and subtle color. Frankincense,
fennel, or saffron might then be added for their scent.

To make the powder usable, it was bound with a little oil or milk so that it could be daubed with feather or finger.[3]

In 2010, French researchers analyzing the traces of powder found in kohl pots discovered that they also contained something even more precious: man-made chemicals, including two kinds of lead chlorides that would have taken around a month to brew. Mystified, they conducted further tests. To their astonishment, these chemicals were found to stimulate the skin around the eye to produce around 240 percent more nitric oxide than usual, significantly reducing the risk of eye infections.[4] In a time before antibiotics, such simple infections could easily lead to cataracts or blindness. Kohl, like the little pot in the shape of the fearsome Bes, was a very practical form of protection.

Payne's gray

"Stalin," an early political opponent once wrote, "gave me the impression . . . of a gray blur which flickered obscurely and left no trace. There is really nothing more to be said about him."[1] It's a stinging line: in our individualistic age it is almost better not to be remembered at all than to be remembered as dull and insubstantial. Of course the opponent could not have been more wrong: Stalin has left a long and burdensome legacy and humanity is unlikely to forget him in a hurry.

One eighteenth-century gentleman, on the other hand, had faded from memory almost before he died. All that remains is the pigeon-plumage shade of gray to which he lent his name. It is still a firm artists' favorite, even if little is known about the man himself. William Payne was born in Exeter in 1760 and raised in Devon before moving to London. Maybe . . . possibly. A pamphlet on the painter produced in 1922 by one Basil Long spends the first 10 pages alternating between putting forward biographical theories and apologizing for a lack of actual evidence.[2]

We do know that after spending some time as a civil engineer Payne traveled to London and began painting full-time. He was a member of the Old Water-Color Society, where he exhibited in the years from 1809 to 1812, and also showed work at the Royal Academy. Joshua Reynolds is even said to have admired some of his landscapes. Payne, however, was most in demand as a teacher. As his contemporary William Henry Pyne put it: his paintings "were no sooner seen than admired, and almost every family of fashion were anxious that their sons and daughters should have the benefit of his tuition."[3] We will never know if it was the strain of dealing with the untalented offspring of London's elite that drove him to find a replacement for true black pigments, but we do know that he was proud enough of this precise mixture of Prussian blue, yellow ocher, and crimson lake to make sure his name stuck to it.

Why is Payne's gray so beloved by artists? It is at least partially because of a phenomenon now known as "atmospheric perspective." Think of hills and mountains fading off into the distance, for example: the farther away things are, the paler and bluer they appear. This effect is caused by particles of dust, pollution, and water droplets scattering the shortest, bluest light wavelengths, and it is exacerbated by fog, rain, and mist. It is small wonder that a landscape painter working in Devon was the first to mix the deep blue-black gray so peculiarly suited for capturing this effect.

Obsidian

There are many intriguing objects in the collection of the British Museum in London, but one of the most mysterious has to be a thick, dark, and highly polished disk with a small, hooped handle. The Aztecs forged the mirror from obsidian in honor of their god Tezcatlipoca (his name means "smoking mirror"), and it was brought over to the Old World after Cortés's conquest of the region that is now Mexico, in the mid-sixteenth century.[1] Obsidian, also known as volcanic glass, is formed when molten lava, erupting from the earth, comes into contact with ice or snow, and cools very quickly.[2] It is very hard, glossy, brittle, and either black or a very dark bronze-green, sometimes with a golden or iridescent sheen caused by layers of tiny gas bubbles that become trapped in the magma as it solidifies. Although there is some doubt about this particular mirror's provenance, Sir Horace Walpole, the British antiquarian who acquired it in 1771, was under no doubt about its previous owner and what it had been used for. On the label attached to the object's handle he wrote a curious inscription: "The Black Stone into which Dr. Dee used to call his spirits."[3]

Dr. John Dee was Elizabethan England's foremost mathematician, astrologer, and natural philosopher. He was a Cambridge graduate, and the queen's philosopher and adviser; he also spent many years talking to angels about the natural order and the end of the world. These conversations were held using his collection of "shewstones"—of which this mirror may have been one—and through several mediums, most famously Edward Kelley. It is not so remarkable that a man of Dee's intelligence believed in the occult—most people did. Indeed, nearly a century later one of the greatest scientific minds in history—belonging to one Isaac Newton—expended the greater part of its energy searching for the philosopher's stone.

What is remarkable is that anything is known about Dee's mystical investigations at all.

He died in 1608 or 1609, disgraced and in poverty, after having had to sell off the majority of his possessions, including most of his famous library. His papers, too, were scattered or destroyed. In 1586 an angel, speaking through Kelley, ordered Dee to burn all 28 volumes of his painstaking records of their previous conversations, which was convenient timing seeing as envoys from the papacy were just about to begin questioning the pair about their involvement with witchcraft, a very serious charge indeed.[4] If they had discovered his obsidian mirror, it might well have been enough to land Dee on the rack or the pyre.

The late sixteenth and early seventeenth centuries witnessed the widespread return of the most disturbing, paranoid, and pessimistic aspects of Christianity: belief in the potency of the devil on earth, and that his envoys—witches—were busy working to overthrow order and bring him to power. In this context blacks of all shades took on disturbing new meanings. Not only was the devil usually depicted (and described by witnesses at witch trials) as black and hairy, but the idea of the sabbat, which so obsessed Europe and later North America, was filled with darkness. From their venues—often forests at night—to their black-clad participants and the retinue of animals that attended Satan—crows, bats, and cats—sabbats were veritable orgies of blackness.[5] Obsidian, a dark rock spewed forth from the fiery bowels of the earth, was naturally deeply suspect.

Obsidian crops up in occult company time and time again. In the fiction of George R. R. Martin and Neil Gaiman, blades made from the volcanic glass have magical powers. Historically, Native American tribes have used it in rituals. As recently as the 1990s, women from the

Obsidian, continued.

Santa Clara Pueblo in New Mexico dressed in black and
carried long obsidian blades in their right hands and
an obsidian spear point, or *tsi wi*, in their left during
witch-destruction ceremonies.[6] Ancient and prehistoric
obsidian artifacts—often blades—have been found around
the Red Sea, Ethiopia, Sardinia, and the Andes. The name
of the Aztec patroness of witches, Itzpapalotl, means
"obsidian butterfly." More damning still for Dee,
Tezcatlipoca, the Aztec god for whom his own mirror
was made, was the god of warriors, rulers, and sorcerers.[7]

Ink

It is one thing for humans to have complex thoughts
and plans; it is quite another to transmit them over long
distances. That requires a system of marks that the sender
knows the receivers can understand. For most cultures
this has meant writing, which in turn has meant creating
decent ink.

Inks have tended to be black because they need to
be very fluid to write with easily—far more so than paint;
most pigments would not be sufficiently legible at such
high levels of dilution.

Sometime around 2600 B.C. in ancient Egypt, Ptahhotep,
a Fifth Dynasty vizier, began to think about retirement.
His reason was old age, and his litany of complaints will be
familiar to anyone with elderly relatives: "Sleep is upon him
in discomfort every day. / Eyes are grown small, ears deaf,
/ Mouth silent, unable to speak." A few lines on he begins
to give touching advice to his son: "Do not be proud on
account of your knowledge, / But discuss with the ignorant
as with the wise. / The limits of art cannot be delivered; /
There is no artist whose talent is fulfilled."[1] (It must have
been good advice: his son later became a vizier himself.)
We know about Ptahhotep, his aches and pains, and his
son because he committed his thoughts to papyrus with
black ink that remains perfectly legible today.[2] It was
made using lampblack, a very fine pigment that was easily
produced by burning a candle or lamp; to this would be
added water and gum arabic, which helped the particles
of lampblack disperse through the water rather than
clumping together.[3]

The Chinese, who ascribed the invention of ink to
Tien-Tchen, who lived between 2697 and 2597 B.C., also
used lampblack for their ink (sometimes also confusingly
known as India ink).[4] The pigment was produced in huge
amounts: row upon row of special funnel-shaped lamps

Ink, continued.

were tended every half hour or so by workers who scraped soot off the sides of the lamps using feathers. For special-occasion ink they used the soot of pine logs, ivory, lacquer resin, or the deposits of dead yeast left over at the end of wine fermentation, but the end product was essentially the same.[5] With the exception of the initial raw material, the recipe for most ink remained stable until the nineteenth century. Even the invention of the printing press had little impact on it. When the 42-line Bible began spilling off Gutenberg's presses in around 1455, the smell of ink in the air would have been much the same as in countless monastic scriptoriums. The principal tweak to the recipe was the use of linseed oil as the base medium, which made for thicker ink that would adhere more easily to the paper.[6]

Other kinds of dark ink involved extracting the bitter tannins from vegetable material. A particularly famous and long-lasting kind, iron-gall ink, was the product of the acrimonious relationship between a wasp and an oak tree. The *Cynips quercusfolii* lays its eggs in the young buds or leaves of the oak tree, along with a chemical that causes the oak to form a hard, nutlike growth around the larvae. This growth—often called an oak apple—is rich in bitter tannic acid. When combined with iron sulfate, water, and gum arabic, the acid produces a velvety blue-black and very permanent ink.[7] A variant on this recipe, recorded by Theophilus in the twelfth century, uses the tannic acid in the sap of crushed buckthorn.[8]

For many cultures, however, the practicalities of ink— legibility, permanency, and consistency—have gone hand in glove with rather more diffuse, emotional, even reverential considerations. The ancient Chinese used inks perfumed with cloves, honey, and musk.[9] The scents, it is true, helped cover the odor of the binders used— yak skin and fish intestines were common—but these inks sometimes also contained powdered rhinoceros horn, pearls, or jasper. In medieval Christian monasteries, the act of copying and illuminating libraries of manuscripts, of putting wisdom and prayer to paper, was seen as a spiritual process in itself.

Black ink also had a devotional relationship with Islam: the Arabic word for ink, *midād*, is closely related to that for divine substance or matter. An early seventeenth-century recipe in a treatise on painters and calligraphers contained 14 ingredients; some, like soot and gallnuts, are obvious enough, but others—saffron, Tibetan musk, and hemp oil— are far less so. The author, Qadi Ahmad, was under little doubt of ink's numinous power. "The ink of the scholar," he wrote, "is more holy than the blood of the martyr."[10]

Charcoal

Émile Cartailhac was a man who could admit when he
was wrong. This was fortunate, because in 1902 the
French prehistorian found himself writing an article for
L'Anthropologie in which he did just that. In "Mea culpa
d'un sceptique" he recanted the views he had spent the
previous 20 years forcefully and scornfully maintaining:
that prehistoric man was incapable of fine artistic
expression and that the cave paintings found in Altamira,
northern Spain, were forgeries.[1]

The Paleolithic paintings at Altamira, which were
produced around 14,000 B.C., were the first examples of
prehistoric cave art to be officially discovered. It happened
by chance in 1879, when a local landowner and amateur
archaeologist was busily brushing away at the floor of the
caves, searching for prehistoric tools. His nine-year-old
daughter, Maria Sanz de Sautuola—a grave little thing
with cropped hair and lace-up booties—was exploring
farther on when she suddenly looked up, exclaiming,
"Look, Papa, bison!" She was quite right: a veritable herd,
subtly colored with black charcoal and ocher, ranged
over the ceiling.[2] When her father published the finding
in 1880, he was met with ridicule. The experts scoffed
at the very idea that prehistoric man—savages really—
could have produced sophisticated polychrome paintings.
The esteemed Monsieur Cartailhac and the majority
of his fellow experts, without troubling to go and see the
cave for themselves, dismissed the whole thing as a fraud.
Maria's father died, a broken and dishonored man, in
1888, four years before Cartailhac admitted his error.[3]

After the discovery of many more caves and hundreds
of lions, handprints, horses, women, hyenas, and bison, the
artistic abilities of prehistoric man are no longer in doubt.
It is thought that these caves were painted by shamans
trying to charm a steady supply of food for their tribes.

Many were painted using the pigment most readily available in the caves at the time: the charred stick remnants of their fires.[4] At its simplest, charcoal is the carbon-rich by-product of organic matter—usually wood—and fire. It is purest and least ashy when oxygen has been restricted during its heating.

As an energy source, charcoal powered the Industrial Revolution. Such vast quantities were used to smelt iron that whole forests were decimated and smoke filled the air around cities. Charcoal is thus indirectly responsible for one of the classic exemplars of natural selection. The *Biston betularia f. typica*, or peppered moth, is usually a speckled white and black. During the nineteenth century a previously unknown variety with an all-black body and bitter chocolate wings began appearing more frequently around northern towns, while numbers of the white-speckled kind declined sharply. By 1895 a study around Manchester found that 95 percent of the peppered moths were dark.[5] Against the bark of the sooty trees, the dark moths were harder for predators to see—hiding, like the Altamira bison, in plain sight.

Jet

In its original sense, the word *jet* may be on the cusp of disappearing. Plug the word into a search engine and squadrons of stumpy airplanes appear. And while people still say "jet black," it is beginning to acquire the worn-thin feeling of something too often repeated.

Actually, the black kind of jet is anything but insubstantial. Also known as lignite, it is a kind of coal formed over millennia from highly pressurized wood; when fine enough, it is so hard it can be carved and polished to an almost glasslike sheen.[1] The most highly prized jet comes from Whitby, a small town on the northeast coast of England.

The Romans were the first to exploit Whitby's jet. It was, until the nineteenth century, so abundant that great lumps could be gathered from the beaches. From there it was probably taken to Eboracum (York), the Roman provincial capital, to be carved and then exported to the rest of the empire. One figurine, found at the beginning of the twentieth century in Westmorland, dates from around A.D. 330, just as the Roman grip on Britain was beginning to slip. The statuette shows a woman leaning on what appears to be a barrel. She wears a mantle that is hitched over her left shoulder, and seems to be wiping away tears with her left hand. If it is, as has been supposed, a depiction of a Roman goddess to be given as an offering when grieving, then it could be the first example of jet's involvement in what became something of a Victorian obsession.[2]

Ancient Greeks and Romans may have started the tradition of wearing special, drab clothes when a friend, relative, or ruler died, but, for the Victorians, rules and conventions governed every color of every stitch of clothing people could wear from the time their loved one died until the niceties of grief were exhausted, up to

two years later. Because glossy pieces of black jet jewelry—
no matter how elaborate the design—could be worn
throughout the mourning period, they became immensely
popular. As with mauve [page 169], Queen Victoria was
at least partially responsible for the trend. Within a week
of Prince Albert's sudden death from typhoid fever on
December 14, 1861, the crown jewelers had been
commissioned to produce commemorative black jewelry,
which the distraught queen continued to press on relatives
for years afterward. She herself remained in mourning for
the rest of her life.[3] (A photograph of the dead prince was
integrated into all royal portraits until 1903.)

In the 1870s, at the height of the cult of mourning,
Whitby's jet industry employed over 1,400 men and boys
at between £3 and £4 a week. Their wares were bought
by the conspicuously bereaved the world over; B. Altman
& Co. department store in New York proudly advertised
its stock of "Whitby jet earrings" in the 1879–80 catalog.[4]

By the 1880s much of the best jet in Whitby had been
consumed—artisans had needed to mine for it from as early
as the 1840s—and the jet carvers were beginning to resort
to the softer, more brittle kind that was inclined to break.
Hardier and cheaper alternatives—like black cut glass,
fancifully known as "French jet"—were used instead. In
1884 the Whitby jet industry could support only 300 jobs
on the paltry weekly wage of 25 shillings. Simultaneously,
the public performance of grief was increasingly seen as
vulgar, rather than refined. Bertram Puckle, in his 1926
book on the history of funerary customs, wrote of "the
hideous lumps of crudely manufactured jet which it is still
considered by some classes of society to be necessary to
wear when 'in mourning.'"[5] In 1936 only five jet workers
remained in business. The First World War had all but
extinguished the West's taste for sartorial grieving.[6]

Melanin

In folklore it is rare for someone or something to get the
better of a black animal, but in one of Aesop's fables,
a fox manages it. Seeing a crow in a tree clasping a hunk
of cheese in its beak, the fox lavishly compliments the
bird's glossy black plumage. Flattered, the crow preens
its feathers, and when the fox asks to hear her sing, she
immediately opens her beak, dropping the cheese down
to the waiting fox.

Perhaps one should not judge the vain crow too
harshly: her coloring is rather special. Unlike plants, the
animal kingdom possesses a pigment, melanin, that allows
for a true black. There are two types, eumelanin and
pheomelanin, which, deployed in varying concentrations,
account for a vast spectrum of skin, fur, and feathers from
roan to tawny and, in the highest concentrations, sable.

In humans, varying levels of eumelanin and
pheomelanin determine skin color. Our earliest ancestors
in Africa evolved to have dark skin with high
concentrations of melanin in order to help protect them
from the harmful ultraviolet wavelengths in the sun's rays.[1]
Descendants of the groups who left Africa some 120,000
years ago gradually developed paler skin as they traveled
northward, because it was a genetic advantage in regions
with less light.[2]

The black animal par excellence, though, is the raven.
Not only are ravens visually striking, but they have long
been known for their intelligence. Because of this they
have always had cultural prominence: ravens, for example,
have attended the Greek god Apollo, the Celtic god Lugus,
and the Norse god Odin. Odin's ravens were particularly
esteemed. Named Huginn (thought) and Muninn
(memory), they traveled the world on his behalf, gathering
information for him and making him all but omniscient.[3]
Early Germanic warriors wore the symbol of the crow on

their clothes, and apparently drank the bird's blood before
battles. So entrenched was this custom that in A.D. 751
Boniface, the archbishop of Mainz, wrote to Pope Zachary
listing the animals eaten by pagan Germans—including
storks, wild horses, and hares—and asking which ones
he should try to ban first. The pope's reply, when it came,
was clear: crows and ravens were at the very top of the list.
Zachary was possibly thinking of Leviticus, where it says
the raven is the bird "which ye shall have in abomination
among the fowls; they shall not be eaten, they are an
abomination."[4]

Metaphorical black animals have also plagued
humanity. In a letter dated June 28, 1783, Samuel Johnson
talked of his depression as a black dog:

*When I rise my breakfast is solitary, the black dog waits to share it,
from breakfast to dinner he continues barking... Night comes at last,
and some hours of restlessness and confusion bring me again to a day of
solitude. What shall exclude the black dog from a habitation like this?*[5]

A century later John Ruskin's horrifying description of the
onset of a psychotic break begins: "A large black cat sprang
forth from behind the mirror."[6] Another man famously
dogged by the specter of depression was Winston
Churchill. He wrote to his wife in July 1911 telling her of
a German doctor who had cured a friend's depression.
"I think this man might be useful to me—if my black dog
returns," writes Churchill. "He seems quite away from me
now—it is such a relief. All the colors come back into
the picture. Brightest of all your dear face."[7]

Pitch black

"In the beginning," the Bible begins, "the earth was without form and void: darkness was upon the face of the deep." Then God said, "'Let there be light,' and there was light." Believer or not, the power of this image—God bringing light to the deep darkness—is undeniable.

Pitch black is the most fearsome kind of darkness. For humans, fear of it, perhaps lingering from the days before we could reliably make fire, is universal and ancient. In the dark we become acutely aware of our limitations as a species: our senses of smell and hearing are too blunt to be of much use in navigating the world, our bodies are soft, and we cannot outpace predators. Without sight, we are vulnerable. Our terror is so visceral we are wont to see nighttime as pitch black, even when it isn't. Thanks to the moon, the stars, and, more recently, fire and electricity, nights so dark that we cannot see anything are rare, and we know that, sooner or later, the sun will rise again. "Pitch" is an appropriate epithet: just as the resinous wood-tar residue might stick to a careless hand, darkness can seem to cling and weigh us down. Perhaps this is why we experience night, figuratively at least, as more than just an absence of light. It is unyielding: a daily helping of death.

Traces of our aversion to night and blackness can be found across cultures and eras. Nyx, the ancient Greek goddess of night, is the daughter of Chaos; her own children include sleep, but also, more ominously, anguish, discord, and death.[1] Nott, a night goddess from Germanic and Scandinavian traditions, wears black and rides in a chariot drawn by a dark horse, pulling darkness across the sky like a drape.[2] Through fear, pitch black has also laid symbolic claim to death, which is, in the most desolate view, a night without end. Both Yama, the Hindu god of death, and Anubis, his ancient Egyptian counterpart, have black skin.

Kali, the fearsome Hindu warrior goddess of both creation and destruction, whose name means "She who is black" in Sanskrit, is usually depicted with dark skin, wearing a necklace of skulls, and brandishing swords and a severed head.[3]

Many cultures have worn black in mourning for the dead. In Plutarch's telling of the legend of the Minotaur, the young tributes that were sacrificed each year to the creature were sent off in a ship with black sails, "since they were heading to certain destruction."[4] Fear of the deepest dark has also left its mark on language: the Latin word for the darkest matte black is *ater* (there is another word, *niger*, reserved for the glossy, benign variety of black), which led to Latin words for ugly, sad, and dirty, and is also the etymological root for the English word *atrocious*.[5]

The most eloquent expression of humanity's fear of pitch black is also one of the oldest. It comes from the Book of the Dead, the Egyptian funerary text used for about 1,500 years until around 50 B.C. Finding himself in the underworld, Osiris, the scribe Ani, describes it thus:

What manner [of land] is this into which I have come? It hath not water, it hath not air; it is deep, unfathomable, it is black as the blackest night, and men wander helplessly therein.[6]

Glossary of other interesting colors

A

Amethyst Violet or purple, from the precious stone

Apricot Soft peach

Aquamarine Blue-green, the color of the sea; also a color of beryl

Asparagus Toned-down spring green

Azure Bright, sky blue, used in heraldry

B

Bastard Warm gold of the light-gels used in stage lighting to suggest sunshine onstage

Beryl A translucent mineral; usually pale green, blue, or yellow

Bister Brownish pigment made from burnt wood

Blackcurrant Deep purple, from the berry

Blood Intense, saturated red, usually with subtle blue undertones

Blush Pinky beige, like flushed cheeks

Bordeaux Deep cherry, from the French wine

Bronze The color of the metal; darker and a bit duller than gold

Burgundy A deep purple-brown, from the French wine

C

Cadet blue Gray-greenish blue, from military uniforms

Café au lait Pale brown, the color of coffee mixed with milk

Capri blue Sapphire; taken from the color of the water in the Grotta Azzurra on the island of Capri

Carmine Mid-crimson red; a pigment made using cochineal

Carnation Originally from Latin *carneus*, "flesh-colored" (used in French heraldry as the color of flesh); now creamy mid-pink

Chartreuse A pale yellow-green; from the liqueur made by the Carthusian monks at La Grande Chartreuse monastery in France

Cherry Deep red with a little pink

Chestnut Red-brown, like the seed of the chestnut tree

Chocolate Rich brown

Cinnabar A bright red mineral; a source of vermilion

Citrine Originally lemon-colored (though the semiprecious stone is warmer); it is often used now as the tertiary color between orange and green

Copper Reddish, rosy gold, like the metal; used to describe hair, it denotes a more intense fiery orange

Coquelicot Bright red with a hint of orange; French for *Papaver rhoeas*, the wild poppy

Coral Soft pinky orange like faded, salt-encrusted reefs (traditionally the most desired shade of coral has been red)

Cornflower A bright blue with a little violet; from the flower

Cream Pale yellow; rich off-white

Crimson Deep red inclined to purple; historically from kermes dye

Cyan Bright blue with a little green

D

Delft blue An inky shade; from the pottery made in the Dutch city of Delft in the eighteenth century

Denim The blue of indigo-dyed jeans

Dove gray Soft, cool-toned mid-gray

Duck egg Blue-green with a little gray

Dun A gray-brown; often used to describe livestock

E

Eau de Nil A pale green thought to resemble the color of the Nile River

Ebony Very dark brown; from the tropical hardwood, usually from the genus *Diospyrus*

Ecru Pale off-white, the color of unbleached cloth; from *crudus*, Latin for "raw"

F

Forest Used by Walter Scott to refer to Lincoln green; now slightly blue mid-green

French gray Very pale gray-green

Fulvous Dull orange; like tawny, often used to describe animal colors, usually birds' plumage

G

Gaudy green Like Lincoln green; cloth dyed with indigo and weld

Glaucous Pale gray blue-green

Goldenrod Strong yellow; after the flower

Grape A violet shade; much brighter than real grapes

Grenadine Originally a peachy orange; now red like the liqueur

Gules Red; from heraldry

Gunmetal Mid-blue-gray

H

Heather Pre–twentieth century a synonym for mottled; now pinky purple

Hooker's green Bright green; Prussian blue mixed with gamboge; named after British illustrator William Hooker (1779–1832)

I

Incarnadine A fierce, saturated pinkish red

J

Jasper Soft green; for the color of the most revered chalcedony

L

Lavender Pale bluish purple; usually a tint much paler than the blooms themselves

Lemon yellow The color of the fruit

Lily white Very pale cream with a bit of warmth

Lime Very bright green; originally after the fruit, but now usually much more luminous, even neon

Lincoln green Color of cloth traditionally made in Lincoln, an English city; worn by Robin Hood and his merry men

Livid From *lividus*, Latin meaning "dull," leaden color; also used to describe the color of bruised flesh

M

Magnolia Pale pink-beige

Mahogany Red brown, after the hardwood

Malachite Glassy bright green; the color of the mineral

Mallow A pinky lilac color; from the flower

Mandarin True orange; from the fruit

Maroon Originally nut brown—*marron* means "chestnut" in French—now brownish dark red

Midnight Dark blue of the night sky

Milk white Pale grayish cream

Moonlight Very pale peach

Morocco Brick red; originally a color of painted leather

Moss Yellowed green; the color of moss

Mouse A gray dun brown, similar to fallow

Mustard Strong yellow, like the condiment

N

Navy Dark blue with a little gray

Nymphea Mid-pinkish purple

O

Ocher Pale yellowish brown; from the earth pigment containing ferric oxide

Old rose Dusty pink with blue undertones

Olive drab Green with plenty of gray and brown; dull olive

Onyx Black; from the chalcedony mineral

Oxblood A dark rust-red

P

Peacock A saturated blue-green

Pea green Fresh springy green

Pearl Very pale lilac-gray

Peridot Sharp green; from the mineral, a kind of olivine

Periwinkle Lilac-blue, after the flower

Phthalo green Piney blue-green, after a synthetic pigment; also comes in deep blue sometimes known as Monastrall

Pistachio A waxy green; the color of the nut kernel and ice cream

Plum Reddish purple; after the fruit

Pomegranate The cranberry-pink color of the fruit

Pompadour Warm pale blue; after the eighteenth-century marquise, mistress of King Louis XV

Pompeian red A dark brick red; from the color of the houses discovered by archaeologists in Pompeii

Poppy A clear brilliant red; from the flower

Primrose Pale yellow with a little green; from the flower

Puke Dark brown; named after a woolen fabric

Q

Quimper Soft cornflower blue; the color of dusk

R

Racing green Dark evergreen; associated with early British car racing

Raspberry Rich pinky red; the color of the berry

Rose Delicate pink or pale crimson

Ruby Rich wine shade of red

S

Sable Black; from heraldry; resembles the fur from the small weasel-like animal of the same name

Salmon A warm pinky orange

Sapphire Dense blue; the color of the precious stone

Shell Pale pink

Shrimp The color of boiled prawn shells

Sienna A yellow-brown; from the ocher mined from the Italian town of the same name; redder when heated: burnt sienna

Slate Mid-azure gray; from the rock

Smalt Glassy blue; from the artists'pigment

Smoke A soft bluish gray

Snow White with a gray-yellow tinge

Strawberry Yellow-toned red; the color of the fruit

Sugar Sweetish pink; the color of cotton candy

T

Tangerine Yellowy orange; from the skin of the fruit

Tawny Tan-colored; orange-brown

Teal Strong green with a dash of blue; after the band on the duck's wing

Tea rose A beige pink

Terra-cotta Brown-red; from the Italian for "baked earth"

Topaz The gemstone comes in many different colors, but the term usually refers to a tawny deep yellow

Turquoise Greenish blue, like a tropical sea

V

Vanilla Pale yellow; the color of custard

Viridian Dusky leek green

W

Walnut Dark brown tone

Watchet Pale blue-gray

Wheat Pale gold

Notes

Color Vision

[1] Incidentally, his rather arbitrary slicing-up of the rainbow into seven color segments was because he wanted it to echo his theories on music.

[2] Other animals have different numbers of cone cells. Dogs, for example, have one fewer, and see the same range of colors as someone we would call color-blind, but many insects, like butterflies, have more. The preying mantis shrimp, a small, iridescent crustacean with eyes like golf balls on stalks, has 16 different types of cone cells, double the number of any other living creature that we know of. This allows it, theoretically, to see the world in colors we cannot even imagine, let alone name.

[3] P. Ball, *Bright Earth: The Invention of Color* (London: Vintage, 2008), p. 163.

[4] J. Gage, *Color and Culture: Practice and Meaning from Antiquity to Abstraction* (London: Thames & Hudson, 1995), p. 129.

[5] K. Stamper, "Seeing Cerise: Defining Colors in Webster's Third," in *Harmless Drudgery: Life from Inside the Dictionary*. Available at: https://korystamper.wordpress.com/2012/08/07/seeing-cerise-defining-colors/

[6] Quoted in D. Batchelor, *Chromophobia* (London: Reaktion Books, 2000), p. 16.

[7] Le Corbusier and A. Ozenfant, "Purism," in R. L. Herbert (ed.), *Modern Artists on Art* (New York: Dover Publications, 2000), p. 63.

[8] Quoted in G. Deutscher, *Through the Language Glass: Why the World Looks Different in Other Languages* (London: Arrow, 2010), p. 42.

[9] Ibid., p. 84.

White

[1] Ball, *Bright Earth*, pp. 169–71.

[2] Ibid., p. 382.

[3] Batchelor, *Chromophobia*, p. 10.

[4] B. Klinkhammer, "After Purism: Le Corbusier and Color," in *Preservation Education & Research*, Vol. 4 (2011), p. 22.

[5] Quoted in Gage, *Color and Culture*, pp. 246–7.

[6] L. Kahney, *Jony Ive: The Genius Behind Apple's Greatest Products* (London: Penguin, 2013), p. 285.

[7] C. Humphries, "Have We Hit Peak Whiteness?," in *Nautilus* (July 2015).

[8] Quoted in V. Finlay, *The Brilliant History of Color in Art* (Los Angeles, CA: Getty Publications, 2014), p. 21.

Lead white

[1] P. Ah-Rim, "Colors in Mural Paintings in Goguryeo Kingdom Tombs," in M. Dusenbury (ed.), *Color in Ancient and Medieval East Asia* (New Haven, CT: Yale University Press, 2015), pp. 62, 65.

[2] Ball, *Bright Earth*, pp. 34, 70.

[3] Ibid., p. 137.

[4] P. Vernatti, "A Relation of the Making of Ceruss," in *Philosophical Transactions*, No. 137, Royal Society (Jan./Feb. 1678), pp. 935–6.

[5] C. Warren, *Brush with Death: A Social History of Lead Poisoning* (Baltimore, MD: Johns Hopkins University Press, 2001), p. 20.

[6] T. Nakashima et al., "Severe Lead Contamination Among Children of Samurai Families in Edo Period Japan," in *Journal of Archaeological Science*, Vol. 32, Issue 1 (2011), pp. 23–8.

[7] G. Lomazzo, *A Tracte Containing the Artes of Curious Paintinge, Caruinge & Buildinge*, trans. R. Haydock (Oxford, 1598), p. 130.

[8] Warren, *Brush with Death*, p. 21.

Ivory

[1] D. Loeb McClain, "Reopening History of Storied Norse Chessmen," in *New York Times* (Sept. 8, 2010).

[2] K. Johnson, "Medieval Foes with Whimsy," in *New York Times* (Nov. 17, 2011).

[3] C. Russo, "Can Elephants Survive a Legal Ivory Trade? Debate Is Shifting Against It," in *National Geographic* (Aug. 30, 2014).

[4] E. Larson, "The History of the Ivory Trade," in *National Geographic* (Feb. 25, 2013). Available at: http://education .nationalgeographic.org/media/history-ivory -trade/ (accessed Apr. 12, 2017).

Silver

[1] F. M. McNeill, *The Silver Bough: Volume One, Scottish Folk-Lore and Folk-Belief*, 2nd edition (Edinburgh: Canongate Classics, 2001), p. 106.

[2] Konstantinos, *Werewolves: The Occult Truth* (Woodbury: Llewellyn Worldwide, 2010), p. 79.

[3] S. Bucklow, *The Alchemy of Paint: Art, Science and Secrets from the Middle Ages* (London: Marion Boyars, 2012), p. 124.

[4] A. Lucas and J. R. Harris, *Ancient Egyptian Materials and Industries*, 4th edition (Mineola, NY: Dover Publications, 1999), p. 246.

[5] Ibid., p. 247.

Whitewash

[1] E. G. Pryor, "The Great Plague of Hong Kong," in *Journal of the Royal Asiatic Society Hong Kong Branch*, Vol. 15 (1975), pp. 61–2.

[2] Wilm, "A Report on the Epidemic of Bubonic Plague at Hongkong in the Year 1896," quoted ibid.

[3] Shropshire Regimental Museum, "The Hong Kong Plague, 1894–95," Available at: www .shropshireregimentalmuseum.co.uk /regimental-history/shropshire-light-infantry /the-hong-kong-plague-1894-95/(accessed Aug. 26, 2015).

[4] "Minutes of Evidence Taken Before the Metropolitan Sanitary Commissioners," in *Parliamentary Papers, House of Commons*, Vol. 32 (London: William Clowes & Sons, 1848).

[5] M. Twain, *The Adventures of Tom Sawyer* (New York: Plain Label Books, 2008), p. 16.

Isabelline

[1] M. S. Sánchez, "Sword and Wimple: Isabel Clara Eugenia and Power," in A. J. Cruz and M. Suzuki (eds.), *The Rule of Women in Early Modern Europe* (Champaign, IL: University of Illinois Press, 2009), pp. 64–5.

[2] Quoted in D. Salisbury, *Elephant's Breath and London Smoke* (Neustadt: Five Rivers, 2009), p. 109.

[3] Ibid., p. 108.

[4] H. Norris, *Tudor Costume and Fashion*, reprinted edition (Mineola, NY: Dover Publications, 1997), p. 611.

[5] W. C. Oosthuizen and P. J. N. de Bruyn, "Isabelline King Penguin Aptenodytes Patagonicus at Marion Island," in *Marine Ornithology*, Vol. 37, Issue 3 (2010), pp. 275–6.

Chalk

[1] R. J. Gettens, E. West Fitzhugh, and R. L. Feller, "Calcium Carbonate Whites," in *Studies in Conservation*, Vol. 19, No. 3 (Aug. 1974), pp. 157, 159–60.

[2] Ibid., p. 160.

[3] G. Field, *Chromatography: Or a Treatise on Colors and Pigments and of Their Powers in Painting, &c.* (London: Forgotten Books, 2012), p. 71.

[4] A. Houbraken, "The Great Theater of Dutch Painters," quoted in R. Cumming, *Art Explained: The World's Greatest Paintings Explored and Explained* (London: Dorling Kindersley, 2007), p. 49.

[5] Ball, *Bright Earth*, p. 163.

[6] H. Glanville, "Varnish, Grounds, Viewing Distance, and Lighting: Some Notes on Seventeenth-Century Italian Painting Technique," in C. Lightweaver (ed.), *Historical Painting Techniques, Materials, and Studio Practice* (New York: Getty Conservation Institute, 1995), p. 15; Ball, *Bright Earth*, p. 100.

[7] C. Cennini, *The Craftsman's Handbook*, Vol. 2, trans. D. V. Thompson (Mineola, NY: Dover Publications, 1954), p. 71.

[8] P. Schwyzer, "The Scouring of the White Horse: Archaeology, Identity, and 'Heritage,'" in *Representations*, No. 65 (Winter 1999), p. 56.

[9] Ibid., p. 56.

[10] Ibid., p. 42.

Beige

[1] Anonymous, "London Society" (Oct. 1889), quoted in Salisbury, *Elephant's Breath and London Smoke*, p. 19.

[2] L. Eiseman and K. Recker, *Pantone: The 20th Century in Color* (San Francisco, CA: Chronicle Books, 2011), pp. 45–7, 188–9, 110–1, 144–5.

[3] K. Glazebrook and I. Baldry, "The Cosmic Spectrum and the Color of the Universe," Johns Hopkins Physics and Astronomy blog. Available at: www.pha.jhu.edu/~kgb/cosspec/ (accessed Oct. 10, 2015).

[4] S. V. Phillips, *The Seductive Power of Home Staging: A Seven-Step System for a Fast and Profitable Sale* (Indianapolis, IN: Dog Ear Publishing, 2009), p. 52.

Yellow

[1] S. Doran, *The Culture of Yellow, or: The Visual Politics of Late Modernity* (New York: Bloomsbury, 2013), p. 2.

[2] C. Burdett, "Aestheticism and Decadence," British Library Online. Available at: www.bl.uk/romantics-and-victorians /articles/aestheticism-and-decadence (accessed Nov. 23, 2015).

[3] Quoted in D. B. Sachsman and D. W. Bulla (eds.), *Sensationalism: Murder, Mayhem, Mudslinging, Scandals and Disasters in 19th-Century Reporting* (New Brunswick, NJ: Transaction Publishers, 2013), p. 5.

[4] Doran, *Culture of Yellow*, p. 52.

[5] R. D. Harley, *Artists' Pigments c. 1600–1835* (London: Butterworth, 1970), p. 101.

[6] Doran, *Culture of Yellow*, pp. 10–1.

[7] Z. Feng and L. Bo, "Imperial Yellow in the Sixth Century," in M. Dusenbury (ed.), *Color in Ancient and Medieval East Asia*, p. 103; J. Chang, *Empress Dowager Cixi: The Concubine Who Launched Modern China* (London: Vintage, 2013), p. 5.

[8] B. N. Goswamy, "The Color Yellow," in *Tribune India* (Sept. 7, 2014).

[9] Ball, *Bright Earth*, p. 85.

[10] "Why Do Indians Love Gold?," in *The Economist* (Nov. 20, 2013). Available at: www.economist.com/blogs/economist -explains/2013/11/economist-explains-11 (accessed Nov. 24, 2015).

Blonde

[1] V. Sherrow, *Encyclopedia of Hair: A Cultural History* (Westport, CN: Greenwood Press, 2006), p. 149.

[2] Ibid., p. 154.

[3] Ibid., p. 148.

[4] "Going Down," in *The Economist* (Aug. 11, 2014). Available at: www.economist.com /blogs/graphicdetail/2014/08/daily-chart-5 (accessed Oct. 25, 2015).

[5] A. Loos, *Gentlemen Prefer Blondes: The Illuminating Diary of a Professional Lady* (New York: Liveright, 1998), p. 37.

[6] "The Case Against Tipping," in *The Economist* (Oct. 26, 2015). Available at: www.economist.com/blogs/gulliver/2015/10 /service-compris (accessed Oct. 26, 2015).

[7] A. G. Walton, "DNA Study Shatters the 'Dumb Blonde' Stereotype," in *Forbes* (June 2, 2014). Available at: www.forbes.com/sites /alicegwalton/2014/06/02/science-shatters -the-blondes-are-dumb-stereotype.

Lead-tin yellow

[1] H. Kühn, "Lead-Tin Yellow," in *Studies in Conservation*, Vol. 13, No. 1 (Feb. 1968), p. 20.

[2] G. W. R. Ward (ed.), *The Grove Encyclopedia of Materials and Techniques in Art* (Oxford, UK: Oxford University Press, 2008), p. 512; N. Eastaugh et al., *Pigment Compendium: A Dictionary and Optical Microscopy of Historical Pigments* (Oxford: Butterworth-Heinemann, 2008), p. 238.

[3] Kühn, "Lead-Tin Yellow," pp. 8–11.

[4] Eastaugh et al., *Pigment Compendium*, p. 238.

[5] Ward (ed.), *Grove Encyclopedia of Materials and Techniques in Art*, p. 512.

[6] Kühn, "Lead-Tin Yellow," p. 8.

[7] This is the method for producing lead-tin yellow type I, which is the more common kind. A second, rarer variety includes silica and is heated to higher temperatures, between 900 and 950˚C.

[8] Ball, *Bright Earth*, p. 137; Kühn, "Lead-Tin Yellow," p. 11.

Indian yellow

[1] B. N. Goswamy, art historian and author; personal correspondence.

[2] *Handbook of Young Artists and Amateurs in Oil Painting*, 1849, quoted in Salisbury, *Elephant's Breath and London Smoke*, p. 106.

[3] Ball, *Bright Earth*, p. 155.

[4] Quoted in Salisbury, *Elephant's Breath and London Smoke*, p. 106.

[5] Harley, *Artists' Pigments*, p. 105.

[6] Field, *Chromatography*, p. 83.

[7] "Indian Yellow," in *Bulletin of Miscellaneous Information* (Royal Botanic Gardens, Kew), Vol. 1890, No. 39 (1890), pp. 45–7.

[8] T. N. Mukharji, "Piuri or Indian Yellow," in *Journal of the Society for Arts*, Vol. 32, No. 1618 (Nov. 1883), p. 16.

[9] Ibid., pp. 16–17.

[10] Finlay, *Color*, pp. 230, 237.

[11] Ibid., pp. 233–40.

[12] C. McKeich, "Botanical Fortunes: T. N. Mukharji, International Exhibitions, and Trade Between India and Australia," in *Journal of the National Museum of Australia*, Vol. 3, No. 1 (Mar. 2008), pp. 2–3.

Acid yellow

[1] See: www.unicode.org/review/pri294 /pri294-emoji-image-background.html

[2] J. Savage, "A Design for Life," in the *Guardian* (Feb. 21, 2009). Available at: www.theguardian.com/artanddesign/2009 /feb/21/smiley-face-design-history (accessed Mar. 4, 2016).

[3] Quoted in J. Doll, "The Evolution of the Emoticon," in the *Wire* (Sept. 19, 2012). Available at: www.thewire.com /entertainment/2012/09/evolution -emoticon/57029/ (accessed Mar. 6, 2016).

Naples yellow

[1] E. L. Richter and H. Härlin, "A Nineteenth-Century Collection of Pigment and Painting Materials," in *Studies in Conservation*, Vol. 19, No. 2 (May 1974), p. 76.

[2] It is so garbled that a translation from German is difficult, but *Neapel* means "Naples" and *Gelb* means "yellow". Richter and Härlin, "A Nineteenth-Century Collection of Pigment and Painting Materials," p. 77.

[3] In the nineteenth and twentieth centuries, though, the term *Naples yellow* was erroneously applied to other yellows too, particularly lead-tin oxides [page 69]. The distinction was not properly cleared up until the 1940s.

[4] Eastaugh et al., *Pigment Compendium*, p. 279.

[5] Field, *Chromatography*, p. 78.

[6] Ball, *Bright Earth*, p. 58, and Lucas and Harris, *Ancient Egyptian Materials and Industries*, p.190.

[7] Quoted in Gage, *Color and Culture*, p. 224.

Chrome yellow

[1] Less than five months later, after Gauguin had moved in, relations between the two broke down. One evening, just before Christmas 1888, Van Gogh walked into a brothel a few doors down from the Yellow House and handed a prostitute a portion of his own ear, wrapped in newspaper. He was committed to first one asylum and then another; on July 27, 1890, he shot himself in the chest; he died the next day.

[2] V. van Gogh, letters to Emile Bernard [letter 665]; Theo van Gogh [letter 666]; and Willemien van Gogh [letter 667]. Available at: http://vangoghletters.org/vg/.

[3] Harley, *Artists' Pigments*, p. 92.

[4] Ball, *Bright Earth*, p. 175; Harley, *Artists' Pigments*, p. 93.

[5] N. L. Vauquelin quoted in Ball, *Bright Earth*, p. 176.

[6] I. Sample, "Van Gogh Doomed His Sunflowers by Adding White Pigments to Yellow Paint," in the *Guardian* (Feb. 14, 2011); M. Gunther, "Van Gogh's Sunflowers May Be Wilting in the Sun," in *Chemistry World* (Oct. 28, 2015). Available at: www.rsc.org/chemistryworld /2015/10/van-gogh-sunflowers-pigment -darkening.

Gamboge

[1] R. Christison, "On the Sources and Composition of Gamboge," in W. J. Hooker (ed.), *Companion to the Botanical Magazine*, Vol. 2 (London: Samuel Curtis, 1836), p. 239.

[2] Harley, *Artists' Pigments*, p. 103.

[3] Field, *Chromatography*, p. 82.

[4] Ball, *Bright Earth*, p. 156.

[5] Finlay, *Color*, p. 243.

[6] Ball, *Bright Earth*, p. 157.

[7] J. H. Townsend, "The Materials of J. M. W. Turner: Pigments," in *Studies in Conservation*, Vol. 38, No. 4 (Nov. 1993), p. 232.

[8] Field, *Chromatography*, p. 82.

[9] Christison, "On the Sources and Composition of Gamboge," in Hooker (ed.), *Companion to the Botanical Magazine*, p. 238.

[10] The way in which the movement of large particles in fluid is affected by the jostling of atoms and molecules.

[11] G. Hoeppe, *Why the Sky Is Blue: Discovering the Color of Life*, trans. J. Stewart (Princeton, NJ: Princeton University Press, 2007), pp. 203–4.

Orpiment

[1] Cennini, *Craftsman's Handbook*, Vol. 2, p. 28.

[2] Eastaugh et al., *Pigment Compendium*, p. 285.

[3] E. H. Schafer, "Orpiment and Realgar in Chinese Technology and Tradition," in *Journal of the American Oriental Society*, Vol. 75, No. 2 (Apr.–June 1955), p. 74.

[4] Cennini, *Craftsman's Handbook*, Vol. 2, pp. 28–9.

[5] Schafer, "Orpiment and Realgar in Chinese Technology and Tradition," pp. 75–6.

[6] Quoted in Finlay, *Color*, p. 242.

[7] Ball, *Bright Earth*, p. 300.

[8] Cennini, *Craftsman's Handbook*, Vol. 2, p. 29.

Imperial yellow

[1] K. A. Carl, *With the Empress Dowager of China* (New York: Routledge, 1905), pp. 6–8.

[2] Chang, *Empress Dowager Cixi*, p. 5.

[3] Carl, *With the Empress Dowager of China*, pp. 8–11.

[4] Feng and Bo, "Imperial Yellow in the Sixth Century," in Dusenbury (ed.), *Color in Ancient and Medieval East Asia*, p. 104–5.

[5] Ibid.

Gold

[1] One gold mine was found in Carmarthenshire in Wales and was exploited by the Romans from the middle of the first century A.D. Another is at Kremnica in what is now Slovakia, which was extensively worked from the beginning of the fourteenth century, leading to a drop in price all over Europe.

[2] Bucklow, *Alchemy of Paint*, p. 176.

[3] Ibid., p. 177.

[4] See: www.britannica.com/biography /Musa-I-of-Mali; Bucklow, *Alchemy of Paint*, p. 179.

[5] Ball, *Bright Earth*, p. 35.

[6] Cennini, *Craftsman's Handbook*, pp. 81, 84.

[7] Making gold paint was no less finicky and expensive than gilding sheets. The metal is so malleable that if one attempts to grind it the pieces will only begin welding together. Instead, it was mixed with fluid mercury to form a paste which, when the excess mercury was squeezed out, became brittle enough to pound to powder in a pestle and mortar. Finally, the mercury could be extracted by gently heating the mixture. This was work for alchemists, who for millennia had been trying to create gold and were well equipped to handle the real thing.

[8] Quoted in Bucklow, *Alchemy of Paint*, p. 184.

Orange

[1] J. Eckstut and A. Eckstut, *The Secret Language of Color* (New York: Black Dog & Leventhal, 2013), p. 72.

[2] Salisbury, *Elephant's Breath and London Smoke*, p. 148.

[3] Quoted in Ball, *Bright Earth*, p. 23.

[4] J. Colliss Harvey, *Red: A Natural History of the Redhead* (London: Allen & Unwin, 2015), p. 2.

[5] Eckstut and Eckstut, *Secret Language of Color*, p. 82.

[6] Rijksmuseum, "William of Orange (1533–1584), Father of the Nation." Available at: https:// www.rijksmuseum.nl/en/explore-the -collection/historical-figures/william-of-orange (accessed Dec. 1, 2015); Eckstut and Eckstut, *Secret Language of Color*, p. 75.

[7] Black, battleship, and warm gray were also considered; warm gray was named the second choice. The CMYK code for GGB international orange is C: 0%; M: 69%; Y: 100%; K: 6%.

[8] L. Eiseman and E. P. Cutter, *Pantone on Fashion: A Century of Color in Design* (San Francisco, CA: Chronicle Books, 2014), p. 16.

[9] Ibid., p. 15.

[10] Quoted in Ball, *Bright Earth*, p. 23.

[11] Quoted in Salisbury, *Elephant's Breath and London Smoke*, p. 149.

Dutch orange

[1] Eckstut and Eckstut, *Secret Language of Color*, p. 76.

[2] Rijksmuseum, "William of Orange, Father of the Nation."

[3] S. R. Friedland (ed.), *Vegetables: Proceedings of the Oxford Symposium on Food and Cooking 2008* (Totnes: Prospect, 2009), pp. 64–5.

[4] Eckstut and Eckstut, *Secret Language of Color*, p. 75.

[5] E. G. Burrows and M. Wallace, *Gotham: A History of New York City to 1898* (Oxford, UK: Oxford University Press, 1999), pp. 82–3.

Saffron

[1] Eckstut and Eckstut, *Secret Language of Color*, p. 82; D. C. Watts, *Dictionary of Plant Lore*, (Burlington, VT: Elsevier, 2007), p. 335.

[2] Saffron is integral to many Spanish dishes, not least paella, but homegrown saffron is not nearly enough to satisfy demand: today Spain is a vast net importer of Iranian saffron.

[3] Finlay, *Color*, pp. 252–3.

[4] Ibid., pp. 253, 260.

[5] Eckstut and Eckstut, *Secret Language of Color*, p. 79.

[6] William Harrison, quoted in Sir G. Prance and M. Nesbitt (eds.), *Cultural History of Plants* (London: Routledge, 2005), p. 309.

[7] Ibid., p. 308.

[8] Watts, *Dictionary of Plant Lore*, p. 335.

[9] Prance and Nesbitt (eds.), *Cultural History of Plants*, p. 308.

[10] Eckstut and Eckstut, *Secret Language of Color*, pp. 80, 82.

[11] Finlay, *Brilliant History of Color in Art*, p. 110.

[12] Quoted in Harley, *Artists' Pigments*, p. 96.

[13] Bureau of Indian Standards, "Flag Code of India." Available at: www.mahapolice.gov.in /mahapolice/jsp/temp/html/flag_code _of_india.pdf (accessed Nov. 28, 2015).

Amber

[1] J. Blumberg, "A Brief History of the Amber Room," Smithsonian.com (July 31, 2007). Available at: www.smithsonianmag.com /history/a-brief-history-of-the-amber -room-160940121/ (accessed Nov. 17, 2015).

[2] Ibid.

[3] M. R. Collings, *Gemlore: An Introduction to Precious and Semi-Precious Stones*, 2nd edition (Rockville, MD: Borgo Press, 2009), p. 19.

[4] M. Gannon, "100-Million-Year-Old Spider Attack Found in Amber," in *LiveScience* (Oct. 8, 2012). Available at: www.livescience .com/23796-spider-attack-found-in-amber .html (accessed Nov. 21, 2015); C. Q. Choi, "230-Million-Year-Old Mite Found in Amber," *LiveScience* (Aug. 27, 2012). Available at: www.livescience.com/22725-ancient-mite -trapped-amber.html (accessed Nov. 21, 2015).

[5] T. Follett, "Amber in Goldworking," in *Archaeology*, Vol. 32, No. 2 (Mar./Apr. 1985), p. 64.

[6] G. V. Stanivukovic (ed.), *Ovid and the Renaissance Body* (Toronto, Canada: University of Toronto Press, 2001), p. 87.

Ginger

[1] Colliss Harvey, *Red*, pp. 1–2, 15.

[2] Quoted in Norris, *Tudor Costume and Fashion*, p. 162.

[3] C. Zimmer, "Bones Give Peek into the Lives of Neanderthals," in *New York Times* (Dec. 20, 2010). Available at: www.nytimes.com /2010 /12/21/science/21neanderthal.html.

[4] Ibid.

Minium

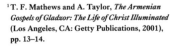

[1] T. F. Mathews and A. Taylor, *The Armenian Gospels of Gladzor: The Life of Christ Illuminated* (Los Angeles, CA: Getty Publications, 2001), pp. 13–14.

[2] Ibid., p. 19. We know at least three artists helped complete the work, because each had a preferred method of painting the faces. One began with primrose yellow before adding details with tiny strokes of green and white. Another favored a base of dull olive, over which he added white and pale pink; a third began with a green ground, and used brown, white, and red to add in the features.

[3] D. V. Thompson, *The Materials and Techniques of Medieval Painting*. Reprinted from the first edition (New York: Dover Publications, 1956), p. 102.

[4] M. Clarke, "Anglo Saxon Manuscript Pigments," in *Studies in Conservation*, Vol. 49, No. 4 (2004), p. 239.

[5] Quoted in F. Delamare and B. Guineau, *Color: Making and Using Dyes and Pigments* (London: Thames & Hudson, 2000), p. 140.

[6] Thompson, *Materials and Techniques of Medieval Painting*, p. 101.

[7] C. Warren, *Brush with Death*, p. 20; Schafer, "The Early History of Lead Pigments and Cosmetics in China," in *T'oung Pao*, Vol. 44, No. 4 (1956), p. 426.

[8] Field, *Chromatography*, p. 95.

Nude

[1] H. Alexander, "Michelle Obama: The 'Nude' Debate," in the *Telegraph* (May 19, 2010).

[2] D. Stewart, "Why a 'Nude' Dress Should Really be 'Champagne' or 'Peach,'" in *Jezebel* (May 17, 2010).

[3] Eiseman and Cutler, *Pantone on Fashion*, p. 20.

[4] See: http://humanae.tumblr.com/.

[5] Crayola, incidentally, was impressively ahead of its time on this issue: their "flesh" crayon was renamed "peach" in 1962, the same year President Kennedy sent troops to protect James Meredith, the first African American student admitted to the segregated University of Mississippi.

Pink

[1] "Finery for Infants," in *New York Times* (July 23, 1893).

[2] Quoted in J. Maglaty, "When Did Girls Start Wearing Pink?," Smithsonian.com (Apr. 7, 2011). Available at: www.smithsonianmag.com/arts-culture/when-did-girls-start-wearing-pink-1370097/ (accessed Oct. 28, 2015).

[3] Ball, *Bright Earth*, p. 157.

[4] In the 1957 film *Funny Face*, a character based on Vreeland performs a five-minute song-and-dance routine called "Think Pink!" Vreeland, after watching a screening, is said to have turned to a junior colleague and muttered: "Never to be discussed."

[5] M. Ryzik, "The Guerrilla Girls, After 3 Decades, Still Rattling Art World Cages," in *New York Times* (Aug. 5, 2015).

[6] Quoted in "The Pink Tax," in *New York Times* (Nov. 14, 2014).

Baker-Miller pink

[1] A. G. Schauss, "Tranquilizing Effect of Color Reduces Aggressive Behavior and Potential Violence," in *Orthomolecular Psychiatry*, Vol. 8, No. 4 (1979), p. 218.

[2] J. E. Gilliam and D. Unruh, "The Effects of Baker-Miller Pink on Biological, Physical and Cognitive Behavior," in *Journal of Orthomolecular Medicine*, Vol. 3, No. 4 (1988), p. 202.

[3] Schauss, "Tranquilizing Effect of Color," p. 219.

[4] Quoted in Ibid., brackets his.

[5] A. L. Alter, *Drunk Tank Pink, and other Unexpected Forces That Shape How We Think, Feel and Behave* (London: Oneworld, 2013), p. 3.

[6] See, for example, Gilliam and Unruh, "Effects of Baker-Miller Pink"; for further examples see T. Cassidy, *Environmental Psychology: Behavior and Experience in Context* (Hove: Routledge Psychology Press, 1997), p. 84.

[7] Cassidy, *Environmental Psychology*, p. 84.

Mountbatten pink

[1] Lord Zuckerman, "Earl Mountbatten of Burma, 25 June 1900–27 August 1979," *Biographical Memoirs of Fellows of the Royal Society*, Vol. 27 (Nov. 1981), p. 358.

[2] A. Raven, "The Development of Naval Camouflage 1914–1945," Part III. Available at: www.shipcamouflage.com/3_2.htm (accessed Oct. 26, 2015).

Puce

[1] H. Jackson, "Color Determination in the Fashion Trades," in *Journal of the Royal Society of the Arts*, Vol. 78, No. 4034 (Mar. 1930), p. 501.

[2] C. Weber, *Queen of Fashion: What Marie Antoinette Wore to the Revolution* (New York: Picador, 2006), p. 117.

[3] *Domestic Anecdotes of a French Nation*, 1800, quoted in Salisbury, *Elephant's Breath and London Smoke*, p. 169.

[4] Quoted in Weber, *Queen of Fashion*, p. 117.

[5] Quoted in Earl of Bessborough (ed.), *Georgiana: Extracts from the Correspondence of Georgiana, Duchess of Devonshire* (London: John Murray, 1955), p. 27.

[6] Weber, *Queen of Fashion*, p. 256.

Fuchsia

[1] Others include: amaranth; mauve; magnolia; cornflower; goldenrod; heliotrope; lavender; and violet, to name a few. In most languages with the exception of English the word for pink is derived from that for the rose.

[2] I. Paterson, *A Dictionary of Color: A Lexicon of the Language of Color* (London: Thorogood, 2004), p. 170.

[3] G. Niles, "Origin of Plant Names," in *The Plant World*, Vol. 5, No. 8 (Aug. 1902), p. 143.

[4] Quoted in M. Allaby, *Plants: Food Medicine and Green Earth* (New York: Facts on File, 2010), p. 39.

[5] Ibid., pp. 38–41.

Shocking pink

[1] M. Soames (ed.), *Winston and Clementine: The Personal Letters of the Churchills* (Boston, MA: Houghton Mifflin, 1998), p. 276.

[2] M. Owens, "Jewelry That Gleams with Wicked Memories," in *New York Times* (Apr. 13, 1997).

[3] Eiseman and Cutler, *Pantone on Fashion*, p. 31.

[4] E. Schiaparelli, *Shocking Life* (London: V&A Museum, 2007), p. 114.

[5] Two years later the Tête de Bélier was stolen from Fellowes's home near Paris as part of a haul worth £36,000. It has not been seen since.

[6] S. Menkes, "Celebrating Elsa Schiaparelli," in *New York Times* (Nov. 18, 2013). Although it is with this pink that Schiaparelli was most associated, her collections were awash with many colors. After "Shocking," each of her perfumes was twinned with its own signature shade: "Zut" with green, "Sleeping" with blue, and "Le Roy Soleil" with gold.

[7] Eiseman and Cutler, *Pantone on Fashion*, p. 31.

Fluorescent pink

[1] H. Greenbaum and D. Rubinstein, "The Hand-Held Highlighter," in *New York Times Magazine* (Jan. 20, 2012).

[2] Schwan Stabilo press release, 2015; Greenbaum and Rubinstein, "Hand-Held Highlighter."

Amaranth

[1] V. S. Vernon Jones (trans.), *Aesop's Fables* (Mineola, NY: Dover Publications, 2009), p. 188.

[2] G. Nagy, *The Ancient Greek Hero in 24 Hours* (Cambridge, MA: Belknap, 2013), p. 408.

[3] J. E. Brody, "Ancient, Forgotten Plant Now 'Grain of the Future,'" in *New York Times* (Oct. 16, 1984).

[4] Brachfeld and Choate, *Eat Your Food,*! p. 199.

[5] Brody, "Ancient, Forgotten Plant Now 'Grain of the Future.'"

[6] Ibid.

[7] Kiple and Ornelas (eds.), *Cambridge World History of Food*, p. 75.

[8] Quoted in Salisbury, *Elephant's Breath and London Smoke*, p. 7.

Red

[1] N. Guéguen and C. Jacob, "Clothing Color and Tipping: Gentlemen Patrons Give More Tips to Waitresses with Red Clothes," in *Journal of Hospitality & Tourism Research*, quoted by Sage Publications/*Science Daily*. Available at: www.sciencedaily.com /releases/2012/08/120802111454.htm (accessed Sept. 20, 2015).

[2] A. J. Elliot and M. A. Maier, "Color and Psychological Functioning," in *Journal of Experimental Psychology*, Vol. 136, No. 1 (2007), pp. 251–2.

[3] R. Hill, "Red Advantage in Sport." Available at: https://community.dur.ac.uk/r.a.hill /red_advantage.htm (accessed Sept. 20, 2015).

[4] Ibid.

[5] M. Pastoureau, *Blue: The History of a Color*, trans. M. I. Cruse (Princeton, NJ: Princeton University Press, 2000), p. 15.

[6] E. Phipps, "Cochineal Red: The Art History of a Color," in *Metropolitan Museum of Art Bulletin*, Vol. 67, No. 3 (Winter 2010), p. 5.

[7] M. Dusenbury, "Introduction," in *Color in Ancient and Medieval East Asia*, pp. 12–13.

[8] Phipps, "Cochineal Red," p. 22.

[9] Ibid., pp. 14, 23–4.

[10] Pastoureau, *Blue*, p. 94.

[11] P. Gootenberg, *Andean Cocaine: The Making of a Global Drug* (Chapel Hill, NC: University of North Carolina Press, 2008), p. 198.

Scarlet

[1] Cloth dyed with kermes was often said to be dyed "scarlet in grain"; this is where we get the word "ingrain," which means to firmly fix or establish.

[2] A. B. Greenfield, *A Perfect Red: Empire, Espionage and the Quest for the Color of Desire* (London: Black Swan, 2006), p. 42.

[3] Gage, *Color and Meaning*, p. 111.

[4] Greenfield, *Perfect Red*, p. 108.

[5] Phipps, "Cochineal Red," p. 26.

[6] G. Summer and R. D'Amato, *Arms and Armor of the Imperial Roman Soldier* (Barnsley: Frontline Books, 2009), p. 218.

[7] Greenfield, *Perfect Red*, p. 183.

[8] Ibid., p. 181.

[9] E. Bemiss, *Dyers Companion*, p 186.

[10] Field, *Chromatography*, p. 89.

[11] Quoted in Salisbury, *Elephant's Breath and London Smoke*, p. 191.

Cochineal

[1] Finlay, *Color*, p. 153.

[2] Phipps, "Cochineal Red," p. 10.

[3] R. L. Lee, "Cochineal Production and Trade in New Spain to 1600," in *The Americas*, Vol. 4, No. 4 (Apr. 1948), p. 451.

[4] Phipps, "Cochineal Red," p. 12.

[5] Quoted ibid., pp. 24–6.

[6] Ibid., p. 27.

[7] Finlay, *Color*, p. 169.

[8] Phipps, "Cochineal Red," pp. 27–40.

[9] Ibid., p. 37.

[10] Finlay, *Color*, pp. 165–76.

Vermilion

[1] Bucklow, *Alchemy of Paint*, p. 87; R. J. Gettens et al., "Vermilion and Cinnabar," in *Studies in Conservation*, Vol. 17, No. 2 (May 1972), pp. 45–7.

[2] Thompson, *Materials and Techniques of Medieval Painting*, p. 106. Conversion rates for Roman currency are notoriously difficult; estimates for comparable rates for 1 sesterce range from $0.50 to $50. Working with a relatively conservative conversion rate of $10 for each sesterce, a pound of cinnabar in Pliny's time cost $70.

[3] Ball, *Bright Earth*, p. 86.

[4] Bucklow, *Alchemy of Paint*, p. 77.

[5] Thompson, *Materials and Techniques of Medieval Painting*, p. 106.

[6] Ibid., pp. 60–1, 108.

[7] Gettens et al., "Vermilion and Cinnabar," p. 49.

[8] Thompson, *Materials and Techniques of Medieval Painting*, p. 30.

[9] One holdout was Renoir, who was famously conservative when it came to his materials. Sometime around 1904 Matisse began trying to persuade him to swap vermilion for cadmium red, but Renoir refused to try even the free sample Matisse gave him.

[10] Quoted in Ball, *Bright Earth*, p. 23.

Rosso corsa

[1] Quoted in L. Barzini, *Pekin to Paris: An Account of Prince Borghese's Journey Across Two Continents in a Motor-Car*, trans. L. P. de Castelvecchio (London: E. Grant Richards, 1907), p. 11.

[2] Ibid., p. 26.

[3] Ibid., p. 40.

[4] Ibid., pp. 58, 396, 569.

[5] Borghese's car is still on display in the Museo dell'Auto in Turin. However, those expecting to see a dashing red machine will be disappointed: the car is now a dull gray color because it was accidentally dropped into a Genoese dock after being displayed at an American motor show. To prevent its rusting it was quickly repainted; the only paint they could find were some tins of battleship gray.

Hematite

1 Phipps, "Cochineal Red," p. 5.

2 E. Photos-Jones et al., "Kean Miltos: The Well-Known Iron Oxides of Antiquity," in *Annual of the British School of Athens*, Vol. 92 (1997), p. 360.

3 E. E. Wreschner, "Red Ocher and Human Evolution: A Case for Discussion," in *Current Anthropology*, Vol. 21, No. 5 (Oct. 1980), p. 631.

4 Ibid.

5 Phipps, "Cochineal Red," p. 5; G. Lai, "Colors and Color Symbolism in Early Chinese Ritual Art," in Dusenbury (ed.), *Color in Ancient and Medieval East Asia*, p. 27.

6 Dusenbury, "Introduction," in *Color in Ancient and Medieval East Asia*, p. 12.

7 Photos-Jones et al., "Kean Miltos," p. 359.

Madder

1 W. H. Perkin, "The History of Alizarin and Allied Coloring Matters, and Their Production from Coal Tar, from a Lecture Delivered May 8th," in *Journal for the Society for Arts*, Vol. 27, No. 1384 (May 1879), p. 573.

2 G. C. H. Derksen and T. A. Van Beek, "Rubia Tinctorum L.," in *Studies in Natural Products Chemistry*, Vol. 26 (2002), p. 632.

3 J. Wouters et al., "The Identification of Haematite as a Red Colorant on an Egyptian Textile from the Second Millennium B.C.," in *Studies in Conservation*, Vol. 35, No. 2 (May 1990), p. 89.

4 Delamare and Guineau, *Color*, pp. 24, 44.

5 Field, *Chromatography*, pp. 97–8.

6 Finlay, *Color*, p. 207.

7 Perkin, "History of Alizarin and Allied Coloring Matters," p. 573.

8 Finlay, *Color*, pp. 208–9.

Dragon's blood

1 Bucklow, *Alchemy of Paint*, p. 155; W. Winstanley, *The Flying Serpent, or: Strange News out of Essex* (London, 1669). Available at: www.henham .org/FlyingSerpent (accessed 19 Sept. 2015).

2 Ball, *Bright Earth*, p. 76.

3 Bucklow, *Alchemy of Paint*, pp. 142, 161.

4 Ball, *Bright Earth*, p. 77.

5 Field, *Chromatography*, p. 97.

Purple

1 Ball, *Bright Earth*, p. 223.

2 Gage, *Color and Culture*, pp. 16, 25.

3 Quoted in Gage, *Color and Culture*, p. 25.

4 Quoted in Eckstut and Eckstut, *Secret Language of Color*, p. 224.

5 J. M. Stanlaw, "Japanese Color Terms, from 400 CE to the Present," in R. E. MacLaury, G. Parameis and D. Dedrick (eds.), *Anthropology of Color* (New York: John Benjamins, 2007), p. 311.

6 Finlay, *Color*, p. 422.

7 S. Garfield, *Mauve: How One Man Invented a Color That Changed the World* (London: Faber & Faber, 2000), p. 52.

Tyrian purple

1 Finlay, *Color*, p. 402.

2 Ball, *Bright Earth*, p. 225.

3 Eckstut and Eckstut, *Secret Language of Color*, p. 223.

4 Gage, *Color and Culture*, p. 16.

5 Ball, *Bright Earth*, p. 255.

6 Finlay, *Color*, p. 403.

7 Gage, *Color and Culture*, p. 25.

8 Ibid.

9 Finlay, *Color*, p. 404.

10 Ball, *Bright Earth*, p. 226.

Archil

[1] E. Bolton, *Lichens for Vegetable Dyeing* (McMinnville, OR: Robin & Russ, 1991), p. 12.

[2] Ibid., p. 9; J. Pereina, *The Elements of Materia, Medica and Therapeutics*, Vol. 2 (Philadelphia, PA: Blanchard & Lea, 1854), p. 74.

[3] Pereina, *Elements of Materia, Medica and Therapeutics*, p. 72.

[4] J. Edmonds, *Medieval Textile Dyeing* (Lulu.com, 2012), p. 39.

[5] Ibid.

[6] And, sometimes, from less far-flung ones: in 1758 production began on an archil-type dye made from a slightly different lichen that had been discovered in Scotland by Dr. Cuthbert Gordon. He called it "cudbear," a corruption of his first name.

[7] Quoted in Edmonds, *Medieval Textile Dyeing*, pp. 40–1.

[8] Bolton, *Lichens for Vegetable Dyeing*, p. 28.

Magenta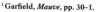

[1] Ball, *Bright Earth*, p. 241.

[2] Garfield, *Mauve*, pp. 79, 81.

[3] Ibid., p. 78.

Mauve

[1] Garfield, *Mauve*, pp. 30–1.

[2] Ibid., p. 32.

[3] Ball, *Bright Earth*, p. 238.

[4] Finlay, *Color*, p. 391.

[5] Garfield, *Mauve*, p. 58.

[6] Quoted ibid., p. 61.

[7] Ball, *Bright Earth*, pp. 240–1.

Heliotrope

[1] N. Groom, *The Perfume Handbook* (Edmunds: Springer-Science, 1992), p. 103.

[2] C. Willet-Cunnington, *English Women's Clothing in the Nineteenth Century* (London: Dover, 1937), p. 314.

[3] Ibid., p. 377.

[4] Of a childhood enemy, she says: "She has just reminded me that we were at school together. I remember it perfectly now. She always got the good conduct prize." Later, saying to the lady herself: "You dislike me, I am quite aware of that, and I have always detested you." And on the vexing issue of higher education for women: "The higher education of men is what I should like to see. Men need it so sadly."

Violet

[1] Quoted in O. Reutersvärd, "The 'Violettomania' of the Impressionists," in *Journal of Aesthetics and Art Criticism*, Vol. 9, No. 2 (Dec. 1950), p. 107.

[2] Quoted ibid., pp. 107–8.

[3] Quoted in Ball, *Bright Earth*, p. 207.

Blue

[1] R. Blau, "The Light Therapeutic," in *Intelligent Life* (May/June 2014).

[2] 2015 National Sleep Foundation poll, see: https://sleepfoundation.org/media-center/press-release/2015-sleep-america-poll; Blau, "Light Therapeutic."

[3] Pastoureau, *Blue*, p. 27.

[4] White clocks in at 32%; red, 28%; black, 14%; gold, 10%; purple, 6%; green, 5%. M. Pastoureau, *Green: The History of a Color*, trans. J. Gladding (Princeton, NJ: Princeton University Press, 2014), p. 39.

[5] M. Pastoureau, *Blue*, p. 50.

[6] Heraldry has its own set of color names, or "tinctures." The basics are or (gold/yellow); argent (silver/white); gules (red); azure (blue); purpure (purple); sable (black); and vert (green).

[7] Pastoureau, *Blue*, p. 60.

[8] Although it is slightly more popular with men, women chose blue more than any other color; *pink* [page 114], incidentally, was no more popular with women than red, purple or green. 2015 YouGov Survey; https://yougov.co.uk /news/2015/05/12/blue-worlds-favourite-color.

Ultramarine

[1] K. Clarke, "Reporters See Wrecked Buddhas," BBC News (Mar. 26, 2001). Available at: http://news.bbc.co.uk/1/hi/world/south _asia/1242856.stm (accessed on Jan. 10, 2016).

[2] Cennini, *Craftsman's Handbook*, Vol. 2, p. 36.

[3] Quoted in Ball, *Bright Earth*, p. 267.

[4] Cennini, *Craftsman's Handbook*, p. 38.

[5] M. C. Gaetani et al., "The Use of Egyptian Blue and Lapis Lazuli in the Middle Ages: The Wall Paintings of the San Saba Church in Rome," in *Studies in Conservation*, Vol. 49, No. 1 (2004), p. 14.

[6] Gage, *Color and Culture*, p. 271.

[7] Ibid., p. 131.

[8] This was particularly the case in southern Europe. In northern Europe, particularly the Netherlands, where ultramarine was scarcer, and where scarlet dye remained the preeminent mark of wealth and distinction, Mary was often clothed in red.

[9] Gage, *Color and Culture*, pp. 129–30.

[10] A similar competition, only with a much smaller prize on offer, had been made by the Royal College of Arts in 1817, with no successful applicants.

[11] Ball, *Bright Earth*, pp. 276–7.

[12] Ibid.

Cobalt

[1] E. Morris, "Bamboozling Ourselves (Part 1)," in *New York Times* (May–June 2009). Available at: http://morris.blogs.nytimes.com/category /bamboozling-ourselves/ (accessed Jan. 1, 2016).

[2] T. Rousseau, "The Stylistic Detection of Forgeries," in *Metropolitan Museum of Art Bulletin*, Vol. 27, No. 6, pp. 277, 252.

[3] Finlay, *Brilliant History of Color in Art*, p. 57.

[4] Ball, *Bright Earth*, p. 178.

[5] Harley, *Artists' Pigments*, pp. 53–4.

[6] Field, *Chromatography*, pp. 110–1.

[7] E. Morris, "Bamboozling Ourselves (Part 3)."

Indigo

[1] Educated guesses as to why plants produce indigo differ. Some suggest it could be a natural insecticide; others have wondered if its bitter taste helps to protect it against the ravages of marauding herbivores.

[2] The pods apparently did not find favor with the early modern herbalist John Parkinson, who described them in 1640 as "hanging downwards, like unto the wormes . . . which we call arseworms, yet somewhat thick and full of black seed." Quoted in J. Balfour-Paul, *Indigo: Egyptian Mummies to Blue Jeans* (London: British Museum Press, 2000), p. 92.

[3] Some cultures traditionally blamed women for indigo crop failures. In ancient Egypt it was believed anyone menstruating near the field might damage it. In one Chinese province, women with flowers in their hair had to stay away from the fermenting-indigo jars. And on Flores Island, Indonesia, if a woman swears while harvesting the plant, it will offend its soul and ruin the dye completely.

[4] Balfour-Paul, *Indigo*, pp. 99, 64.

[5] Because these blocks are so hard, many classical authors, and even some early modern ones, thought it was mineral in origin, possibly a semiprecious stone related to lapis lazuli. Delamare and Guineau, *Color*, p. 95.

[6] Balfour-Paul, *Indigo*, p. 5.

[7] Pastoureau, *Blue*, p. 125.

[8] Balfour-Paul, *Indigo*, pp. 7, 13.

[9] Eckstut and Eckstut, *Secret Language of Color*, p. 187.

10 Balfour-Paul, *Indigo*, p. 23.

11 Ibid., pp. 28, 46.

12 Ibid., pp. 44–5, 63.

13 Delamare and Guineau, *Color*, p. 92.

14 Balfour-Paul, *Indigo*, p. 5.

15 *Jean* is believed to descend from bleu de Gênes, or Genoa blue, a cheap indigo dye popular for sailors' uniforms.

16 Just Style, "Just-Style Global Market Review of Denim and Jeanswear—Forecasts to 2018" (Nov. 2012). Available at www.just-style.com /store/samples/Global%20Market%20for%20 Denim%20and%20Jeanswear%2Single _brochure.pdf (accessed Jan. 3, 2016), p. 1.

Prussian blue

1 Ball, *Bright Earth*, p. 273; Delamare and Guineau, *Color*, p. 76.

2 Ball, *Bright Earth*, pp. 272–3.

3 Field, *Chromatography*, p. 112.

4 Woodwood received a tip-off from a German man called Caspar Neumann, a debtor to the Royal Society who apparently wanted to reingratiate himself. Neumann sent the method, in Latin, to Woodwood in a letter from Leipzig dated 17 November 1723. The revelation ruined Dippel, who fled to Scandinavia where he became the physician to the Swedish King Frederick I before being expelled from the country and spending some time in a Danish gaol. A. Kraft, "On Two Letters from Caspar Neumann to John Woodward Revealing the Secret Method for Preparation of Prussian Blue," in *Bulletin of the History of Chemistry*, Vol. 34, No. 2 (2009), p. 135.

5 Quoted in Ball, *Bright Earth*, p. 275.

6 Finlay, *Color*, pp. 346–7.

7 Eckstut and Eckstut, *Secret Language of Color*, p. 187.

8 Quoted in Ball, *Bright Earth*, p. 274.

Egyptian blue

1 Lucas and Harris, A*ncient Egyptian Materials and Industries*, p. 170.

2 Delamare and Guineau, *Color*, p. 20; Lucas and Harris, *Ancient Egyptian materials and Industries*, p. 188; V. Daniels et al., "The Blackening of Paint Containing Egyptian Blue," in *Studies in Conservation*, Vol. 49, No. 4 (2004), p. 219.

3 Delamare and Guineau, *Color*, p. 20.

4 Daniels et al., "Blackening of Paint Containing Egyptian Blue," p. 217.

5 M. C. Gaetani et al., "Use of Egyptian Blue and Lapis Lazuli in the Middle Ages," p. 13.

6 Ibid., p. 19.

7 Although it now looks as if ultramarine and Egyptian blue were used concurrently longer than was thought: the two pigments have been found mixed together in the murals at one eighth-century church in Rome.

Woad

1 J. Edmonds, *The History of Woad and the Medieval Woad Vat* (Lulu.com, 2006), p. 40.

2 Ibid., p. 13; Delamare and Guineau, *Color*, p. 44.

3 Delamare and Guineau, *Color*, p. 44.

4 Quoted in Balfour-Paul, *Indigo*, p. 30.

5 Pastoureau, *Blue*, p. 63.

6 Ibid., p. 64.

7 Quoted in Balfour-Paul, *Indigo*, p. 34.

8 Pastoureau, *Blue*, p. 125.

9 Quoted in Edmonds, *History of Woad*, pp. 38–9.

10 Pastoureau, *Blue*, p. 130; Balfour-Paul, *Indigo*, p. 56–7.

Electric blue

[1] *New Scientist* interview with Alexander Yuvchenko, "Cheating Chernobyl" (Aug. 21, 2004).

[2] M. Lallanilla, "Chernobyl: Facts About the Nuclear Disaster," in *LiveScience* (Sept. 25, 2013). Available at: www.livescience.com /39961-chernobyl.html (accessed Dec. 30, 2015).

[3] A few hours later, Yuvchenko found himself in the local hospital, paralyzed with radiation sickness, watching as one by one his fellow nuclear plant workers died around him. He is one of the few survivors from the plant.

[4] *New Scientist* interview with Alexander Yuvchenko, "Cheating Chernobyl."

[5] Quoted in Salisbury, *Elephant's Breath and London Smoke*, p. 75.

Cerulean

[1] S. Heller, "Oliver Lincoln Lundquist, Designer, Is Dead at 92," in *New York Times* (Jan. 3, 2009).

[2] Pantone press release, 1999: www.pantone .com/pages/pantone/pantone .aspx?pg=20194&ca=10.

[3] Ball, *Bright Earth*, p. 179. The pigment took its name from the word *caeruleus*, used by later Roman writers to describe the Mediterranean Sea.

[4] Ibid.

[5] Brassaï, *Conversations with Picasso*, trans. J. M. Todd (University of Chicago Press, 1999), p. 117.

Green

[1] Finlay, *Color*, pp. 285–6.

[2] Pastoureau, *Green*, pp. 20–4.

[3] Eckstut and Eckstut, *Secret Language of Color*, pp. 146–7.

[4] Pastoureau, *Green*, p. 65.

[5] Ball, *Bright Earth*, pp. 73–4.

[6] Ibid., pp. 14–5.

[7] Quoted in Pastoureau, *Green*, p. 42.

[8] Quoted ibid., p. 116.

[9] Quoted in Ball, *Bright Earth*, p. 158.

[10] Pastoureau, *Green*, p. 159.

[11] Quoted in ibid., p. 200.

Verdigris

[1] P. Conrad, "Girl in a Green Gown: The History and Mystery of the Arnolfini Portrait by Carola Hicks," in the *Guardian* (Oct. 16, 2011). The portrait has had an eventful history too. It was owned by Philip II of Spain, the sixteenth-century Habsburg monarch. His descendant Carlos III hung it in the royal family's bathroom. It was coveted by Napoleon and, later, Hitler, and spent much of the Second World War with many other National Gallery treasures in a top-secret bunker hidden in the Blaenau Ffestiniog slate quarry in Snowdonia in Wales. (This was just as well: the National Gallery later suffered a direct hit by the Luftwaffe during an air raid.)

[2] C. Hicks, *Girl in a Green Gown: The History and Mystery of the Arnolfini Portrait* (London: Vintage, 2012), pp. 30–2.

[3] Pastoureau, *Green*, pp. 112, 117.

[4] The glowing green mineral malachite is also formed of copper carbonate.

[5] Eckstut and Eckstut, *Secret Language of Color*, p. 152.

[6] Ball, *Bright Earth*, p. 113.

[7] Delamare and Guineau, *Color*, p. 140.

[8] Cennini, *Craftsman's Handbook*, p. 33.

[9] Ball, *Bright Earth*, p. 299.

[10] Quoted in Pastoureau, *Green*, p. 190.

[11] This mixture is often called copper resinate, really an umbrella term for a wide range of mixtures made with verdigris and resins.

Absinthe

[1] K. MacLeod, introduction to M. Corelli, *Wormwood: A Drama of Paris* (New York: Broadview, 2004), p. 44.

[2] P. E. Prestwich, "Temperance in France: The Curious Case of Absinth," in *Historical Reflections*, Vol. 6, No. 2 (Winter 1979), p. 302.

[3] Ibid., pp. 301–2.

[4] "Absinthe," in *The Times* (May 4, 1868).

[5] "Absinthe and Alcohol," in *Pall Mall Gazette* (Mar. 1, 1869).

[6] Prestwich, "Temperance in France," p. 305.

[7] F. Swigonsky, "Why Was Absinthe Banned for 100 Years?," Mic.com (June 22, 2013). Available at: http://mic.com/articles/50301 /why-was-absinthe-banned-for-100-years-a -mystery-as-murky-as-the-liquor-itself #.NXpx3nWbh (accessed Jan. 8, 2016).

Emerald

[1] Avarice—green; envy and jealousy—yellow; pride and lust—red; anger—black; sloth—blue or white. Pastoureau, *Green*, p. 121.

[2] Ibid., pp. 56, 30.

[3] B. Bornell, "The Long, Strange Saga of the 180,000-carat Emerald: The Bahia Emerald's Twist-Filled History," in *Bloomberg Businessweek* (Mar. 6, 2015).

Kelly green

[1] Kelly, a common Irish surname from which the color takes its name, has a much-disputed etymology. Some believe it originally indicated a warrior; others, a religious person.

[2] For the full text see www.confessio.ie.

[3] A. O'Day, *Reactions to Irish Nationalism 1865–1914* (London: Hambledon Press, 1987), p. 5.

[4] Pastoureau, *Green*, pp. 174–5.

[5] O'Day, *Reactions to Irish Nationalism*, p. 3.

Scheele's green

[1] Ball, *Bright Earth*, p. 173.

[2] Ibid.

[3] P. W. J. Bartrip, "How Green Was My Valence? Environmental Arsenic Poisoning and the Victorian Domestic Ideal," in *The English Historical Review*, Vol. 109, No. 433 (Sept. 1994), p. 895.

[4] "The Use of Arsenic as a Color," *The Times* (Sept. 4, 1863).

[5] Bartrip, "How Green Was My Valence?," pp. 896, 902.

[6] G. O. Rees, Letter to *The Times* (June 16, 1877).

[7] Harley, *Artists' Pigments*, pp. 75–6.

[8] Quoted in Pastoureau, *Green*, p. 184.

[9] Bartrip, "How Green Was My Valence?," p. 900.

[10] W. J. Broad, "Hair Analysis Deflates Napoleon Poisoning Theories," in *New York Times* (June 10, 2008).

Terre verte

[1] Eastaugh et al., *Pigment Compendium*, p. 180.

[2] Field, *Chromatography*, p. 129.

[3] Delamare and Guineau, *Color*, pp. 17–8.

[4] Cennini, *Craftsman's Handbook*, p. 67.

[5] Ibid., pp. 93–4.

[6] Ibid., p. 27.

Avocado

[1] K. Connolly, "How U.S. and Europe Differ on Offshore Drilling," BBC (May 18, 2010).

[2] Eiseman and Recker, *Pantone*, pp. 135, 144.

[3] Pastoureau, *Green*, p. 24.

[4] J. Cartner-Morley, "The Avocado Is Overcado: How #Eatclean Turned It into a Cliché," in the *Guardian* (Oct. 5, 2015).

Celadon

[1] L. A. Gregorio, "Silvandre's Symposium: The Platonic and the Ambiguous in L'Astrée," in *Renaissance Quarterly*, Vol. 53, No. 3 (Autumn 1999), p. 783.

[2] Salisbury, *Elephant's Breath and London Smoke*, p. 46.

[3] S. Lee, "Goryeo Celadon." Available at http://www.metmuseum.org/toah/hd/cela/hd_cela.htm (accessed Mar. 20, 2016).

[4] Ibid.

[5] J. Robinson, "Ice and Green Clouds: Traditions of Chinese Celadon," in *Archaeology*, Vol. 40, No. 1 (Jan.–Feb. 1987) pp. 56–8.

[6] Finlay, *Color*, p. 286.

[7] Robinson, "Ice and Green Clouds: Traditions of Chinese Celadon," p. 59; quoted in Finlay, *Color*, p. 271.

[8] Finlay, *Color*, p. 273.

Brown

[1] Genesis 3:19.

[2] Ball, *Bright Earth*, p. 200.

[3] Eastaugh et al., *Pigment Compendium*, p. 55.

[4] M. P. Merrifield, *The Art of Fresco Painting in the Middle Ages and Renaissance* (Mineola, NY: Dover Publications, 2003).

[5] Quoted in "Miracles Square," OpaPisa website. Available at: www.opapisa.it/en/miracles-square/sinopie-museum/the-recovery-of-the-sinopie.html (accessed Oct. 20, 2015).

[6] Ball, *Bright Earth*, p. 152.

[7] Martin Boswell, Imperial War Museum; private correspondence.

Khaki

[1] This was particularly true of their chemical industry, thanks to technical advances in the manufacture of aniline dyes. Britain had become so reliant on German's dye industry that at times during the war Britain found itself almost unable to dye its own uniforms khaki: it was Germany who produced the colorants.

[2] Richard Slocombe, Imperial War Museum; private correspondence.

[3] J. Tynan, *British Army Uniform and the First World War: Men in Khaki* (London: Palgrave Macmillan, 2013), pp. 1–3.

[4] William Hodson, second in command of the Guides, quoted in ibid., p. 2.

[5] Martin Boswell, Imperial War Museum; private correspondence.

[6] J. Tynan, "Why First World War Soldiers Wore Khaki," in *World War I Centenary from the University of Oxford*. Available at: http://ww1centenary.oucs.ox.ac.uk/material/why-first-world-war-soldiers-wore-khaki/(accessed Oct. 11, 2015). In 1914, officers were easily distinguishable from regular soldiers by special clothing, such as long leather boots and, as Paul Fussell puts it in *The Great War and Modern Memory* (Oxford University Press, 2013), "melodramatically cut riding breeches." These made them special targets; they soon donned regular khaki uniforms like all the rest.

[7] A. Woollacott, "'Khaki Fever' and Its Control: Gender, Class, Age and Sexual Morality on the British Homefront in the First World War," in *Journal of Contemporary History*, Vol. 29, No. 2 (Apr. 1994), pp. 325–6.

[8] Marie Lloyd, known as the queen of the music hall, frequently sang the popular "Now You've Got Yer Khaki On" when performing in 1915, the gist of which was that wearing khaki could make a man seem more attractive.

Buff

[1] Salisbury, *Elephant's Breath and London Smoke*, p. 36.

[2] Norris, *Tudor Costume and Fashion*, pp. 559, 652.

3 G. C. Stone, *A Glossary of the Construction, Decoration and Use of Arms and Armor in All Countries and in All Times* (Mineola, NY: Dover Publications, 1999), p. 152.

4 Quoted in E. G. Lengel (ed.), *A Companion to George Washington* (London: Wiley-Blackwell, 2012).

5 Up to this point the colonies had relied on Britain for much of their cloth; uniforms were hard to reliably source for the Americans during the war and there was a constant struggle to keep the men clothed. When, on New Year's Day 1778, HMS *Symmetry* was captured while loaded with supplies including "Scarlett, Blue & Buff Cloth, sufficient to Cloath all the officers of the Army," there was general rejoicing (followed by intense squabbling over where the cloth would end up).

6 J. C. Fitzpatrick (ed.), *The Writings of George Washington from the Original Manuscript Sources, 1745–1799*, Vol. 7 (Washington, DC: Government Printing Office, 1939), pp. 452–3.

7 B. Leaming, *Jack Kennedy: The Education of a Statesman* (New York: W. W. Norton, 2006), p. 360.

Fallow

1 P. F. Baum (trans.), *Anglo-Saxon Riddles of the Exeter Book* (Durham, NC: Duke University Press, 1963), p. v.

2 Riddle 44: "Splendidly it hangs by a man's thigh, / under the master's cloak. In front is a hole. / It is stiff and hard . . ." Answer? A key.

3 J. I. Young, "Riddle 15 of the Exeter Book," in *Review of English Studies*, Vol. 20, No. 80 (Oct. 1944), p. 306.

4 Baum (trans.), *Anglo-Saxon Riddles of the Exeter Book*, p. 26.

5 Maerz and Paul, *Dictionary of Color*, pp. 46–7.

6 J. Clutton-Brock, *A Natural History of Domesticated Mammals* (Cambridge, UK: Cambridge University Press, 1999), pp. 203–4.

7 Baum (trans.), *Anglo-Saxon Riddles of the Exeter Book*, pp. 26–7.

8 Young, "Riddle 15 of the Exeter Book," p. 306.

Russet

1 Maerz and Paul, *Dictionary of Color*, pp. 50–1.

2 Quoted in S. K. Silverman, "The 1363 English Sumptuary Law: A Comparison with Fabric Prices of the Late Fourteenth Century," graduate thesis for Ohio State University (2011), p. 60.

3 R. H. Britnell, *Growth and Decline in Colchester, 1300–1525* (Cambridge, UK: Cambridge University Press, 1986), p. 55.

4 Although *russet* was used in the adjectival sense as a color from the 1400s, it wasn't until the sixteenth century that it became more of a brown than a gray. The Franciscans, an order of priests very active in Europe during the Middle Ages, gained their nickname, the grayfriars, from their habit of wearing russet cloth, and as late as 1611 "light russet" was given as a translation for the French *gris* in Cotgrave's dictionary.

5 G. D. Ramsay, "The Distribution of the Cloth Industry in 1561–1562," in *English Historical Review*, Vol. 57, No. 227 (July 1942), pp. 361–2, 366.

6 Quoted in Britnell, *Growth and Decline in Colchester*, p. 56.

7 S. C. Lomas (ed.), *The Letters and Speeches of Oliver Cromwell, with Elucidations by Thomas Carlyle*, Vol. 1 (New York: G. P. Putnam's Sons, 1904), p. 154.

Sepia

1 R. T. Hanlon and J. B. Messenger, *Cephalopod Behavior* (Cambridge, UK: Cambridge University Press, 1996), p. 25.

2 C. Ainsworth Mitchell, "Inks, from a Lecture Delivered to the Royal Society," in *Journal of the Royal Society of Arts*, Vol. 70, No. 3637 (Aug. 1922), p. 649.

3 Ibid.

4 M. Martial, *Selected Epigrams*, trans. S. McLean (Madison, WI: University of Wisconsin Press, 2014), pp. xv–xvi.

5 Ibid., p. 11.

6 C. C. Pines, "The Story of Ink," in *American Journal of Police Science*, Vol. 2, No. 4 (July/Aug. 1931), p. 292.

7 Field, *Chromatography*, pp. 162–3.

Umber

1 A. Sooke, "Caravaggio's Nativity: Hunting a Stolen Masterpiece," BBC.com (Dec. 23, 2013). Available at: www.bbc.com/culture/story /20131219-hunting-a-stolen-masterpiece (accessed Oct. 13, 2015); J. Jones, "The Masterpiece That May Never Be Seen Again," in the *Guardian* (Dec. 22, 2008). Available at: www.theguardian.com/artanddesign/2008 /dec/22/caravaggio-art-mafia-italy (accessed Oct. 13, 2015).

2 Ball, *Bright Earth*, pp. 151–2.

3 Field, *Chromatography*, p. 143.

4 Finlay, *Brilliant History of Color in Art*, pp. 8–9.

5 Ball, *Bright Earth*, pp. 162–3.

6 Jones, "Masterpiece That May Never Be Seen Again."

7 *Nativity* remains on the FBI's list of unsolved art crimes.

Mummy

1 S. Woodcock, "Body Color: The Misuse of Mummy," in *The Conservator*, Vol. 20, No. 1 (1996), p. 87.

2 Lucas and Harris, *Ancient Egyptian Materials and Industries*, p. 303.

3 Giovanni d'Athanasi recorded the sad fate of the insufficiently distinguished body of the governor of Thebes in his book published in 1836: "An English traveler, had just bought the fellow mummy of the governor of Thebes, but having taken it into his head, while on his road to Cairo, that there might be some gold coins in this mummy, he caused it to be opened, and not finding any thing in it of the nature he sought, he threw it into the Nile . . . Such was the fate of the mortal remains of the governor of Thebes" (p. 51).

4 P. McCouat, "The Life and Death of Mummy Brown," in *Journal of Art in Society* (2013). Available at: www.artinsociety.com /the-life-and-death-of-mummy-brown.html (accessed Oct. 8, 2015).

5 Ibid.

6 Quoted ibid.

7 Woodcock, "Body Color," p. 89.

8 G. M. Languri and J. J. Boon, "Between Myth and Reality: Mummy Pigment from the Hafkenscheid Collection," in *Studies in Conservation*, Vol. 50, No. 3 (2005), p. 162; Woodcock, "Body Color," p. 90.

9 Languri and Boon, "Between Myth and Reality," p. 162.

10 McCouat, "Life and Death of Mummy Brown."

11 R. White, "Brown and Black Organic Glazes, Pigments and Paints," in *National Gallery Technical Bulletin*, Vol. 10 (1986), p. 59; E. G. Stevens (1904), quoted in Woodcock, "Body Color," p. 89.

12 Criticism of the use of mummies in medicine had begun much earlier. In 1658 the philosopher Sir Thomas Browne had called it "dismal vampirism": "The Egyptian mummies, which Cambyses or time hath spared, avarice now consumeth. Mummie is become Merchandise."

13 Diary of Georgiana Burne-Jones, quoted in Woodcock, "Body Color," p. 91.

14 Quoted in McCouat, "Life and Death of Mummy Brown."

15 Quoted in "Techniques: The Passing of Mummy Brown," *Time* (Oct. 2, 1964). Available at: http://content.time.com/time /subscriber/article/0,33009,940544,00.html (accessed Oct. 9, 2015).

Taupe

1 "The British Standard Color Card," in *Journal of the Royal Society of Arts*, Vol. 82, No. 4232 (Dec. 1933), p. 202.

2 The history of organizing and charting color in a systematic way has been a long and frustrating one, beginning with the first color wheel in Newton's *Opticks* (1704) and continuing to the present day. A detailed account can be found in Ball, *Bright Earth*, pp. 40–54.

3 Maerz and Paul, *Dictionary of Color*, p. v.

4 "The British Standard Color Card," p. 201.

5 Maerz and Paul, *Dictionary of Color*, p. 183.

Black

[1] M. Pastoureau, *Black: The History of a Color*, trans. J. Gladding (Princeton, NJ: Princeton University Press, 2009), p. 12.

[2] Quoted in Ball, *Bright Earth*, p. 206.

[3] J. Harvey, *Story of Black*, p. 25.

[4] Quoted in E. Paulicelli, *Writing Fashion in Early Modern Italy: From Sprezzatura to Satire* (Farnham: Ashgate, 2014), p. 78.

[5] Pastoureau, *Black*, pp. 26, 95–6.

[6] Ibid., p. 102.

[7] L. R. Poos, *A Rural Society After the Black Death: Essex 1350–1525* (Cambridge, UK: Cambridge University Press, 1991), p. 21.

[8] Pastoureau, *Black*, p. 135.

[9] Black has remained popular—with most people at least: Oscar Wilde wrote to the *Daily Telegraph* in 1891 to complain of this "black uniform . . . a gloomy, drab, and depressing color."

[10] Quoted in S. Holtham and F. Moran, "Five Ways to Look at Malevich's Black Square," Tate Blog. Available at: www.tate .org.uk/context-comment/articles /five-ways-look-Malevich-Black-Square (accessed Oct. 8, 2015).

Kohl

[1] T. Whittemore, "The Sawâma Cemetries," in *Journal of Egyptian Archaeology*, Vol. 1, No. 4 (Oct. 1914), pp. 246–7.

[2] R. Kreston, "Ophthalmology of the Pharaohs: Antimicrobial Kohl Eyeliner in Ancient Egypt," *Discovery Magazine* (Apr. 2012). Available at: http://blogs.discovermagazine.com /bodyhorrors/2012/04/20/ophthalmology-of -the-pharaohs/ (accessed Sept. 24, 2015).

[3] Ibid.

[4] K. Ravilious, "Cleopatra's Eye Makeup Warded Off Infections?," *National Geographic News* (Jan. 15, 2010). Available at: http://news .nationalgeographic.com/news/2010/01 / 100114- cleopatra-eye-makeup-ancient -egyptians/ (accessed Sept. 24, 2015); Kreston, "Ophthalmology of the Pharaohs."

Payne's gray

[1] Quoted in A. Banerji, *Writing History in the Soviet Union: Making the Past Work* (New Delhi: Esha Béteille, 2008), p. 161.

[2] B. S. Long, "William Payne: Water-Color Painter Working 1776–1830," in *Walker's Quarterly*, No. 6 (Jan. 1922). Available at: https://archive.org/stream/williampaynewate 00longuoft, pp. 3–13.

[3] Quoted in ibid., pp. 6–8.

Obsidian

[1] British Museum, "Dr. Dee's Mirror," www.britishmuseum.org/explore/highlights /highlight_objects/pe_mla/d/dr_dees_mirror .aspx (accessed 6 Oct. 2015).

[2] J. Harvey, *The Story of Black* (London: Reaktion Books, 2013), p. 19.

[3] British Museum, "Dr. Dee's Mirror."

[4] C. H. Josten, "An Unknown Chapter in the Life of John Dee," in *Journal of the Warburg and Courtauld Institutes*, Vol. 28 (1965), p. 249. Dee missed some that had been concealed in a secret drawer. When these were discovered after his death a kitchen maid began using them to line her pie dishes. Miraculously enough, some of the papers did survive the flames and pie crusts, including Dee's pitiable account of this destruction—he calls it a holocaust. A full transcript of this section can be found in ibid., pp. 223–57.

[5] Pastoureau, *Black*, pp. 137–9.

[6] J. A. Darling, "Mass Inhumation and the Execution of Witches in the American Southwest," in *American Anthropologist*, Vol. 100, No. 3 (Sept. 1998), p. 738; See also S. F. Hodgson, "Obsidian, Sacred Glass from the California Sky," in Piccardi and Masse (eds.), *Myth and Geology*, pp. 295–314.

[7] R. Gulley, *The Encyclopedia of Demons and Demonology* (New York: Visionary Living, 2009), p. 122; British Museum, "Dr. Dee's Mirror."

Ink

[1] Translation from UCL online; see: ucl.ac.uk /museums-static/digitalegypt/literature /ptahhotep.html.

[2] Delamare and Guineau, *Color*, pp. 24–5.

[3] Ibid., p. 25.

[4] C. C Pines, "The Story of Ink," in *The American Journal of Police Science*, Vol. 2, No. 4 (July/Aug. 1931), p. 291.

[5] Finlay, *Color*, p. 99.

[6] Pastoureau, *Black*, p. 117.

[7] Rijksdienst voor het Cultureel Erfgoed, The Iron Gall Ink Website. Available at: http:// irongallink.org/igi_indexc752.html (accessed Sept. 29, 2015), p. 102.

[8] Delamare and Guineau, *Color*, p. 141.

[9] Finlay, *Color*, p. 102.

[10] Bucklow, *Alchemy of Paint*, pp. 40–1.

Charcoal

[1] P. G. Bahn and J. Vertut, *Journey Through the Ice Age* (Berkley, CA: University of California Press, 1997), p. 22.

[2] M. Rose, "'Look, Daddy, Oxen!': The Cave Art of Altamira," in *Archaeology*, Vol. 53, No. 3 (May/June 2000), pp. 68–9.

[3] H. Honour and J. Flemming, *A World History of Art* (London: Laurence King, 2005), p. 27; Bahn and Vertut, *Journey Through the Ice Age*, p. 17.

[4] Honour and Flemming, *A World History of Art*, pp. 27–8.

[5] A. Bhatia, "Why Moths Lost Their Spots, and Cats Don't Like Milk: Tales of Evolution in Our Time," in *Wired* (May 2011).

Jet

[1] A. L. Luthi, *Sentimental Jewelery: Antique Jewels of Love and Sorrow* (Gosport: Ashford Colour Press, 2007), p. 19.

[2] J. Munby, "A Figure of Jet from Westmorland," in *Britannia*, Vol . 6 (1975), p. 217.

[3] Luthi, *Sentimental Jewelery*, p. 17.

[4] L. Taylor, *Mourning Dress: A Costume and Social History* (London: Routledge Revivals, 2010), p. 129.

[5] Quoted ibid., p. 130.

[6] Ibid., p. 129.

Melanin

[1] It has been estimated that incidences of skin cancer among white people double for every 10-degree decrease in latitude.

[2] R. Kittles, "Nature, Origin, and Variation of Human Pigmentation," in *Journal of Black Studies*, Vol. 26, No. 1 (Sept. 1995), p. 40.

[3] Harvey, *Story of Black*, pp. 20–1.

[4] Pastoureau, *Black*, pp. 37–8.

[5] Quoted in Knowles (ed.), *The Oxford Dictionary of Quotations*, p. 417.

[6] Quoted in Harvey, *Story of Black*, p. 23.

[7] Quoted in M. Gilbert, *Churchill: A Life* (London: Pimlico, 2000), p. 230.

Pitch black

[1] Ancient Greeks referred to the "black Nyx," and she could also be described as "black-winged" or "sable-vestured." Over a millennium later, Shakespeare drew on startlingly similar imagery: he called it "sable Night" and referred to its "black mantle."

[2] Pastoureau, *Black*, pp. 21, 36.

[3] Harvey, *Story of Black*, pp. 29, 32. Defying her frightening appearance, if Kali's devotees feel she has failed them, they can visit her temples in order to fling, in place of garlands and incense, curses and shit.

[4] Quoted ibid., p. 41.

[5] Pastoureau, *Black*, p. 28.

[6] Quoted in Harvey, *Story of Black*, p. 29.

Bibliography and suggested further reading

Those interested in learning more about the science of color and the heady rush of the aniline revolution should read Philip Ball's *Bright Earth* and Simon Garfield's *Mauve*. For those who want to be taken to find extraordinary colors across the world in eloquent companys look no further than *Color* by Victoria Finlay. And those with a particular interest in the dark side could do no better than reading Michel Pastoureau's illuminating monograph *Black*—my favorite of his single-color books—and John Harvey's *The Story of Black*.

A

Ainsworth, C. M., "Inks, from a Lecture Delivered to the Royal Society," in *Journal of the Royal Society of Arts*, Vol. 70, No. 3637 (Aug. 1922), pp. 647–60.

Albers, J., *Interaction of Color*. 50th Anniversary Edition (New Haven, CT: Yale University Press, 1963).

Alexander, H., "Michelle Obama: The 'Nude' Debate," in the *Telegraph* (May 19, 2010).

Allaby, M., *Plants: Food Medicine and Green Earth* (New York: Facts on File, 2010).

Allen, N., "Judge to Decide who Owns £250 Million Bahia Emerald," in the *Telegraph* (Sept. 24, 2010).

Aristotle, *Complete Works* (New York: Delphi Classics, 2013).

Alter, A. L., *Drunk Tank Pink, and Other Unexpected Forces That Shape How We Think, Feel and Behave* (London: Oneworld, 2013).

B

Bahn, P. G., and J. Vertut, *Journey Through the Ice Age* (Berkeley, CA: University of California Press, 1997).

Balfour-Paul, J., *Deeper Than Indigo: Tracing Thomas Machell, Forgotten Explorer* (Surbiton: Medina, 2015).

Balfour-Paul, J., *Indigo: Egyptian Mummies to Blue Jeans* (London: British Museum Press, 2000).

Ball, P., *Bright Earth: The Invention of Color* (London: Vintage, 2008).

Banerji, A., *Writing History in the Soviet Union: Making the Past Work* (New Delhi: Esha Béteille, 2008).

Bartrip, P. W. J., "How Green Was My Valence? Environmental Arsenic Poisoning and the Victorian Domestic Ideal," in *The English Historical Review*, Vol. 109, No. 433 (Sept.1994).

Barzini, L., *Pekin to Paris: An Account of Prince Borghese's Journey Across Two Continents in a Motor-Car*. Trans. L. P. de Castelvecchio (London: E. Grant Richards, 1907).

Batchelor, D., *Chromophobia* (London: Reaktion Books, 2000).

Baum, P. F. (trans.), *Anglo-Saxon Riddles of the Exeter Book* (Durham, NC: Duke University Press, 1963).

Beck, C. W., "Amber in Archaeology," in *Archaeology*, Vol. 23, No. 1 (Jan. 1970), pp. 7–11.

Bemis, E., *The Dyers Companion*. Reprinted from 2nd edition (Mineola, NY: Dover Publications,1973).

Berger, K., "Ingenious: Mazviita Chirimuuta," in *Nautilus* (July 2005).

Bessborough, Earl of (ed.), *Georgiana: Extracts from the Correspondence of Georgiana, Duchess of Devonshire* (London: John Murray, 1955).

Bhatia, A., "Why Moths Lost their Spots, and Cats Don't Like Milk: Tales of Evolution in Our Time," in *Wired* (May 2011).

Billinge, R., and L. Campbell, "The Infra-Red Reflectograms of Jan van Eyck's Portrait of Giovanni(?) Arnolfini and His Wife Giovanna Cenami(?)," in *National Gallery Technical Bulletin*, Vol. 16 (1995), pp. 47–60.

Blau, R., "The Light Therapeutic," in *Intelligent Life* (May/June 2014), pp. 62–71.

Blumberg, J., "A Brief History of the Amber Room," Smithsonian.com (July 31, 2007).

Bolton, E., *Lichens for Vegetable Dyeing* (McMinnville, OR: Robin & Russ, 1991).

Bornell, B., "The Long, Strange Saga of the 180,000-Carat Emerald: The Bahia Emerald's Twist-Filled History," in *Bloomberg Businessweek* (Mar. 6, 2015).

Brachfeld, A., and M. Choate, *Eat Your Food! Gastronomical Glory from Garden to Glut.* (Colorado: Coastalfields, 2007).

Brassaï, *Conversations with Picasso.* Trans. J. M. Todd (Chicago: University of Chicago Press, 1999).

British Museum, "Dr. Dee's Mirror."

Britnell, R. H., *Growth and Decline in Colchester, 1300–1525* (Cambridge, UK: Cambridge University Press, 1986).

Broad, W. J., "Hair Analysis Deflates Napoleon Poisoning Theories," in *New York Times* (June 10, 2008).

Brody, J. E., "Ancient, Forgotten Plant Now 'Grain of the Future,'" in *New York Times* (Oct. 16, 1984).

Brunwald, G., "Laughter Was Life," in *New York Times* (Oct. 2, 1966).

Bucklow, S., *The Alchemy of Paint: Art, Science and Secrets from the Middle Ages* (London: Marion Boyars, 2012).

Burdett, C., "Aestheticism and Decadence," https://www.bk.uk/romantics-and-victorians/articles/aestheticism-and-decadence.

Bureau of Indian Standards, "Flag Code of India."

Burrows, E. G., and M. Wallace, *Gotham: A History of New York City to 1898* (Oxford, UK: Oxford University Press, 1999).

C

Carl, K. A., "A Personal Estimate of the Character of the Late Empress Dowager, Tze-'is," in *Journal of Race Development*, Vol. 4, No. 1 (July 1913), pp. 58–71.

Carl, K. A., *With the Empress Dowager of China* (New York: Routledge, 1905).

Cartner-Morley, J., "The Avocado Is Overcado: How #Eatclean Turned It into a Cliché," in the *Guardian* (Oct. 5, 2015).

Carus-Wilson, E. M., "The English Cloth Industry in the Late Twelfth and Early Thirteenth Centuries," in *Economic History Review*, Vol. 14, No. 1 (1944), pp. 32–50.

Cassidy, T., *Environmental Psychology: Behavior and Experience in Context* (Hove: Routledge Psychology Press, 1997).

Cennini, C., *The Craftsman's Handbook*, Vol. 2. Trans. D. V. Thompson (Mineola, NY: Dover Publications, 1954).

Chaker, A. M., "Breaking Out of Guacamole to Become a Produce Star," in *Wall Street Journal* (Sept. 18, 2012).

Chang, J., *Empress Dowager Cixi: The Concubine Who Launched Modern China* (London: Vintage, 2013).

Chirimutta, M., *Outside Color: Perceptual Science and the Puzzle of Color in Philosophy.* (Cambridge, MA: MIT Press, 2015).

Choi, C. Q., "230-Million-Year-Old Mite Found in Amber," in *LiveScience* (Aug. 27, 2012).

Clarke, K., "Reporters See Wrecked Buddhas," BBC News (Mar. 26, 2001).

Clarke, M., "Anglo Saxon Manuscript Pigments," in *Studies in Conservation*, Vol. 49, No. 4 (2004), pp. 231–44.

Clutton-Brock, J., *A Natural History of Domesticated Mammals* (Cambridge, UK: Cambridge University Press, 1999).

Collings, M. R., *Gemlore: An Introduction to Precious and Semi-Precious Stones*, 2nd edition (Rockville, MD: Borgo Press, 2009).

Colliss Harvey, J., *Red: A Natural History of the Redhead* (London: Allen & Unwin, 2015).

Connolly, K., "How U.S. and Europe Differ on Offshore Drilling," BBC News (May 18, 2010).

Conrad, P., "Girl in a Green Gown: The History and Mystery of the Arnolfini Portrait by Carola Hicks," in the *Guardian* (Oct. 16, 2011).

Copping, J., "Beijing to Paris Motor Race Back on Course," in the *Daily Telegraph* (May 27, 2007).

Corelli, M., *Wormwood: A Drama of Paris* (New York: Broadview, 2004).

Cowper, M. (ed.), *The Words of War: British Forces' Personal Letters and Diaries During the Second World War* (London: Mainstream Publishing, 2009).

Cumming, R., *Art Explained: The World's Greatest Paintings Explored and Explained* (London: Dorling Kindersley, 2007).

D

Daniels, V., R. Stacey, and A. Middleton,
"The Blackening of Paint Containing Egyptian
Blue," in *Studies in Conservation*, Vol. 49, No. 4
(2004), pp. 217–30.

Darling, J. A., "Mass Inhumation and the
Execution of Witches in the American
Southwest," in *American Anthropologist*,
Vol. 100, No. 3 (Sept. 1998), pp. 732–52.

D'Athanasi, G., *A Brief Account of the
Researches and Discoveries in Upper Egypt,
Made Under the Direction of Henry Salt, Esq.*
(London: John Hearne, 1836).

Delamare, F., and B. Guineau, *Color: Making
and Using Dyes and Pigments* (London: Thames
& Hudson, 2000).

Delistraty, C. C., "Seeing Red," in *The Atlantic*
(Dec. 5, 2014).

Derksen, G. C. H., and T. A.Van Beek,
"Rubia Tinctorum L.," in *Studies in Natural
Products Chemistry*, Vol. 26 (2002),
pp. 629–84.

Deutscher, G., *Through the Language Glass:
Why the World Looks Different in Other
Languages* (London: Arrow, 2010).

Doll, J., "The Evolution of the Emoticon,"
in *The Wire* (Sept. 19, 2012).

Doran, S., *The Culture of Yellow, or: The Visual
Politics of Late Modernity* (New York:
Bloomsbury, 2013).

Dusenbury, M. (ed.), *Color in Ancient and
Medieval East Asia* (New Haven, CT:
Yale University Press, 2015).

E

Eastaugh, N., V. Walsh, T. Chaplin, and
R. Siddall, *Pigment Compendium: A Dictionary
and Optical Microscopy of Historical Pigments*
(Oxford: Butterworth-Heinemann, 2008).

Eckstut, J., and A. Eckstut, *The Secret Language
of Color* (New York: Black Dog & Leventhal,
2013).

The Economist, "Bones of Contention"
(Aug. 29, 2015).

The Economist, "The Case Against Tipping"
(Oct. 26, 2015).

The Economist, "Going Down" (Aug. 11, 2014).

The Economist, "Why do Indians Love Gold?"
(Nov. 20, 2013).

Edmonds, J., *The History of Woad and the
Medieval Woad Vat* (Lulu.com, 2006).

Edmonds, J., *Medieval Textile Dyeing*
(Lulu.com, 2012).

Edmonds, J., *Tyrian or Imperial Purple Dye*
(Lulu.com, 2002).

Eiseman, L., and E. P. Cutler, *Pantone on
Fashion: A Century of Color in Design*
(San Francisco, CA: Chronicle Books, 2014).

Eiseman, L., and K. Recker, *Pantone: The 20th
Century in Color* (San Francisco, CA:
Chronicle Books, 2011).

Eldridge, L., *Face Paint: The Story of Makeup*
(New York: Abrams Image, 2015).

Elliot, A. J., and M. A. Maier, "Color and
Psychological Functioning," in *Journal of
Experimental Psychology*, Vol. 136, No. 1
(2007), pp. 250–4.

F

Field, G., *Chromatography: Or a Treatise on
Colors and Pigments and of Their Powers in
Painting, &c.* (London: Forgotten Books, 2012).

Finlay, V., *The Brilliant History of Color in Art*
(Los Angeles, CA: Getty Publications, 2014).

Finlay, V., *Color: Travels Through the Paintbox*
(London: Sceptre, 2002).

Fitzpatrick, J. C. (ed.), *The Writings of George
Washington from the Original Manuscript
Sources, 1745–1799*, Vol. 7 (Washington, DC:
Government Printing Office, 1939).

Follett, T., "Amber in Goldworking," in *Archaeology*,
Vol. 38 No. 2 (Mar./Apr. 1985), pp. 64–5.

Franklin, R., "A Life in Good Taste: The Fashions
and Follies of Elsie de Wolfe," in *The New Yorker*
(Sept. 27, 2004), p. 142.

Fraser, A., *Marie Antoinette: The Journey*
(London: Phoenix, 2001).

Friedman, J., *Paint and Color in Decoration*
(London: Cassell Illustrated, 2003).

Friedland, S. R. (ed.), *Vegetables: Proceedings of
the Oxford Symposium on Food and Cooking 2008*
(Totnes: Prospect, 2009).

Fussell, P., *The Great War and Modern Memory*
(Oxford, UK: Oxford University Press, 2013).

G

Gaetani, M. C., U. Santamaria, and C. Seccaroni,
"The Use of Egyptian Blue and Lapis Lazuli
in the Middle Ages: The Wall Paintings of the
San Saba Church in Rome," in *Studies in
Conservation*, Vol. 49, No. 1 (2004), pp. 13–22.

Gage, J., *Color and Culture: Practice and
Meaning from Antiquity to Abstraction*
(London: Thames & Hudson, 1995).

Gage, J., *Color and Meaning: Art, Science and
Symbolism* (London: Thames & Hudson, 2000).

Gage, J., *Color in Art* (London: Thames &
Hudson, 2006).

Gannon, M., "100-Million-Year-Old Spider Attack Found in Amber," in *LiveScience* (Oct. 8, 2012).

Garfield, S., *Mauve: How One Man Invented a Color that Changed the World* (London: Faber & Faber, 2000).

Gettens, R. J., R. L. Feller, and W. T. Chase, "Vermilion and Cinnabar," in *Studies in Conservation*, Vol. 17, No. 2 (May 1972), pp. 45–60.

Gettens, R. J., E. West Fitzhugh, and R. L. Feller, "Calcium Carbonate Whites," in *Studies in Conservation*, Vol. 19, No. 3 (Aug. 1974), pp. 157–84.

Gilbert, M., *Churchill: A Life* (London: Pimlico, 2000).

Gilliam, J. E., and D. Unruh, "The Effects of Baker-Miller Pink on Biological, Physical and Cognitive Behavior," in *Journal of Orthomolecular Medicine*, Vol. 3, No. 4 (1988), pp. 202–6.

Glazebrook, K., and I. Baldry, "The Cosmic Spectrum and the Color of the Universe," www.astro.ljmu.ac.uk/~ikb/Cosmic-Spectrum .html.

Goethe, J. W., *Theory of Colors*. Trans. C. L. Eastlake (London: John Murray, 1840).

Gootenberg, P., *Andean Cocaine: The Making of a Global Drug* (Chapel Hill, NC: University of North Carolina Press, 2008).

Gorton, T., "Vantablack Might Not Be the World's Blackest Material," in *Dazed* (Oct. 27, 2014).

Goswamy, B. N., "The Color Yellow," in *Tribune India* (Sept. 7, 2014).

Goswamy, B. N., *The Spirit of Indian Painting: Close Encounters with 101 Great Works 1100–1900* (London: Allen Lane, 2014).

Govan, F., "Spanish Saffron Scandal as Industry Accused of Importing Cheaper Foreign Varieties," in the *Telegraph* (Jan. 31, 2011).

Greenbaum, H., and D. Rubinstein, "The Hand-Held Highlighter," in *New York Times Magazine* (Jan. 20, 2012).

Greenfield, A. B., *A Perfect Red: Empire, Espionage and the Quest for the Color of Desire* (London: Black Swan, 2006).

Greenwood, K., *100 Years of Color: Beautiful Images and Inspirational Palettes from a Century of Innovative Art, Illustration and Design* (London: Octopus, 2015).

Groom, N., *The Perfume Handbook* (London: Springer-Science, 1992).

Guéguen, N., and C. Jacob, "Clothing Color and Tipping: Gentlemen Patrons Give More Tips to Waitresses with Red Clothes," in *Journal of Hospitality & Tourism Research*, quoted by Sage Publications/*Science Daily* (Aug. 2012).

Guillim, J., *A Display of Heraldrie: Manifesting a More Easie Access to the Knowledge Therof Then Hath Hitherto been Published by Any, Through the Benefit of Method*. 4th edition. (London: T. R., 1660).

Gulley, R., *The Encyclopedia of Demons and Demonology* (New York: Visionary Living, 2009).

Gunther, M., "Van Gogh's Sunflowers May Be Wilting in the Sun," in *Chemistry World* (Oct. 28, 2015).

H

Hanlon, R. T., and J. B. Messenger, *Cephalopod Behavior* (Cambridge University Press, 1996).

Harkness, D. E., *John Dee's Conversations with Angels: Cabala, Alchemy, and the End of Nature* (Cambridge University Press, 1999).

Harley, R. D., *Artists' Pigments c. 1600–1835* (London: Butterworths, 1970).

Harvard University Library Open Collections Program, "California Gold Rush."

Harvey, J., *The Story of Black* (London: Reaktion Books, 2013).

Heather, P. J., "Color Symbolism: Part I," in *Folklore*, Vol. 59, No. 4 (Dec. 1948), pp. 165–83.

Heather, P. J., "Color Symbolism: Part IV," in *Folklore*, Vol. 60, No. 3 (Sept. 1949), pp. 316–31.

Heller, S., "Oliver Lincoln Lundquist, Designer, Is Dead at 92," in *New York Times* (Jan. 3, 2009).

Herbert, Reverend W., *A History of the Species of Crocus* (London: William Clower & Sons, 1847).

Hicks, C., *Girl in a Green Gown: The History and Mystery of the Arnolfini Portrait* (London: Vintage, 2012).

Hodgson, S. F., "Obsidian, Sacred Glass from the California Sky," in L. Piccardi and W. B. Masse (eds.), *Myth and Geology* (London: Geographical Society, 2007), pp. 295–314.

Hoeppe, G., *Why the Sky Is Blue: Discovering the Color of Life*. Trans. J. Stewart (Princeton, NJ: Princeton University Press, 2007).

Holtham, S., and F. Moran, "Five Ways to Look at Malevich's Black Square," www.tate.org.uk /context-comment/articles/five-ways-look -Malevich-Black-Square.

Honour, H., and J. Flemming, *A World History of Art* (London: Laurence King, 2005).

Hooker, W. J. (ed.), *Companion to the Botanical Magazine*, Vol. 2 (London: Samuel Curtis, 1836).

Humphries, C., "Have We Hit Peak Whiteness?," in *Nautilus* (July 2015).

I

Iron Gall Ink, irongallink.org.

J

Jackson, H., "Color Determination in the Fashion Trades," in *Journal of the Royal Society of the Arts*, Vol. 78, No. 4034 (Mar. 1930), pp. 492–513.

Johnson, K., "Medieval Foes with Whimsy," in *New York Times* (Nov. 17, 2011), p. 23.

Jones, J., "The Masterpiece That May Never Be Seen Again," in the *Guardian* (Dec. 22, 2008).

Josten, C. H., "An Unknown Chapter in the Life of John Dee," in *Journal of the Warburg and Courtauld Institutes*, Vol. 28 (1965), pp. 223–57.

Journal of the Royal Society of Arts, "The British Standard Color Card," Vol. 82, No. 4232 (Dec. 1933), pp. 200–2.

Just Style, "Just-Style Global Market Review of Denim and Jeanswear—Forecasts to 2018" (Nov. 2012).

K

Kahney, L., *Jony Ive: The Genius Behind Apple's Greatest Products* (London: Penguin, 2013).

Kapoor, A., Interview with *Artforum* (April 3, 2015).

Kiple, K. F., and K. C. Ornelas (eds.), *The Cambridge World History of Food*, Vol. 1 (Cambridge University Press, 2000).

Kipling, R., *Something of Myself and Other Autobiographical Writings*. Ed. T. Pinney (Cambridge University Press, 1991).

Kittles, R., "Nature, Origin, and Variation of Human Pigmentation," in *Journal of Black Studies*, Vol. 26, No. 1 (Sept. 1995), pp. 36–61.

Klinkhammer, B., "After Purism: Le Corbusier and Color," in *Preservation Education & Research*, Vol. 4 (2011), pp. 19–38.

Konstantinos, *Werewolves: The Occult Truth* (Woodbury: Llewellyn Worldwide, 2010).

Kowalski, M. J., "When Gold Isn't Worth the Price," in *New York Times* (Nov. 6, 2015), p. 23.

Kraft, A., "On Two Letters from Caspar Neumann to John Woodward Revealing the Secret Method for Preparation of Prussian Blue," in *Bulletin of the History of Chemistry*, Vol. 34, No. 2 (2009), pp. 134–40.

Kreston, R., "Ophthalmology of the Pharaohs: Antimicrobial Kohl Eyeliner in Ancient Egypt," *Discovery Magazine* (Apr. 2012).

Kühn, H., "Lead-Tin Yellow," in *Studies in Conservation*, Vol. 13, No. 1 (Feb. 1968), pp. 7–33.

L

Lallanilla, M., "Chernobyl: Facts About the Nuclear Disaster," in *LiveScience* (Sept. 25, 2013).

Languri, G. M., and J. J. Boon, "Between Myth and Reality: Mummy Pigment from the Hafkenscheid Collection," in *Studies in Conservation*, Vol. 50, No. 3 (2005), pp. 161–78.

Larson, E., "The History of the Ivory Trade," in *National Geographic* (Feb. 25, 2013).

Leaming, B., *Jack Kennedy: The Education of a Statesman* (New York: W. W. Norton, 2006).

Le Corbusier and A. Ozenfant, "Purism," in R. L. Herbert (ed.), *Modern Artists on Art* (Mineola, NY: Dover Publications, 2000) pp. 63-4.

Lee, R. L., "Cochineal Production and Trade in New Spain to 1600," in *The Americas*, Vol. 4, No. 4 (Apr. 1948), pp. 449–73.

Le Gallienne, R., "The Boom in Yellow," in *Prose Fancies* (London: John Lane, 1896).

Lengel, E. G. (ed.), *A Companion to George Washington* (London: Wiley-Blackwell, 2012).

Lightweaver, C. (ed.), *Historical Painting Techniques, Materials, and Studio Practice* (New York: Getty Conservation Institute, 1995).

Litzenberger, C., *The English Reformation and the Laity: Gloucestershire, 1540–1589* (Cambridge University Press, 1997).

Loeb McClain, D., "Reopening History of Storied Norse Chessmen," in *New York Times* (Sept. 8, 2010), p.2.

Lomas, S. C. (ed.), *The Letters and Speeches of Oliver Cromwell, with Elucidations by Thomas Carlyle*, Vol. 1 (New York: G. P. Putnam's Sons, 1904).

Lomazzo, G., *A Tracte Containing the Artes of Curious Paintinge, Caruinge & Buildinge*. Trans. R. Haydock (Oxford, 1598).

Long, B. S., "William Payne: Water-Color Painter Working 1776–1830," in *Walker's Quarterly*, No. 6 (Jan. 1922), pp. 3–39.

Loos, A., *Gentlemen Prefer Blondes: The Illuminating Diary of a Professional Lady* (New York: Liveright, 1998).

Lucas, A., and J. R. Harris, *Ancient Egyptian Materials and Industries*, 4th edition (Mineola, NY: Dover Publications, 1999).

Luthi, A. L., *Sentimental Jewelery: Antique Jewels of Love and Sorrow* (Gosport: Ashford Color Press, 2007).

M

Madeley, G., "So Is Kate Expecting a Ginger Heir?," *Daily Mail* (Dec. 20, 2012).

Maerz, A., and M. R. Paul, *A Dictionary of Color* (New York: McGraw-Hill, 1930).

Maglaty, J., "When Did Girls Start Wearing Pink?," Smithsonian.com (Apr. 7, 2011).

Martial, M., *Selected Epigrams*. Trans. S. McLean (Madison, WI: University of Wisconsin Press, 2014).

Mathews, T. F., and A. Taylor, *The Armenian Gospels of Gladzor: The Life of Christ Illuminated* (Los Angeles, CA: Getty Publications, 2001).

McCouat, P., "The Life and Death of Mummy Brown," in *Journal of Art in Society* (2013), www.artinsociety.com.

McKeich, C., "Botanical Fortunes: T. N. Mukharji, International Exhibitions, and Trade Between India and Australia," in *Journal of the National Museum of Australia*, Vol. 3, No. 1 (Mar. 2008), pp. 1–12.

McKie, R., and V. Thorpe, "Top Security Protects Vault of Priceless Gems," in the *Guardian* (Nov. 11, 2007).

McNeill, F. M., *The Silver Bough: Volume One, Scottish Folk-Lore and Folk-Belief*, 2nd edition (Edinburgh: Canongate Classics, 2001).

McWhorter, J., *The Language Hoax: Why the World Looks the Same in Any Language* (Oxford University Press, 2014).

Menkes, S., "Celebrating Elsa Schiaparelli," in *New York Times* (Nov. 18, 2013), p. 12.

Merrifield, M. P., *The Art of Fresco Painting in the Middle Ages and Renaissance* (Mineola, NY: Dover Publications, 2003).

"Minutes of Evidence Taken Before the Metropolitan Sanitary Commissioners," in *Parliamentary Papers, House of Commons*, Vol. 32 (London: William Clowes & Sons, 1848).

"Miracles Square," www.opapisa.it/en/square-of-miracles.

Mitchell, L., *The Whig World: 1760–1837* (London: Hambledon Continuum, 2007).

Morris, E., "Bamboozling Ourselves (Parts 1–7)," in *New York Times* (May–June 2009).

Mukharji, T. N., "Piuri or Indian Yellow," in *Journal of the Society for Arts*, Vol. 32, No. 1618 (Nov. 1883), pp. 16–7.

Munby, J., "A Figure of Jet from Westmorland," in *Encyclopaedia Britannia*, Vol . 6 (1975), pp. 216–8.

N

Nabokov, N., *Speak, Memory* (London: Penguin Classics, 1998).

Nakashima, T., K. Matsuno, M. Matsushita, and T. Matsushita, "Severe Lead Contamination Among Children of Samurai Families in Edo Period Japan," in *Journal of Archaeological Science*, Vol. 32, Issue 1 (2011), pp. 23–8.

Nagy, G., *The Ancient Greek Hero in 24 Hours* (Cambridge, MA: Belknap, 2013).

Neimeyer, C. P., *The Revolutionary War* (Westport, CN: Greenwood Press, 2007).

New York Times, "Baby's First Wardrobe," (Jan. 24, 1897).

New York Times, "Finery for Infants," (July 23, 1893), p. 11.

New York Times, "The Pink Tax," (Nov. 14, 2014).

Newton, I., "A Letter to the Royal Society Presenting a New Theory of Light and Colors," in *Philosophical Transactions*, No. 7 (Jan. 1672), pp. 3075–3087.

Niles, G., "Origin of Plant Names," in *The Plant World*, Vol. 5, No. 8 (Aug. 1902), pp. 141–4.

Norris, H., *Tudor Costume and Fashion*. Reprinted edition (Mineola, NY: Dover Publications, 1997).

O

O'Day, A., *Reactions to Irish Nationalism 1865–1914* (London: Hambledon Press, 1987).

Olson, K., "Cosmetics in Roman Antiquity: Substance, Remedy, Poison," in *The Classical World*, Vol. 102, No. 3 (Spring 2009), pp. 291–310.

Oosthuizen, W. C., and P. J. N. de Bruyn, "Isabelline King Penguin Aptenodytes Patagonicus at Marion Island," in *Marine Ornithology*, Vol. 37, Issue 3 (2010), pp. 275–6.

Owens, M., "Jewelry That Gleams with Wicked Memories," in *New York Times* (Apr. 13, 1997), Arts & Leisure p. 41.

P

Pall Mall Gazette, "Absinthe and Alcohol," (Mar. 1, 1869).

Pastoureau, M., *Black: The History of a Color*. Trans. J. Gladding (Princeton, NJ: Princeton University Press, 2009).

Pastoureau, M., *Blue: The History of a Color*. Trans. M. I. Cruse (Princeton University Press, 2000).

Pastoureau, M., *Green: The History of a Color*. Trans. J. Gladding (Princeton University Press, 2014).

Paterson, I., *A Dictionary of Color: A Lexicon of the Language of Color* (London: Thorogood, 2004).

Paulicelli, E., *Writing Fashion in Early Modern Italy: From Sprezzatura to Satire* (Farnham: Ashgate, 2014).

R

Peplow, M., "The Reinvention of Black," in *Nautilus* (Aug. 2015).

Pepys, S., *Samuel Pepys' Diary*, www.pepysdiary .com.

Pereina, J., *The Elements of Materia, Medica and Therapeutics*, Vol. 2 (Philadelphia, PA: Blanchard & Lea, 1854).

Perkin, W. H., "The History of Alizarin and Allied Coloring Matters, and Their Production from Coal Tar, from a Lecture Delivered May 8th," in *Journal for the Society for Arts*, Vol. 27, No. 1384 (May 1879), pp. 572–608.

Persaud, R., and A. Furnham, "Hair Color and Attraction: Is the Latest Psychological Research Bad News for Redheads?," *Huffington Post* (Sept. 25, 2012).

Phillips, S. V., *The Seductive Power of Home Staging: A Seven-Step System for a Fast and Profitable Sale* (Indianapolis, IN: Dog Ear Publishing, 2009).

Phipps, E., "Cochineal Red: The Art History of a Color," in *Metropolitan Museum of Art Bulletin*, Vol. 67, No. 3 (Winter 2010), pp. 4–48.

Photos-Jones, E., A Cottier, A. J. Hall, and L. G. Mendoni, "Kean Miltos: The Well-Known Iron Oxides of Antiquity," in *Annual of the British School of Athens*, Vol. 92 (1997), pp. 359–71.

Pines, C. C., "The Story of Ink," in *American Journal of Police Science*, Vol. 2, No. 4 (Jul./Aug. 1931), pp. 290–301.

Pitman, J., *On Blondes: From Aphrodite to Madonna: Why Blondes Have More Fun* (London: Bloomsbury, 2004).

Poos, L. R., *A Rural Society After the Black Death: Essex 1350–1525* (Cambridge University Press, 1991).

Prance, Sir G., and M. Nesbitt (eds.), *The Cultural History of Plants* (London: Routledge, 2005).

Prestwich, P. E., "Temperance in France: The Curious Case of Absinth," in *Historical Reflections*, Vol. 6, No. 2 (Winter 1979), pp. 301–19.

Profi, S., B. Perdikatsis, and S. E. Filippakis, "X-Ray Analysis of Greek Bronze Age Pigments from Thea," in *Studies in Conservation*, Vol. 22, No. 3 (Aug. 1977), pp. 107–15.

Pryor, E. G., "The Great Plague of Hong Kong," in *Journal of the Royal Asiatic Society Hong Kong Branch*, Vol. 15 (1975), pp. 61–70.

Q

Quito, A., "Pantone: How the World Authority on Color Became a Pop Culture Icon," in *Quartz* (Nov. 2, 2015).

Ramsay, G. D., "The Distribution of the Cloth Industry in 1561–1562," in *English Historical Review*, Vol. 57, No. 227 (July 1942), pp. 361–9.

Raven, A., "The Development of Naval Camouflage 1914–1945, Part III," in *Plastic Ship Modeler*, Vol. 13, No. 1 (1997).

Ravilious, K., "Cleopatra's Eye Makeup Warded Off Infections?," *National Geographic News*, (Jan. 15, 2010).

Rees, G. O., Letter to *The Times* (June 16, 1877).

Regier, T., and P. Kay, "Language, Thought, and Color: Whorf Was Half Right," in *Trends in Cognitive Sciences*, Vol. 13, No. 10 (Oct. 2009), pp. 439–46.

Reutersvärd, O., "The 'Violettomania' of the Impressionists," in *Journal of Aesthetics and Art Criticism*, Vol. 9, No. 2 (Dec. 1950), pp. 106–10.

Richter, E. L., and H. Härlin, "A Nineteenth Century Collection of Pigment and Painting Materials," in *Studies in Conservation*, Vol. 19, No. 2 (May 1974), pp. 76–92.

Rijksmuseum, "William of Orange (1533–1584), Father of the Nation."

Roberson, D., J. Davidoff, I. R. L. Davies, and L. R. Shapiro, "Color Categories and Category Acquisition in Himba and English," in N. Pitchford and C. P. Bingham (eds.), *Progress in Color Studies: Psychological Aspects* (Amsterdam: John Benjamins Publishing, 2006).

Rose, M., "'Look, Daddy, Oxen!': The Cave Art of Altamira," in *Archaeology*, Vol. 53, No. 3 (May/June 2000), pp. 68–9.

Rousseau, T., "The Stylistic Detection of Forgeries," in *Metropolitan Museum of Art Bulletin*, Vol. 27, No. 6 (Feb. 1968), pp. 247–52.

Royal Botanic Gardens, Kew, "Indian Yellow," in *Bulletin of Miscellaneous Information*, Vol. 1890, No. 39 (1890), pp. 45–50.

Ruskin, J., *Selected Writings*, D. Birch (ed.) (Oxford University Press, 2009).

Ruskin, J., *The Two Paths: Being Lectures on Art, and Its Application to Decoration and Manufacture, Delivered in 1858–9* (New York: John Wiley & Son, 1869).

Russo, C., "Can Elephants Survive a Legal Ivory Trade? Debate Is Shifting Against It," in *National Geographic* (Aug. 30, 2014).

Ryzik, M., "The Guerrilla Girls, After 3 Decades, Still Rattling Art World Cages," in *New York Times* (Aug. 5, 2015).

S

Sachsman, D. B., and D. W. Bulla (eds.), *Sensationalism: Murder, Mayhem, Mudslinging, Scandals and Disasters in 19th-Century Reporting* (New Brunswick, NJ: Transaction Publishers, 2013).

Salisbury, D., *Elephant's Breath and London Smoke* (Neustadt: Five Rivers, 2009).

Sample, I., "Van Gogh Doomed His Sunflowers by Adding White Pigments to Yellow Paint," in the *Guardian* (Feb. 14, 2011).

Samu, M., "Impressionism: Art and Modernity," Heilbrunn Timeline of Art History (Oct. 2004).

Sánchez, M. S., "Sword and Wimple: Isabel Clara Eugenia and Power," in A. J. Cruz and M. Suzuki (eds.), *The Rule of Women in Early Modern Europe* (Champaign, IL: University of Illinois Press, 2009), pp. 64–79.

Savage, J., "A Design for Life," in the *Guardian* (Feb. 21, 2009).

Schafer, E. H., "The Early History of Lead Pigments and Cosmetics in China," in *T'oung Pao*, Vol. 44, No. 4 (1956), pp. 413–38.

Schafer, E. H., "Orpiment and Realgar in Chinese Technology and Tradition," in *Journal of the American Oriental Society*, Vol. 75, No. 2 (Apr.–June 1955), pp. 73–80.

Schauss, A. G., "Tranquilizing Effect of Color Reduces Aggressive Behavior and Potential Violence," in *Orthomolecular Psychiatry*, Vol. 8, No. 4 (1979), pp. 218–21.

Schiaparelli, E., *Shocking Life* (London: V&A Museum, 2007).

Schwyzer, P., "The Scouring of the White Horse: Archaeology, Identity, and 'Heritage,'" in *Representations*, No. 65 (Winter 1999), pp. 42–62.

Seldes, A., J. E. Burucúa, G. Siracusano, M. S. Maier, and G. E. Abad, "Green, Yellow and Red Pigments in South American Painting, 1610–1780," in *Journal of the American Institute for Conservation*, Vol. 41, No. 3 (Autumn/Winter 2002), pp. 225–42.

Sherrow, V., *Encyclopedia of Hair: A Cultural History* (Westport, CN: Greenwood Press, 2006).

Shropshire Regimental Museum, "The Hong Kong Plague, 1894–95."

Silverman, S. K., "The 1363 English Sumptuary Law: A Comparison with Fabric Prices of the Late Fourteenth Century." Graduate thesis for Ohio State University (2011).

Slive, S., "Henry Hexham's 'Of Colors': A Note on a Seventeenth-Century List of Colors," in *Burlington Magazine*, Vol. 103, No. 702 (Sept. 1961), pp. 378–80.

Soames, M. (ed.), *Winston and Clementine: The Personal Letters of the Churchills* (Boston, MA: Houghton Mifflin, 1998).

Sooke, A., "Caravaggio's Nativity: Hunting a Stolen Masterpiece," BBC.com (Dec. 23, 2013).

Stamper, K., "Seeing Cerise: Defining Colors in Webster's Third," in *Harmless Drudgery: Life from Inside the Dictionary* (Aug. 2012).

Stanivukovic, G. V. (ed.), *Ovid and the Renaissance Body* (Toronto, Canada: University of Toronto Press, 2001).

Stanlaw, J. M., "Japanese Color Terms, from 400 CE to the Present," in R. E. MacLaury, G. Paramei, and D. Dedrick (eds.), *Anthropology of Color* (New York: John Benjamins, 2007), pp. 297–318.

Stephens, J. (ed.), *Gold: Firsthand Accounts from the Rush That Made the West* (Helena, MT: Twodot, 2014).

Stewart, D., "Why a 'Nude' Dress Should Really Be 'Champagne' or 'Peach,'" in *Jezebel* (May 17, 2010).

Stone, G. C., *A Glossary of the Construction, Decoration and Use of Arms and Armor in All Countries and in All Times* (Mineola, NY: Dover Publications, 1999).

Summer, G., and R. D'Amato, *Arms and Armor of the Imperial Roman Soldier* (Barnsley: Frontline Books, 2009).

Summers, M., *The Werewolf in Lore and Legend* (Mineola, NY: Dover Occult, 2012).

Swigonski, F., "Why Was Absinthe Banned for 100 Years?" (Mic.com, June 22, 2013).

T

Tabuchi, H., "Sweeping Away Gender-Specific Toys and Labels," in *New York Times* (Oct. 27, 2015).

Taylor, L., *Mourning Dress: A Costume and Social History* (London: Routledge Revivals, 2010).

The Times, "Absinthe" (May 4, 1868).

The Times, "The Use of Arsenic as a Color" (Sept. 4, 1863).

Thompson, D. V., *The Materials and Techniques of Medieval Painting. Reprinted from the first edition* (Mineola, NY: Dover Publications, 1956).

Time, "Techniques: The Passing of Mummy Brown" (Oct. 2, 1964).

Townsend, J. H., "The Materials of J. M. W. Turner: Pigments," in *Studies in Conservation*, Vol. 38, No. 4 (Nov. 1993), pp. 231–54.

Tugend, A., "If Your Appliances Are Avocado, They Probably Aren't Green," in *New York Times* (May 10, 2008).

Twain, M., *The Adventures of Tom Sawyer* (New York: Plain Label Books, 2008).

Tynan, J., *British Army Uniform and the First World War: Men in Khaki* (London: Palgrave Macmillan, 2013).

Tynan, J., "Why First World War Soldiers Wore Khaki," in *World War I Centenary* from the University of Oxford.

U

UCL, Digital Egypt for Universities, "Teaching of Ptahhotep."

ur-Rahman, A. (ed.), *Studies in Natural Products Chemistry: Volume 26: Bioactive Natural Products (Part G)* (Amsterdam: Elsevier Science, 2002).

V

Vasari, G., *The Lives of the Artists*, J. Conaway Bondanella and P. Bondanella trans. (Oxford, UK: Oxford University Press, 1998).

Vernatti, P., "A Relation of the Making of Ceruss," in the Royal Society, *Philosophical Transactions*, No. 137 (Jan./Feb. 1678), pp. 935–6.

Vernon Jones, V. S. (trans.), *Aesop's Fables* (Mineola, NY: Dover Publications, 2009).

W

Wald, C., "Why Red Means Red in Almost Every Language," in *Nautilus* (July 2015).

Walker, J., *The Finishing Touch: Cosmetics Through the Ages* (London: British Library, 2014).

Walton, A. G., "DNA Study Shatters the 'Dumb Blonde' Stereotype," in *Forbes* (June 2, 2014).

Ward, G. W. R. (ed.), *The Grove Encyclopedia of Materials and Techniques in Art* (Oxford, UK: Oxford University Press, 2008).

Warren, C., *Brush with Death: A Social History of Lead Poisoning* (Baltimore, MD: Johns Hopkins University Press, 2001).

Watts, D. C., *Dictionary of Plant Lore* (Burlington, VT: Elsevier, 2007).

Weber, C., *Queen of Fashion: What Marie Antoinette Wore to the Revolution* (New York: Picador, 2006).

Webster, R., *The Encyclopedia of Superstitions* (Woodbury: Llewellyn Worldwide, 2012).

White, R., "Brown and Black Organic Glazes, Pigments and Paints," in *National Gallery Technical Bulletin*, Vol. 10 (1986), pp. 58–71.

Whittemore, T., "The Sawâma Cemeteries," in *Journal of Egyptian Archaeology*, Vol. 1, No. 4 (Oct. 1914), pp. 246–7.

Willett Cunnington, C., *English Women's Clothing in the Nineteenth Century* (London: Dover, 1937).

Winstanley, W., *The Flying Serpent, or: Strange News out of Essex* (London, 1669).

Woodcock, S., "Body Color: The Misuse of Mummy," in *The Conservator*, Vol. 20, No. 1 (1996), pp. 87–94.

Woollacott, A., "'Khaki Fever' and Its Control: Gender, Class, Age and Sexual Morality on the British Homefront in the First World War," in *Journal of Contemporary History*, Vol. 29, No. 2 (Apr. 1994), pp. 325–47.

Wouters, J., L. Maes, and R. Germer, "The Identification of Haematite as a Red Colorant on an Egyptian Textile from the Second Millennium B.C.," in *Studies in Conservation*, Vol. 35, No. 2 (May 1990), pp. 89–92.

Wreschner, E. E., "Red Ocher and Human Evolution: A Case for Discussion," in *Current Anthropology*, Vol. 21, No. 5 (Oct. 1980), pp. 631–44.

Y

Young, J. I., "Riddle 15 of the Exeter Book," in *Review of English Studies*, Vol. 20, No. 80 (Oct. 1944), pp. 304–6.

Young, P., *Peking to Paris: The Ultimate Driving Adventure* (Dorchester: Veloce Publishing, 2007).

Z

Ziegler, P., *Diana Cooper: The Biography of Lady Diana Cooper* (London: Faber, 2011).

Zimmer, C., "Bones Give Peek into the Lives of Neanderthals," in *New York Times* (Dec. 20, 2010).

Zuckerman, Lord, "Earl Mountbatten of Burma, 25 June 1900–27 August 1979," *Biographical Memoirs of Fellows of the Royal Society*, Vol. 27 (Nov. 1981), pp. 354–64.

Acknowledgments

I am hugely grateful to the many people who took the time to help me with individual color stories and to point me in the direction of relevant research. Particular thanks go to Cédric Edon, director of communication at Schiaparelli; Martin Boswell, curator of uniforms, and Richard Slocombe, senior curator of art, at the Imperial War Museum. To Professors Raman Siva Kumar and B. N. Goswamy, and to Dr. Mark Nesbitt, curator at Royal Botanical Gardens, Kew, and the staff at Museum Victoria for helping me delve into the mystery of Indian yellow. And to Henning Rader at the Munich Museum and Sabrina Hamann at Stabilo.

Thank you also to Mrs. Herries and to Jenny and Piers Litherland, for the loan of their wonderful home where I spent a very happy six weeks writing, and to Carla Bennedetti for looking after me while I was there. Thank you to my British editors at John Murray, Georgina Laycock and Kate Miles; to the talented James Edgar, who looked after this book's design; and to Imogen Pelham, for all her work getting me from proposal to publication. My respect and gratitude also go to the team at Penguin Books in America, particularly Meg Leder and Shannon Kelly, and to the copyeditor, who patiently and painstakingly weeded out every "u" from every "color," all while making the text clearer, tighter, better. Thank you. Special thanks also to Michelle Ogundehin and Amy Bradford at *Elle Decoration* for taking the pitch for the original column. Thank you also to all the friends who have offered support, advice, research suggestions, and glasses of wine when they were required. Special mention must also go to Tim Cross and to my brother Kieren for reading through various drafts; to my dad, for always coming to my rescue; and to Fiammetta Rocco for her unfailing kindness and advice.

Thank you, finally, to Olivier, not only for bringing me coffee each morning, but also for the read-throughs, suggestions, patience when I was sure I was going insane, cheerleading, thoughtful criticism, and boundless encouragement.

Index

Page numbers of main color entries are indicated in **bold**.